Great
Old-Fashioned
American
Desserts

OTHER BOOKS BY BEATRICE OJAKANGAS

The Great Scandinavian Baking Book
Great Whole Grain Breads
New Ideas for Casseroles
Scandinavian Cooking
The Best of the Liberated Cook
The Complete Fondue Party Book
Gourmet Cooking for Two
The Finnish Cookbook

Great
Old-Fashioned
American Desserts

Beatrice
Ojakangas

E. P. DUTTON  NEW YORK

This paperback edition of *Great Old-Fashioned American Desserts* first published in 1989
by E. P. Dutton.

Published in the United States by E. P. Dutton,
a division of Penguin Books USA Inc.,
2 Park Avenue, New York, N.Y. 10016.

Published simultaneously in Canada by Fitzhenry and Whiteside, Limited, Toronto.

Library of Congress Cataloging-in-Publication Data
Ojakangas, Beatrice.
Great old-fashioned American desserts.
Includes index.
1. Desserts.   2. Cookery, American.   I. Title.
TX773.O35   1987   641.8'6   86-24401
ISBN: 0-525-24534-0 (cloth)
ISBN: 0-525-48504-X (paper)

Designed by Mark O'Connor

1 2 3 4 5 6 7 8 9 10

For dessert lovers everywhere

Contents

ACKNOWLEDGMENTS   *ix*

Introduction   *I*

Easy-to-Fix Desserts with Fresh Fruits and Berries   *4*

Cooked Fruit and Berry Desserts   *20*

Simple Cooked Puddings   *56*

Old-style Baked and Steamed Puddings   *75*

Pastries, Pancakes, Baked Dumplings, and Fried Doughs   *108*

Old-time Icebox Desserts and Cakes   *138*

Ice Creams, Sherbets, and Ices   *154*

Country Dairy Desserts: Custards, Soufflés, and Creams   *168*

All-American Pies   *185*

All-American Cakes   *214*

Cookie-Jar Cookies and Pan Bars   *263*

INDEX   *283*

Acknowledgments

To try to name all the friends, colleagues, and relatives who generously provided me with ideas, encouragement, recipes, stories, and anecdotes would be a book in itself. Many shared family cookbooks or old family favorites with me. They ate and evaluated and kept me going as I worked on the book, and I thank them all.

I also wish to thank the researchers at Duluth Public Library, who willingly dug through their sources and found information for me. In addition, I am grateful to my many colleagues in home economics who helped by sharing interesting bits of information from their files, which I otherwise would not have had access to. Among them are the home economists at Kraft, Borden, Pillsbury Mills, General Mills, General Foods, Best Foods, Pet and Carnation, the American Egg Board, and the National Dairy Council.

Introduction

From California to New York, from Vermont to Florida, the aroma of an apple pie baking, its juices bubbling through the slits in the crust, of chocolate cake fresh from the oven, or of buttery cookies cooling on a rack evokes a special response in us. We are a nation that loves desserts!

Since the birth of this country, desserts have been a major part of American cooking. Colonial aristocrats competed with one another to see who could create the most delicious and intricate desserts, while early country cooks delighted their families with heart- and hearth-warming crisps, cobblers, buckles, bettys, pies, and cakes. Because of the rich diversity of influences in America, what we consider a dessert can be anything from fresh fruit to ice cream, dumplings, or a cake. To this patchwork of influences are added a fundamental respect for the abundance of the land and a practical use of the ingredients that are common to the region. No other country can boast such a wide variety of desserts, and unlike the Europeans, we usually prepare our own rather than buy them. What our cakes, tortes, and pies may lose in finesse we gain in freshness and expression.

Although many American desserts originated in other countries, we have developed uniquely American desserts as well, aided by our ingenuity. We bake pies in slope-sided pans and cakes in special layer pans. Angel food and sponge-cake pans, as we know them, are truly American. Ingredients such as condensed milk, marshmallows, chocolate chips, and peanut butter are unique to our shelves, as is the wide variety of convenience products available. Baking contests, magazines, newspaper booklets, and flyers filled with recipes, directions, and tips ensure that we keep no new idea a secret.

The search for the great old-fashioned American desserts has led me to old cookbooks and recipe boxes of early New England, the old South, the Prairie states, the Southwest, the Gold Rush settlers of California, and the Upper Middle West, as well as the conservative and stoic Shakers, Amish, and Pennsylvania Dutch. It has been fascinating—invaluable, in fact—to dig into the old and antique cookbooks in my own personal collection, in my friends' personal collections, and in libraries and research centers. In many of them, there is little more than a listing of recipes and ingredients, but even with such scant information, I was able to tell a great deal about the culture of the era and locale.

Most of the Colonial cookbooks I found were, of course, British; their dessert sections were filled with steamed and boiled puddings, cakes, jellies, and creams. It was more difficult to find records in the language of the later immigrants: Germans, Italians, French, Spanish, Swedes, Norwegians, Finns, and Danes. These cooks brought with them family books written in their own languages; over time, the names of the recipes changed and ingredient substitutions were made.

Our grandmothers often cooked without recipes for the main courses of their meals, relying on judgment, taste, and available ingredients. But when it came to a dessert, a "formula" was written down, since baking, for instance, is a more "scientific" process. These formulas for pastries and cakes, pies, and puddings were recorded and passed on to younger cooks. Many of these recipes have endured the test of time, have been handed down from one generation to the next, and now make up a large part of traditional American desserts.

In this book I have tried to include the best of the most authentic and traditional desserts, from every corner of the country. Mostly old favorites, but with a few popular modern additions, the range of recipes is as diverse as the country that gave birth to them. Fresh fruit and fresh berry concoctions as well as cooked fruit and cooked berry desserts are an essential part of any collection of truly American desserts. Puddings—top-of-the-stove, baked, and steamed—are really as American as apple pie, and pastries, pancakes, dumplings, and doughnuts are served as desserts in many parts of the country. Icebox desserts, which followed the invention of the first non-electric refrigerator, are still enjoyed today, and ice creams, sherbets, and ices have become, of course, an American standard. I have also included some classic dairy desserts, in addition to what no American desserts collection should be without: all-American cakes, pies, and cookies.

The recipes that follow have all been tested and revised for today's ingredients and today's equipment. When possible, I have simplified the recipes by changing the order of preparation, but I have altered methods or ingredients only when it is possible to do so without lowering the quality of the result.

Even in today's exercise- and calorie-conscious world, Americans still love to end their meals with something sweet. This book does offer some desserts for weight watchers—satisfying end-of-the-meal dishes that are relatively low-calorie—as well as the better known, ever popular, sinfully delicious, great old-fashioned American desserts.

Easy-to-Fix Desserts with Fresh Fruits and Berries

When berries and fruits are in the peak of the season, we're as likely today to buy them "cents off," using a supermarket coupon, as we are to go out and pick them ourselves. Nonetheless, each of them has its own season. It's usually a feast or famine extreme. The first carton of strawberries in season probably gets eaten out of hand. The next might make it to a dessert planned for either a family or company meal. After that, the price really goes down, and it is hard to resist buying a whole case! So it is as raspberries, apricots, peaches, blueberries, melons, pears, and apples begin to come into season.

True, not all of us grow fruits in our own backyards. But most of us are near the source of one or another fresh fruit at some time during the summer season. In California, an apricot tree in the back of the house presents a challenge to the householder; when the fruit is ripe, it must be used before it is lost. In Phoenix, a backyard fig tree presents the same challenge to its owner. In our area in Minnesota, strawberries, raspberries, and blueberries in season look so voluptuous on the fruit stand that one cannot resist them. It's *time* to go beyond eating them out of hand. Especially when the price is right. The quick and simple recipes in this chapter can be adapted to be used with almost any fresh fruit. Minimal cooking equals maximum flavor. Maximum flavor comes also when fruit is fully ripe and in season.

What would you do with a basket of fresh berries? How you answer the question may depend on what you've done before, what you have seen somebody else do, or what you've just read in a magazine. Maybe you would do what your grandmother would have done.

In this chapter are basic ideas for preparing delicious desserts with fresh fruits. The recipes are examples of the ingenuity of many great American cooks. The original ideas came from women's club cookbooks, church cookbooks, and farmer's wives' collections. Sometimes a single-line entry described the procedure, but it sounded interesting enough to warrant further experimentation. An example is the Michigan Black Cherry Dessert, which was just listed as "Black Cherry Sauce" in *The New Buckeye Cookbook*. It read: "To every pound of well-ripened, stoned cherries add a half pound sugar, melted, and poured over boiling hot. Put on ice till cold and serve." The idea sounded interesting enough to me to do a little experimenting. I found that Michigan black cherries, whether fresh or frozen, work well. When I tried pouring caramelized sugar over the cherries, the cherries oozed their juices and blended with the flavor of the darkened sugar to make a pleasing cherry saucelike dessert.

Who can resist eating the succulent strawberries of early spring just plain with cream and sugar? Fresh wild strawberries picked from grassy meadows are the ultimate, but we won't turn down those picked at the local markets when they're in midseason abundance. That's when they are the best.

A Midwestern farmhouse cook with a Scandinavian background might serve the fresh berries with a thin, eggy custard sauce, even though there's lots of cream from her own farm available. A dairy farmer in New England might fold the berries into whipped cream. A California vintner might serve them in champagne (which seems terribly extravagant to most of us). In the South they might be served in a compote to add color to an orange ambrosia.

The cranberries of autumn have been used for all kinds of simple desserts from cranberry "sauce," which is served over ice cream or rice pudding, to cranberry puddings and pies. It is a good idea to freeze extra bags of cranberries when they are in season, to make delightful iced cranberries in hot caramel sauce for dessert when time is limited and you want an easy, yet rather light dessert.

Historically, it has been the American country cook who has been creative with the abundance of fruits in season. As seasons fluctuate and overlap each other, the tail end of last month's abundance is still around as the next fruit in season comes to the front. Strawberries and rhubarb are ripe at almost the same time, so they are often combined. Just at their tail end, they overlap raspberries, apricots, and peaches, which later overlap the various melons of late summer and early autumn.

Here are just a few notes about buying fresh fruits. Purchase berries and fruits in season, fully ripe. There are many varieties of berries, which vary from one area of the country to another. Spring-time brings strawberries, followed by raspberries, blueberries, blackberries, currants, gooseberries, and cranberries.

Because berries are highly perishable and bruise easily, refrigerate and use them within a day or two after you buy them. You can also freeze them for later use. To freeze, lay them in single layers, unwashed but picked over, on cookie sheets. Freeze until solid, then pack into containers. They will keep for 2 months in a refrigerator's freezer, or up to a year in a deep freeze at 0°F. or lower.

Fresh Berries and Vanilla Cream Sauce

MAKES 6 SERVINGS

We usually think of serving fresh berries with cream, but this recipe is a favorite dairy farmer's recipe. One would at first think that dairy farmers would use cream with abandon; not so, as cream is the most valuable part of the milk. For special Sunday desserts, berries might be simply folded into cream to make a "berry fool," but a vanilla cream sauce such as this one, which is a thin custard that pours like cream, points out the bright flavor of juicy berries. Try this sauce also with baked fruit desserts such as apples, crisps, crumbles, or cobblers.

Fresh raspberries, strawberries, blueberries
6 egg yolks
⅔ cup sugar
2½ cups milk
1 teaspoon vanilla

Pick over the berries. In a large bowl, beat the egg yolks with ⅓ cup of the sugar. In a heavy saucepan, combine the remaining sugar with the milk; heat to boiling. Whisk about ½ cup of the boiling mixture into the yolks. Return the yolk mixture to the saucepan and cook over medium heat, whisking, until the custard is thick enough to coat the back of a wooden spoon (about 160°F.). Turn the heat off and stir for 2 to 3 minutes. Do not boil or custard will curdle. Add the vanilla and pour through a fine mesh strainer into a serving bowl. Chill, covered.

To serve, pour or ladle sauce over servings of fresh berries.

Fresh Berry Fool

MAKES 4 SERVINGS

The word *fool* is an old-fashioned term of endearment. This old-fashioned dessert favorite is a combination of fruit and cream. Fools are made with either fresh berries or cooked fruit.

2 *cups fresh strawberries or raspberries*
¼ to ⅓ *cup powdered sugar*
1 *cup heavy cream*
3 *tablespoons fruit-flavored liqueur, or* 1 *teaspoon vanilla*
Fresh berries for garnish

Pick over the berries; remove stems from strawberries and combine in a bowl with the sugar. Let stand 10 minutes. Whip the cream until stiff and flavor with the liqueur or vanilla. Fold into the berries and chill until ready to serve. Spoon into dessert dishes and garnish with an additional fresh berry.

Cooked Fruit Fool

MAKES 4 SERVINGS

1 *cup heavy cream*
1 *cup cooked fruit purée, such as applesauce, cooked rhubarb, cooked apricots, currants, or cooked, strained gooseberries*
½ *teaspoon almond extract, or* 2 *teaspoons Amaretto*

Whip the cream until stiff and fold in the fruit purée. Flavor with the almond extract or Amaretto. Chill until ready to serve.

Fresh Berry Tumble

MAKES 6 SERVINGS

A great last-minute dessert, perfect in the summertime when fresh berries are in the markets. Select whichever berries look the best and combine them just before serving. It works well served with crunchy nut wafers or sponge or angel food cake. When fresh berries are not available, purchase individually frozen, unsugared berries.

3 *cups of any combination of fresh blueberries, raspberries,*
   strawberries, red currants, blackberries, or loganberries
1 *cup heavy cream*
1/4 *cup powdered sugar*
1 *teaspoon vanilla*
Grated rind of 1/2 *lemon*

Pick over the berries and combine them in a bowl. Just before serving, whip the cream and add the sugar, vanilla, and lemon rind. Fold the whipped cream into the berries, and turn into individual dessert dishes or into a pretty glass serving bowl.

Frozen Cranberries with Hot Caramel Sauce

MAKES 6 SERVINGS

Buy extra cranberries when they are in season and freeze them. When you need a spectacular last-minute dessert, make the caramel sauce and keep it hot. Serve the hot sauce over the frozen, chopped berries in stemmed dessert dishes. This recipe originates with Scandinavian cooks who, in the old country, froze lingonberries and served them with this sauce, which is made from easily available dairy ingredients.

2 *cups fresh, raw cranberries*
2 *tablespoons sugar*
Hot Caramel Sauce (see following recipe)

Wash and dry the cranberries. Turn into a bowl and freeze until solid (about 4 hours). Put cranberries into a food processor with the steel blade in place and process, or turn out onto a board and chop with a knife, until berries are coarsely chopped. Blend with the sugar and keep frozen until ready to serve.

To serve, spoon about ⅓ cup of the frozen, chopped berries into each dessert dish. Top with the Hot Caramel Sauce and serve immediately.

Hot Caramel Sauce

MAKES ABOUT 1½ CUPS

1 *cup sugar*
1 *cup heavy cream*
2 *teaspoons dark corn syrup*
2 *teaspoons butter*
2 *teaspoons vanilla*

Combine the sugar, heavy cream, and corn syrup in a saucepan. Bring to a boil and cook for 5 minutes, or until sauce is slightly thickened and light tan in color. Add the butter and vanilla. Reheat before serving.

Orange Ambrosia

MAKES 6 SERVINGS

In an 1879 Virginia housewives' cookbook, ambrosia was entered twice. "Pare and slice as many oranges as you choose, and put them in a glass bowl. Sprinkle sugar and grated coconut over each layer." The second version is more elaborate: fresh pineapple and orange slices are alternated with sugar and coconut to form a pyramid. Then, "if you like," pour good Madeira or sherry wine over all. Today, ambrosia is a favorite dessert in the South, and it is often found on the menus of country inns and plantations that are open to guests. Ambrosia is always topped with coconut.

3 *seedless oranges*
3 *bananas*
¼ *cup shredded or flaked coconut*

Cut the peel from the oranges and remove the sections. Cut each section into thirds. Slice the bananas and combine with the oranges. Chill. Spoon into dessert dishes. Top with coconut before serving.

Yankee Apple Snow

MAKES 4 SERVINGS

This old-fashioned dessert from northern New England used to be tedious to make, as it had to be whisked by hand to frothy lightness. Today, with an electric mixer, we can make it in minutes!

1 *large Granny Smith apple, or 2 small tart apples*
1 *tablespoon lemon juice*
¾ *cup powdered sugar*
2 *egg whites*
Vanilla Cream Sauce (see recipe)

Pare the apple and grate it into the large bowl of an electric mixer (you should have about 1 cup grated apple). Stir in the lemon juice. Add the sugar and egg whites. Beat at high speed until the pudding is light and frothy, about 5 minutes. Heap into a glass dish and serve with Vanilla Cream Sauce.

Old-fashioned Strawberry Whip

MAKES 10 TO 12 SERVINGS

This will absolutely amaze you! It reminds me of a diet dessert I once made called "smashing spoof." The strawberries, powdered sugar, and egg white whisk up to voluminously fill a 3-quart serving bowl. Serve it as a topping for sliced fresh berries.

1½ *cups fresh, juicy strawberries, cleaned and hulled*
1 *cup powdered sugar*
1 *egg white*

Mash the strawberries in the large bowl of an electric mixer. Add the sugar and egg white and beat with mixer at high speed, until stiff enough to hold its shape, about 8 to 10 minutes. It will multiply in volume many times, becoming light and fluffy.

Shaker Strawberry Sauce

MAKES ABOUT 6 SERVINGS

The Shakers, a Utopian community in America, had their origin in French Protestantism. They merged with the radical Quakers in England and in 1787 settled in New Lebanon, New York, to establish religious freedom. Ingenuity and simplicity are the marks of Shaker tradition. Their furniture, for instance, is classic. Much of Yankee design and many inventions—such as the buzz saw, rotary harrow, the threshing machine, apple corer, and the common clothespin—are credited to the Shakers. Shakers also believed in simplicity in food, although they ate well. This fluffy, fresh-tasting strawberry sauce can be served as is, over plain white cake, or over plain rice pudding. Shaker cooks would make this on a platter so that plenty of air could be beaten into the sauce. This takes a lot of energy and a strong arm when using a flat whisk!

1 *egg white*
1 *cup fresh strawberries, mashed*
1 *cup powdered sugar*
4 *tablespoons butter, at room temperature*

In a large mixing bowl, beat the egg white until very stiff. Add the crushed berries and beat until light and fluffy. Gradually add the sugar and beat until the mixture stands in peaks, about 5 minutes. Beat in the butter until it is worked into the foam. Serve immediately.

Iced Cantaleupes

MAKES 2 SERVINGS

Cantaloupes and watermelon have been garden fruits associated with the South. However, in an early Virginia cookbook, the author must have felt the need to explain how to serve them: "Cut out carefully the end with the stem, making a hole large enough to admit an apple. With a spoon, remove the seed. Fill with ice, replace the round piece taken out, and place on end. Eat with powdered sugar, salt, and pepper." Because most cantaloupes are larger than the one that was described, we get 2 servings from 1 melon.

1 *medium cantaloupe*
Crushed ice
Powdered sugar
Salt and pepper to taste (optional)

Cut the cantaloupe in half. Remove the seeds and pack the cavities with ice. Fit the two halves together again and let stand 30 minutes, until chilled. Remove the ice and place each half on a serving dish. Sprinkle with powdered sugar, salt, and pepper. Serve immediately.

Honeydew and Fresh Peach Compote

MAKES 4 SERVINGS

Peaches that ripen and are available in midsummer are a natural combination with melons. Because of the color contrast, this makes a pretty fruit salad that is popular for picnics and outings, and serving it as suggested here enhances the natural beauty of this dessert. The addition of sweet vermouth, which is optional, brings out the flavors of the fruits.

2 large, ripe peaches, peeled, pitted, and sliced
2 tablespoons fresh lemon juice
1½ tablespoons sugar
Eight ½-inch-thick wedges honeydew melon, seeded, peel removed
½ cup sweet vermouth (optional)
Fresh mint sprigs for garnish

In a mixing bowl, combine the peaches, lemon juice, and sugar. Arrange 2 wedges of melon on each serving plate to make a ring. Divide the peach slices among the 4 plates, and pour 2 tablespoons sweet vermouth over each, if desired. Garnish with fresh mint sprigs.

Minted Orange Cup

MAKES 4 SERVINGS

Our country home is overrun by mint! Once it gets "loose," you can hardly contain it. In the fall, dig up a spadeful of mint, and put it in a large planter; then you will have fresh mint all winter.

4 *large seedless oranges*
2 *tablespoons powdered sugar*
2 *tablespoons minced fresh mint*
1 *tablespoon sherry*
Fresh mint sprigs for garnish

Cut oranges in half. Using a grapefruit knife, loosen segments. Remove pulp with a pointed spoon. Combine orange pulp in a bowl with the sugar, mint, and sherry. Chill. Serve in sherbet glasses and garnish with additional fresh mint.

Old-fashioned Fruit Tumble

MAKES 8 SERVINGS

Golden Delicious apples will survive a year of storage so that they can add their texture to a compote of fresh summer fruits. Early American cooks would often just "tumble" together a variety of fruits to make a simple dessert.

2 *Golden Delicious apples, pared, cored, and thinly sliced*
4 *peaches, peeled and thinly sliced*
2 *tablespoons fresh lemon juice*
1 *cantaloupe, seeded*
2 *cups strawberries, hulled*
1 *cup blueberries*
⅓ *cup honey*
2 *tablespoons dark rum*
3 *tablespoons sweet butter*
Fresh mint leaves for garnish

In a bowl, combine the apple and peach slices with the lemon juice. Scoop out balls of the cantaloupe and add them to the bowl, along with the strawberries and blueberries. Combine the honey, rum, and butter in a saucepan; heat until the butter is melted. Turn the fruit mixture into a serving bowl, or divide among 8 serving dishes. Spoon the sauce over the fruit and garnish with fresh mint leaves.

Strawberries in Champagne

MAKES 4 TO 6 SERVINGS

This recipe came from a vintner's wife in California, who suggests that instead of rinsing the berries in water, rinse them in white wine; this adds flavor rather than making them watery. Another way to clean the berries is to hull them and polish them with a terry-cloth towel. Just put 6 or 8 large ripe, juicy berries into a towel, and, holding both ends with both hands, roll the berries back and forth until they are shiny.

1 *quart large strawberries, hulled*
4 *tablespoons brandy*
4 *tablespoons superfine sugar*
1 *bottle brut champagne, chilled*

Divide strawberries among 4 to 6 tall champagne flutes or stemmed balloon wineglasses. Drizzle with the brandy and sugar. Chill until ready to serve. Before serving, pour champagne over the berries.

Michigan
Black Cherry Dessert

MAKES 6 SERVINGS

Cherry orchards in Michigan produce a great share of the nation's black and red pie cherries. Well-ripened, almost overripe cherries are delicious when made into a simple, stewed dessert. It is delicious served over a scoop of ice cream or plain white cake.

1 *pound very ripe black cherries, pitted*
1 *cup sugar*

Put the cherries into a large stainless-steel mixing bowl. Sprinkle the sugar in an even layer onto the bottom of a cast-iron skillet. Place over medium heat and stir with a wooden spoon, until the sugar is melted. Pour molten sugar evenly over the cherries. Place over a bowl of ice and let stand until almost all of the crystallized sugar has melted into the cherry juice.

Spoon into dessert dishes and serve plain, with cream, or over cake or ice cream.

Fancy Pears

MAKES 4 SERVINGS

Edward Harris Heth in *The Country Kitchen Cookbook* described a dessert made with fresh pears, which he prepared for the "rich lady" who moved out to the country for the summer. The sauce is one that goes well on all kinds of fresh fruits and berries. But in this combination, the sweetness of the sauce counterbalances the bitterness of the cocoa and brings out the flavor of the pears. Although Comice pears are ideal, try them with spicy Bosc or Anjous as well. The sauce must be made at least 4 hours before serving so that it can chill and thicken.

THE SAUCE

1 *egg*
1 *cup powdered sugar*
5 *tablespoons melted butter*
1 *cup heavy cream*
¼ *cup brandy or light rum*

THE PEARS

4 *ripe Comice pears*
4 *tablespoons dark unsweetened cocoa*

In the small bowl of an electric mixer, beat the egg until frothy; add the powdered sugar and butter and beat until light. In another bowl, whip the cream until stiff, and fold into the egg mixture. Blend in the brandy or rum. Chill 4 hours.

Pare and core the pears. Place on individual dessert plates and fill the hole of each pear with the cocoa. Spread one-quarter of the sauce over each pear.

Cooked Fruit and Berry Desserts

This all-American category of desserts goes beyond fresh fruit brought simply and quickly to the table in the height of its season. Fresh berries and soft fruits require little cooking. Apples require more cooking, but they are also more durable and more stowable; so the variety of apple desserts is voluminous because they can be made year-round.

Early American cooks were masters at fruit puddings, dumplings, cobblers, pandowdies, crisps, fruit grunts, buckles, slumps, bettys, and roly-polies that have doughs and batters on top or are rolled in dough. There is as much variety in the names of the desserts as there are opinions about how they should be made. It is impossible to define or distinguish, for example, a cobbler from a buckle, or a slump from a fruit grunt. Yet, there are those who would defend with their life the name of their favorite grunt or buckle! Misinterpretation and

20

change of name happen easily in a country where we have people from many different backgrounds.

Similar desserts that appear in historical and folk cookbooks beyond the East are simply called "pudding," though they might have the same ingredients as a unique-sounding pudding from New England. One difference: Cooks of the East are more likely to steam or boil their puddings; recipes from the Midwest and West are generally baked in the oven. In this chapter are "puddings" that are baked and steamed or boiled and include fruits and berries. These recipes come from the Shakers, Pennsylvania Dutch, New England Yankees, frontier cooks, and the cooks of the Far West. They are simple and filling, and sometimes have been considered a meal in themselves. Served steaming hot from the oven for Sunday-night supper with a glass of cold milk, old-fashioned fruit puddings—grunts, slumps, dowdies, crisps—are a satisfying and nourishing meal.

Poached Apples
with Maple Cream

MAKES 4 SERVINGS

Apple orchards abound throughout our country. The varieties grown in each area depend so much on the climate that it's hard to give just one suggestion for the best apple for poaching! Select a firm, flavorful apple, such as Golden Delicious, Melrose, Winesap, Jonathan, Rome Beauty, or Granny Smith. Although we usually think first of Vermont when maple syrup is mentioned, there are other areas throughout the country where the delicious syrup is produced—Ohio, Minnesota, Wisconsin, Michigan, just to name a few.

Because the apples are pared before cooking, they will cook very quickly. Certain varieties might even get mushy all of a sudden. Watch them *very* carefully while cooking; it just takes *minutes*. This dessert is delicious and beautiful when you serve one whole apple on a plate surrounded with the maple-and-cream sauce.

4 *large, firm apples*
1 *cup maple syrup*
½ *cup water*
1 *tablespoon butter*
1 *teaspoon all-purpose flour*
½ *cup light cream or half-and-half*

Pare and core the apples.

In a saucepan, combine the syrup and water. Bring to a boil and simmer 3 minutes. Add the apples and cover. Simmer until the apples are tender but not mushy, 3 to 8 minutes. With slotted spoon, lift the apples onto individual dessert dishes or plates. Boil syrup until reduced to ¾ cup. Pour syrup into a measuring cup. Melt butter in the saucepan. Blend in the flour, cream, and then the syrup. Boil, uncovered, until reduced to 1 cup, about 3 minutes. Serve warm, or at room temperature.

Stewed Fruits

MAKES 4 SERVINGS

Pears, apples, plums, figs, rhubarb, peaches, apricots, quinces, and most berries can be easily stewed to make a simple dessert. Dried fruits make excellent stewed desserts, but more water must be added.

To stew fruits, peel the fruit, if necessary, and/or remove seeds. Add just enough water to keep the fruit from sticking to the bottom of the pan; add sugar to taste. Simmer, covered, until the fruit is just tender but not mushy. Cool. Add a fruit-flavored liqueur, if desired, to dress up stewed fruit for a "company" dessert, and serve it in stemmed glasses for an elegant presentation. Stewed fruit is good served with whipped cream or cream poured over it. Here is a general recipe.

4 cups peeled sliced pears, quinces, or apples, halved and pitted
    plums, rhubarb cut into 1-inch pieces, quartered peaches, or
    halved apricots or figs
½ cup water
½ to 1 cup sugar
Rum, brandy, or fruit-flavored liqueur (optional)
Heavy cream or whipped cream (optional)

Place the fruit in a saucepan; add the water and sugar. Place over medium heat and cook 10 to 20 minutes, or until fruit is tender. Cover and cool.

If desired, add rum, brandy, or fruit-flavored liqueur to taste, spoon into dessert dishes, and top with cream.

Pears Poached
with Raspberries

MAKES 4 SERVINGS

Raspberries lend a pretty pink color in this method of poaching pears.

One 10-ounce package frozen raspberries, thawed
½ cup framboise (raspberry-flavored liqueur) or crème de cassis
4 firm but ripe pears
Chopped pistachio nuts for garnish

Purée the raspberries and strain through a sieve to remove the seeds. Combine with the framboise or crème de cassis.

Peel the pears, leaving the stems intact. Remove the cores and seeds from the bottom side. Arrange pears standing upright in a saucepan. Pour the raspberry mixture over the pears. Bring to a boil, cover, and simmer until pears are tender, 8 to 10 minutes. Remove pears and cool, then chill.

Boil the cooking liquid until reduced to a thick syrup, 10 to 12 minutes over medium heat. Cool syrup.

To serve, arrange pears on individual plates and drizzle syrup evenly over them. Sprinkle with chopped pistachios.

Homemade Applesauce

Puréed, cooked apples have the most delicate and distinctive flavor if cooked covered, over low heat. You can make applesauce from any variety of apples; however, mild, less flavorful apples will produce a mild, less flavorful sauce. For the best flavor, select fresh, tart, full-flavored apples that will cook down in a short time. Your yield will depend on the juiciness of the apples used, and you may wish to blend varieties of apples to get the flavor and consistency you desire. Greenings, McIntosh, Cortland, Gravenstein, Wealthy, Winesap, and Jonathan are among the apples that make good applesauce.

Apples, quartered
Sugar to taste
Lemon juice to taste

Wash and cut the apples into quarters. Remove cores. Place in a deep pot and partly cover with water. Apples that have been stored will be less juicy than fresh autumn apples and will require a bit more liquid. Slowly bring to a simmer and cook until tender. Press through a purée strainer or blend, skin and all, in food processor or blender to get the prettiest color. Add sugar and lemon juice to taste.

Baked Apples
Stuffed with Dates and Walnuts

MAKES 4 SERVINGS

An old-time favorite! The tops of the apples are cut off before coring and used as a lid.

4 *large, tart cooking apples*
½ *cup chopped dates*
¼ *cup chopped walnuts*
½ *teaspoon cinnamon*
⅓ *cup tightly packed brown sugar*
2 *tablespoons butter*
Heavy cream or Vanilla Cream Sauce (see recipe)

Preheat oven to 400°F.

Cut off the tops of the apples about one-quarter of the way down; reserve tops with stems intact. Remove cores, being careful not to cut all the way through the bottoms. With a spoon, widen the center cores. Score each apple all around the middle with the tip of a paring knife to prevent wrinkling and sinking while baking. Combine the dates, walnuts, and cinnamon. Stuff the centers of the apples with the mixture, and replace the tops. Place apples in a shallow baking dish and pour ⅓ cup water into the dish. Sprinkle each apple with brown sugar and top with a little piece of butter. Bake 35 to 45 minutes, or until apples are cooked.

Serve warm with cream or Vanilla Cream Sauce.

Baked Pears
with Mint Cream

MAKES 6 SERVINGS

Simple and elegant! Just cut the pears in half lengthwise, bake, and serve them dusted with powdered sugar and topped with a dollop of mint-flavored whipped cream. At holiday time, these are spectacular when served in a pretty bowl and garnished with tiny pine boughs stuck between the pear halves. In the summertime, when wild mint is plentiful, use fresh mint instead of the pine boughs.

6 Bosc, Anjou, or Bartlett pears
Fresh lemon juice
Powdered sugar
1 cup heavy cream
¼ cup superfine sugar
2 tablespoons green crème de menthe
A few drops green food coloring (optional)

Preheat oven to 375°F.

Scrub the pears, dry them, and halve them lengthwise. With a melon baller or a small measuring spoon, scoop out the center seeds, but leave the core intact (only one half will have the stem). Place the pears with the cut side up in a baking pan in a single layer. Brush with lemon juice. Bake for 45 minutes, or until the pears are just tender. Remove from the oven and cool completely. Dust heavily with powdered sugar. Arrange on a serving tray or in a bowl, and dust again with powdered sugar. Whip the cream, adding the superfine sugar and crème de menthe. Add food coloring, if desired. Serve the cream on the side to spoon over individual servings of the pears, two halves per serving.

Old Oregon Baked Pears

MAKES 4 SERVINGS

The cookery of the West Coast has always been simple and elegant. Although pears are not indigenous to Oregon, they do very well there. In the forties, the late Helen Evans Brown, respected food writer of the West, included this recipe in a collection of simple classics.

4 *Comice, D'Anjou, or Bosc pears*
⅓ *cup fresh lime juice*
⅓ *cup honey*
⅓ *cup rum*
⅓ *cup water*
2 *to 3 tablespoons chopped almonds*
½ *to 1 cup sour cream*

Preheat oven to 350°F.

Butter a shallow baking dish. Halve the pears and remove cores. Arrange the pear halves with the cut side up in a baking dish. Put 1 teaspoon lime juice, 1 teaspoon honey, and 1 teaspoon rum into the cavity of each pear half. Combine the remaining lime juice, honey, and rum with the water. Bake pears for 1 hour, basting with the mixture until it is all used up. Sprinkle the baked pears with almonds and place under the broiler until almonds are browned. Serve warm with sour cream.

Baked Peaches Flambé

MAKES 4 SERVINGS

This is great with fresh peaches when in season, but out of season, use your own home-canned peaches. Or, if necessary, use commercially canned peaches.

8 *peach halves, peeled*
1 *tablespoon fresh lemon juice*
½ *cup tightly packed brown sugar*
¼ *teaspoon nutmeg*
¼ *cup brandy, rum, or kirsch*
Whipped cream or heavy cream

Preheat oven to 350°F.

Arrange the peach halves in a shallow baking dish with the cut side up. Brush with the lemon juice and sprinkle with brown sugar and nutmeg. Bake for 30 minutes. Just before serving, heat the brandy, rum, or kirsch in a metal ladle or small pan, until barely warm. Ignite and pour over the peaches. Transfer peaches to serving dishes, spoon the pan juices over them, and top with whipped cream or heavy cream.

Baked Pie Plant (Rhubarb)

MAKES 6 TO 8 SERVINGS

Rhubarb or "pie plant" is the unsung hero of American cooks, an effortlessly grown fruit that offers its thick, juicy stalks from the early spring through June. From *The New Buckeye Cookbook,* the advice is to bake it in a deep bean pot with a cover, using "a teacup of sugar to a quart of pie plant" to make a superior sauce. Covering it during baking doubles the baking time but contains the aroma of the fruit. I like to add a small chunk of fresh ginger to the rhubarb. It is good topped with cream or Vanilla Cream Sauce.

4 cups cubed rhubarb (1-inch pieces)
1 cup sugar
One 1-inch piece fresh ginger (optional)

Preheat oven to 325°F.
Combine the rhubarb, sugar, and ginger (if used), in a 1½-quart casserole or bean pot with a cover. Cover and bake for 1 hour, until rhubarb is stewed and soft. Serve warm.

Bananas Foster

MAKES 4 SERVINGS

A classic in the South, "fried or flamed" bananas were first prepared in the cook houses behind plantation homes. They became well known, due to the popularity of New Orleans restaurants that regularly feature this dessert.

½ *cup brown sugar*
¼ *cup butter*
4 *bananas, peeled, halved crosswise and lengthwise*
A dash of cinnamon
¼ *cup banana liqueur*
⅓ *cup light rum*
4 *scoops vanilla ice cream*

In a flat chafing dish or wide skillet, blend the brown sugar and butter; heat until mixture bubbles. Add the bananas and sauté until tender. Sprinkle with cinnamon. Combine the banana liqueur and rum. Heat slightly, ignite, and pour over the bananas. Baste with the flaming liquid until the flame burns out. Serve immediately over ice cream.

Applesauce Crisp

MAKES 4 TO 6 SERVINGS

Freshly made applesauce from flavorful, tart apples is, of course, the very best for this dessert. A good-quality commercially produced applesauce can also be used.

2 cups applesauce
1 to 2 tablespoons fresh lemon juice
½ cup tightly packed brown sugar
¼ cup raisins
½ teaspoon cinnamon
1 cup all-purpose flour
½ cup granulated sugar
½ cup butter, chilled
½ cup chopped pecans or walnuts
Vanilla Cream Sauce (see recipe)

Preheat oven to 375°F.
Combine the applesauce, lemon juice, brown sugar, raisins, and cinnamon. Turn into an ungreased, shallow, 1-quart casserole.
Blend the flour, granulated sugar, and butter until crumbly. Add the nuts. Sprinkle this mixture evenly over the applesauce mixture. Bake for 25 minutes, or until golden brown. Serve with Vanilla Cream Sauce.

Almond Peach Crisp

MAKES 4 TO 6 SERVINGS

Peaches have a natural affinity for the flavor of almonds, and though this may seem like regular peach crisp or peach cobbler, it isn't.

4 *large ripe peaches, peeled and sliced*
½ *cup tightly packed light or dark brown sugar*
½ *cup all-purpose flour*
½ *teaspoon cinnamon*
¼ *teaspoon nutmeg*
⅓ *cup butter*
½ *cup slivered or sliced almonds*
Heavy cream (optional)

Preheat oven to 375°F.

Butter a 9-inch-square pan or a 10-inch shallow porcelain quiche pan. Arrange peach slices in the pan. Combine brown sugar, flour, cinnamon, and nutmeg. Cut in the butter until mixture is crumbly. Sprinkle mixture over the peaches in the pan. Top with the almonds. Bake 30 minutes, until topping is crisp. Serve warm with cream to pour over it, if desired.

Apple Crunch

MAKES 4 TO 6 SERVINGS

Apples baked with a crunchy topping is a favorite all-American family dessert, quick to make and delicious served warm with cream or whipped cream. Autumn apples are juicier than those that have been stored for winter and spring consumption. If your apples are juicy, use less water or none at all.

4 large, tart cooking apples, pared, cored, and sliced
½ cup water (optional)
1 teaspoon cinnamon
1 cup crushed cornflakes
1 cup tightly packed brown sugar
½ cup butter, melted
Heavy cream or whipped cream

Preheat oven to 375°F.
Butter a shallow 2-quart casserole and arrange the apples in it. Add water, if needed. In a bowl, blend the cinnamon, cornflake crumbs, sugar, and butter. Pat the mixture over the apples. Bake until the apples are tender and the crust is browned, about 30 to 45 minutes. Serve warm with cream or whipped cream.

Old-fashioned Fruit Cobbler

∽

MAKES 6 SERVINGS

An old-fashioned cobbler is made with a rich shortcake topping.

THE FRUIT MIXTURE

2 *cups fresh pared, cored, and sliced apples, fresh pitted or canned peaches, blackberries, loganberries, blueberries, or pitted cherries*
¼ *cup sugar*
1 *tablespoon quick-cooking or minute tapioca*
3 *to 4 tablespoons butter*

THE COBBLER TOPPING

2 *cups all-purpose flour*
4 *teaspoons baking powder*
½ *teaspoon salt*
¼ *cup sugar*
⅓ *cup butter*
1 *egg, lightly beaten*
⅓ *cup milk*

Preheat oven to 425°F.

Butter a shallow 1½-quart baking dish and arrange the fruit in the dish in an even layer. Sprinkle with ¼ cup sugar and the tapioca. Dot with 3 to 4 tablespoons butter.

In a bowl, or in the work bowl of a food processor with the steel blade in place, combine the flour, baking powder, salt, and ¼ cup sugar. Blend in ⅓ cup butter, until mixture resembles moist crumbs. Combine the egg and the milk, and stir into the flour mixture.

Pat out the dough to about a ¾-inch thickness, and cut into

34

rounds. Place rounds on top of the fruit mixture in the pan. Bake for 30 minutes, or until the cobbler is bubbly around the edges and the topping is lightly browned.

Blueberry
Brown Betty

MAKES 6 SERVINGS

A *betty* is a fruit dessert that features fruit topped with a crumb mixture or fruit and a crumb mixture in alternating layers. The actual origin of the term *betty* is unknown, but recipes for fruit bettys were mentioned in print as far back as 1864. Apple brown betty is made by using apples instead of the blueberries. The *very best* version is to bake this with fresh wild blueberries, second choice is with fresh cultivated blueberries, and the third choice is with frozen berries.

4 cups fresh blueberries, or frozen, unthawed berries
½ cup sugar
½ cup all-purpose flour
¼ teaspoon salt
¼ cup butter

Preheat oven to 325°F.
Place blueberries in a 1½-quart baking dish or 6 individual ramekins that can go into the oven. Combine sugar, flour, and salt. Cut in the butter, until the mixture resembles coarse crumbs. Sprinkle mixture over the blueberries. Bake 35 minutes, or until the top is crisp and golden.

Plum Duff

MAKES 4 SERVINGS

The original Plum Duff was named by seamen. Webster describes *duff* as a stiff flour pudding that is boiled in a bag and contains fruits, nuts, and spices. In colonial times, duffs became very popular, and there developed a succession of lighter varieties, as is illustrated by the following recipes for New England Apple Duff and Blackberry Duff.

½ cup brown sugar

¼ cup butter, melted

1 egg, well beaten

1 cup cooked, seeded, and mashed unsweetened prunes

½ cup all-purpose flour

¼ teaspoon baking soda

¼ teaspoon baking powder

¼ teaspoon salt

1 tablespoon milk

Foamy Sauce (see following recipe)

Preheat oven to 350°F. Butter 4 custard cups well.

In a bowl, combine the brown sugar and melted butter. Stir in the egg and prunes. Stir together the flour, baking soda, baking powder, and salt, and add to the prune mixture along with the milk. Divide the mixture between the custard cups, filling them two-thirds full. Bake for 25 minutes. Serve warm with Foamy Sauce.

Foamy Sauce

MAKES ABOUT 1 CUP

½ cup sugar
½ cup butter
2 teaspoons water
1 egg, beaten
½ teaspoon vanilla

Combine the sugar, butter, and water in a saucepan over low heat, until well blended. Keep warm. Just before serving, stir in the beaten egg and vanilla.

New England Apple Duff

MAKES 6 SERVINGS

A duff of apples, such as this one, is far lighter than the original and more of a soufflé-like pudding. It is best served as soon as it comes out of the oven.

2 *pounds tart cooking apples, pared and cored*
¾ *cup hard cider*
1½ *tablespoons quick-cooking tapioca*
1 *cup plus* 6 *tablespoons sugar*
2 *eggs, separated*
Salt
¼ *teaspoon cream of tartar*
½ *teaspoon vanilla extract*
6 *tablespoons all-purpose flour*
¼ *teaspoon almond extract*

Preheat oven to 325°F. Butter a 2-quart casserole.

Cut the apples into eighths and place in a large saucepan. Combine the cider, tapioca, and 1 cup sugar, and stir until sugar is dissolved; pour over the apples. Bring to a boil, lower heat, and simmer for 10 to 12 minutes, until apples are soft but not mushy. Turn into the prepared casserole.

In a bowl, beat the egg yolks with a dash of salt and 6 tablespoons sugar; set aside. Beat the egg whites with another dash of salt, until foamy. Add the cream of tartar and whisk until stiff but not dry. Fold the egg yolk mixture into the egg whites. Add the vanilla, and fold in the flour and almond extract. Pour batter over the apples and bake 35 to 45 minutes, or until puffed and golden brown.

Blackberry Duff

MAKES 6 SERVINGS

This is cooked in the top of a double boiler. When fresh blackberries are not available, use frozen, unsugared berries without thawing them first.

2 *cups all-purpose flour*
2 *teaspoons baking powder*
1/2 *teaspoon salt*
1 *cup milk*
2 *eggs, beaten*
1 *cup sugar*
2 *cups blackberries*
Eggnog Sauce (see following recipe)

In a bowl, combine the flour, baking powder, and salt. Mix the milk with the eggs, and combine with the flour mixture. Set aside. Sprinkle the sugar over the blackberries and let stand 30 minutes. Stir the berries into the batter. Turn mixture into the top of a 2-quart double boiler, cover, and cook over boiling water for 2 hours. Do not stir. Serve warm with Eggnog Sauce.

Eggnog Sauce

MAKES ABOUT 2 1/2 CUPS

This is a great sauce for a lot of different fruit puddings, as well as for fresh sliced fruit.

2 *cups half-and-half*
1/2 *cup sugar*
4 *egg yolks*
A dash of salt
1/2 *teaspoon vanilla*
2 *tablespoons rum*

Scald the half-and-half, and stir the sugar into it. Beat the egg yolks with a dash of salt and the vanilla. Whisk in the scalded cream and cook over hot water, stirring constantly until thickened; do not boil. Flavor with the rum and serve warm.

Cranberry Pudding

MAKES 6 SERVINGS

Serving this with Brandy Butter Sauce makes a sweet contrast to the tartness of the berries.

½ cup butter

1½ cups cranberries

¼ cup coarsely chopped walnuts

¾ cup sugar

1 egg

½ cup all-purpose flour

½ cup whipped cream or Brandy Butter Sauce (see following recipe)

Preheat oven to 325°F. Spread 2 tablespoons of the butter over the bottom and sides of an 8- or 9-inch pie pan.

Wash the cranberries and pat dry. Spread the cranberries in an even layer in the bottom of the buttered pie pan. Top with the walnuts and half the sugar. In a mixing bowl, beat the egg with the remaining sugar, until the mixture is thick and creamy. Add the flour, a little at a time. Melt the remaining butter, and add to the batter. Pour batter over the cranberries and nuts. Bake for 45 minutes, or until the top is golden and a cake tester comes out clean. Cool to room temperature. Cut into wedges and lift with pie server onto serving plates, inverting each piece so the cranberries are on top. Serve with whipped cream or Brandy Butter Sauce.

Brandy Butter Sauce

MAKES ABOUT 2 CUPS

This sauce should be served hot. If you make it ahead, cover and refrigerate until a few minutes before serving. Return to high heat and stir until sauce comes to a boil.

1 *cup sugar*
½ *cup heavy cream*
½ *cup butter*
2 *tablespoons brandy*
2 *teaspoons vanilla*

Combine sugar, cream, and butter in a heavy saucepan. Over high heat, stirring constantly, bring mixture to a boil. Boil 3 minutes, continuing to stir. Remove from heat and add the brandy and vanilla.

Baked Lemon Pudding

MAKES 6 SERVINGS

This pudding bakes into two layers, a cakelike top with a soft lemon custard beneath.

1½ cups sugar
½ cup all-purpose flour
½ teaspoon baking powder
¼ teaspoon salt
3 eggs, separated
2 teaspoons grated lemon rind
¼ cup fresh lemon juice
2 tablespoons melted butter
1½ cups milk
1 cup heavy cream

Preheat oven to 350°F. Butter a 2-quart soufflé dish.

In a bowl, combine 1 cup of the sugar with the flour, baking powder, and salt. In another bowl, beat the egg yolks with the lemon rind and lemon juice, butter, and milk until foamy. Blend in the flour mixture and beat until smooth.

Whip the egg whites until stiff, and add the remaining sugar, a tablespoon at a time. Fold the stiff meringuelike mixture into the egg yolk mixture. Turn into the prepared baking dish. Set in another pan filled with about 1 inch of hot water. Bake for 45 minutes, until set. Chill 1 hour or more. Before serving, whip the cream until stiff and spread over the top of the pudding.

Old Maine Blueberry Batter Cake

MAKES ABOUT 8 SERVINGS

Although this sounds like it belongs in the category of cakes, it is really a delicious saucy blueberry baked pudding, which is wonderful served warm with cream to pour over it. It has a cakelike top with a blueberry sauce beneath. It is easier to make than blueberry pie, but the flavors are similar.

2 *cups fresh or frozen unsugared blueberries*
4 *tablespoons lemon juice*
1¾ *cups sugar*
1 *cup all-purpose flour*
1 *teaspoon baking powder*
¼ *teaspoon salt*
3 *tablespoons butter, at room temperature*
½ *cup milk*
1 *tablespoon cornstarch*
1 *cup boiling water*

Preheat oven to 350°F.

Butter a 9-inch-square or an 11-by-7-inch baking dish, and sprinkle the blueberries in an even layer over the bottom of the dish. Drizzle with lemon juice. In the large bowl of an electric mixer, combine ¾ cup sugar, the flour, baking powder, salt, and butter. Mix 1 minute until blended. Add the milk. Mix just until blended, and spoon this batter over the blueberries in the dish. Combine the remaining 1 cup sugar with the cornstarch, and sprinkle it over the batter. Pour the boiling water over it. Bake for 1 hour, until the top is golden and the blueberry sauce is bubbly around the edges. Serve warm.

Apple Pandowdy

MAKES 8 SERVINGS

There are at least three definite versions of pandowdy recorded in old cookbooks. All are native to the eastern part of the United States and all are baked apple puddings. One version goes like this: "Fill a heavy pot heaping full of pleasant apples, sliced. Add 1 cup molasses, 1 cup sugar, 1 cup water, 1 teaspoon cloves, 1 teaspoon cinnamon. Cover with baking powder biscuit crust, sloping it over the sides. Bake overnight. In the morning cut the hard crust into the apple. Eat with yellow cream or plain."

Another version is also called Apple Jonathan or Apple Pot Pie. This version includes 5 apples, 3 tablespoons each of sugar and molasses, nutmeg, cinnamon, and salt. The apples are baked until soft, then topped with a rich biscuit dough and served with hard sauce, lemon sauce, or nutmeg sauce.

In Maine, the old recipe starts with 3 slices of home-raised salt pork covered with apples, water, and molasses. This is cooked on top of the stove, and dumplings are added as for soup. In still another version, bread crumbs are combined with sugar and layered with the apples, and in still another, the apples are covered with a rich short crust. All are called Apple Pandowdy.

The version here is my favorite, a pandowdy made with a rich pastry that is inverted onto a serving plate after it is baked. It is rather simple to make and resembles an upside-down apple pie.

THE FILLING

4 *medium tart apples*
½ *cup sugar*
½ *teaspoon ground cinnamon*
¼ *teaspoon salt*
¼ *cup molasses or tightly packed brown sugar*
½ *cup water*

THE PASTRY

1 *cup all-purpose flour*
1 ½ *teaspoons baking powder*
¼ *teaspoon salt*
½ *cup butter or shortening*
⅓ *cup milk*

Preheat oven to 450°F. Lightly butter a shallow 1 ½- to 2-quart baking dish.

Pare the apples and slice. Place in bottom of the baking dish. Sprinkle with the sugar, cinnamon, and ¼ teaspoon salt. Mix molasses and water and pour over the apples.

In a mixing bowl, combine flour, baking powder, and ¼ teaspoon salt. Cut in butter or shortening, until mixture resembles coarse crumbs. Add milk and mix until dough holds together in a ball. On a lightly floured board, roll out dough to a thickness of about ⅓ inch to fit the top of the casserole. Place over the apples. Cut vents in the top. Bake 20 to 25 minutes, until golden.

Bird's Nest Pudding

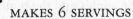

MAKES 6 SERVINGS

About the only agreement I could find as to what Bird's Nest Pudding should be like is that it includes apples. In Connecticut, a baked-custard mixture was poured over the apples before baking. In Vermont, the "home" of maple sugar, they serve a sour sauce over the pudding; while in Massachusetts, where there are fewer maple trees, it is served with maple sugar. In the old *White House Cookbook,* a historical document of American cookery of 1887, a Bird's Nest

45

Pudding recipe is given like this: "Core and peel eight apples, put in a dish, fill the places from which the cores have been taken with sugar and a little grated nutmeg; cover and bake. Beat the yolks of four eggs light, add two teacupfuls of flour, with three even teaspoonfuls of baking powder sifted with it, one pint of milk with a teaspoonful of salt; then add the whites of the eggs well beaten, pour over the apples and bake one hour in a moderate oven. Serve with sauce."

Contrast that recipe with this one from Vermont.

THE APPLES

8 *tart apples, pared and sliced*
¾ *cup sugar*
½ *teaspoon cinnamon*

THE BISCUIT TOPPING

2 *cups all-purpose flour*
½ *teaspoon baking soda*
1 *teaspoon cream of tartar*
½ *teaspoon salt*
¼ *cup lard*
1 *cup milk*

Sour Sauce (see following recipe)

Preheat oven to 350°F.

Butter a deep 2-quart casserole. Turn the apples into the buttered dish. Mix the sugar with the cinnamon, and sprinkle over the apples.

In a mixing bowl, mix the flour with the baking soda, cream of tartar, and salt. Cut in the lard, until blended into the flour. Add the milk to make a soft dough. Turn out onto a lightly floured board and knead 2 or 3 strokes. Pat to a 1-inch thickness, and fit over the apples. Bake 40 minutes, until the apples are done and the biscuit topping is golden. Serve with Sour Sauce.

Sour Sauce

MAKES ABOUT 1 CUP

½ *cup sugar*
1 *tablespoon all-purpose flour*
¾ *cup water*
2 *tablespoons butter*
2 *to* 3 *tablespoons white vinegar*

In a saucepan, combine the sugar, flour, water, and butter. Cook over medium to high heat, stirring constantly, until mixture comes to a boil and thickens. Add vinegar to taste.

Early American Apple Grunt

MAKES 6 SERVINGS

This version of apple grunt is baked, but in Colonial days, it was cooked in a Dutch oven hanging over an open fire. The name *grunt* presumably came from the sound the pudding made as it bubbled and grunted beneath the biscuitlike topping. If desired, this very same pudding also may be cooked over an open fire. Just cover it tightly and simmer for 1 hour.

4 *tablespoons butter*
⅓ *cup tightly packed brown sugar*
2 *cups pared, cored, and sliced fresh apples*
¾ *cup chopped walnuts*
1 *egg*
½ *cup granulated sugar*
⅓ *cup milk*
⅛ *teaspoon salt*
1 *teaspoon baking powder*
1 *cup all-purpose flour*
Whipped cream or ice cream

Preheat oven to 375°F.

Melt butter in an 8-inch baking pan. Remove 2 tablespoons of the butter and place in a mixing bowl. Add the brown sugar to the pan and stir until dissolved. Arrange apples over the brown sugar. Sprinkle with walnuts. Add egg, granulated sugar, and milk to the bowl with the 2 tablespoons butter. Mix in the salt and baking powder, then add the flour, mixing until smooth. Pour batter over the apples. Bake for 35 minutes. Loosen cake from sides of pan with spatula and invert onto a serving platter. Serve with whipped cream or ice cream.

Cape Cod Blueberry Grunt

MAKES 6 SERVINGS

Grunts are traditionally steamed or simmered rather than baked. Although sources disagree as to exactly *how* grunts are to be cooked, this version is steamed in a dish that is set in a pan of boiling water. This is also called Blueberry Slump.

2 *cups blueberries*
½ *cup water*
¼ *cup sugar*
2 *cups all-purpose flour*
4 *teaspoons baking powder*
1 *teaspoon salt*
2 *tablespoons shortening, at room temperature*
⅔ *cup milk*
Heavy cream

Butter a deep soufflé dish or baking dish. It should be a dish that will fit into a larger saucepan or pot for steaming. Combine the berries, water, and sugar in the dish.

In a bowl, mix the flour, baking powder, and salt. Blend in the shortening until it is evenly distributed. Stir in the milk until the dough is soft but not sticky. Turn out the dough onto a lightly floured board. Pat down with floured hands until about ¾ inch thick and about the same circumference as the baking dish containing the berries. Place the dough on top of the berries in the dish. Set dish on a rack in a pan or pot of boiling water. Cover pan or pot and cook 1 hour, keeping the water simmering constantly and adding more water as needed to keep it within 1 inch of the top of the dish. Serve warm with cream spooned over the grunt.

Louisa May Alcott's Apple Slump

MAKES 6 SERVINGS

The author of *Little Women* was so fond of this apple dessert that she named her Concord, Massachusetts, house Apple Slump.

6 *cups pared, cored, and sliced apples*
1 *cup sugar*
1 *teaspoon cinnamon*
½ *cup water*
1 ½ *cups sifted all-purpose flour*
¼ *teaspoon salt*
1 ½ *teaspoons baking powder*
½ *cup milk*
New England Nutmeg Sauce (see following recipe) or heavy cream

Combine apple slices, sugar, cinnamon, and water in a saucepan with a tight-fitting lid. Heat to boiling. Mix flour, salt, and baking powder in a bowl. Stir in enough milk to make a soft dough. Drop dough from a tablespoon onto the apple mixture. Cover and cook over low heat for 30 minutes. Serve warm with New England Nutmeg Sauce or heavy cream.

New England Nutmeg Sauce

MAKES ABOUT 1½ CUPS

1 *cup sugar*
1 *tablespoon flour*
1 *cup boiling water*
1 *tablespoon butter*
1 *teaspoon nutmeg*

Mix sugar and flour. Add the boiling water and cook, stirring, until sauce bubbles and thickens. Add butter and simmer 5 minutes. Remove from the heat and stir in nutmeg. Serve hot.

York County Farm Apple Mystery Pudding

MAKES 6 TO 8 SERVINGS

The farm kitchen is a busy place, and sometimes there's only enough time to stir up a quick dessert like this. This pudding tastes much like an apple pie and is served similarly.

¾ cup all-purpose flour

1 cup tightly packed light or dark brown sugar

1½ teaspoons baking powder

½ teaspoon salt

A dash of mace

A dash of cinnamon

2 eggs

1½ teaspoons vanilla

1½ cups pared, cored, and chopped tart apples

¾ cup chopped walnuts

Whipped cream

Cinnamon for topping

Preheat oven to 350°F. Butter a 9-inch pie pan.

In a large mixing bowl, combine the flour, brown sugar, baking powder, salt, mace, and cinnamon. Stir in the eggs and vanilla. Blend well. Fold in the apples and walnuts. Turn mixture into the pie pan and bake 25 to 30 minutes, or until browned and crusty on top. Serve with whipped cream and sprinkle with cinnamon.

Baked Apple Dumplings

MAKES 8 SERVINGS

Original apple dumplings were tied in muslin squares that had been dipped in water and floured on the inside. Then the dumplings were boiled in water for 1 hour. In other versions, the dumplings were steamed, but the modern preference is to bake them.

2 cups all-purpose flour
2 1/2 teaspoons baking powder
1/2 teaspoon salt
3/4 cup plus 8 teaspoons butter, chilled
3/4 cup milk
8 small apples, pared and cored
1/2 cup sugar
Apple jelly
Cinnamon sugar
Heavy cream or Cinnamon Hard Sauce (see following recipe)

Preheat oven to 375°F.
In a bowl, combine the flour, baking powder, and salt. Cut 3/4 cup butter into the flour mixture, until it is the size of peas. Add the milk, and stir with a fork until the dough holds together in a ball. Knead 2 or 3 times to make a smooth dough. Divide into 8 parts. On a floured board, roll out each piece of dough to 1/8-inch thickness. Place an apple on each part. Fill each hollow with 1 tablespoon sugar, 1 teaspoon butter, and a dab of apple jelly. Fold dough up over the apple, pressing the edges together. Place dumplings on a baking pan and sprinkle with cinnamon sugar. Make a vent hole, with a fork or the tip of a knife, on the top of each dumpling. Bake 30 to 40 minutes, until golden and the apples test done. Serve with cream or Cinnamon Hard Sauce.

Cinnamon Hard Sauce

MAKES ¾ CUP

¼ *cup butter*
1 *cup powdered sugar*
A *dash of salt*
½ *teaspoon cinnamon*
1 *tablespoon heavy cream*
1 *teaspoon vanilla*

Cream the butter and add the sugar gradually, mixing until fluffy. Add the salt, cinnamon, heavy cream, and vanilla. Beat well. Shape into a roll about 2 inches thick, and chill. Cut into slices and place a slice on top of each hot apple dumpling.

Rhubarb Pudding

MAKES 12 TO 15 SERVINGS

This soufflé-like pudding, with rhubarb on top of a buttery crust, is a perfect dessert for a crowd. One of its best features is that it can be made ahead of time.

THE CRUST

2 *cups all-purpose flour*
10 *tablespoons powdered sugar*
1 *cup butter*

THE FILLING

6 eggs
2½ cups granulated sugar
½ cup all-purpose flour
2 teaspoons baking powder
2 teaspoons vanilla
4 to 5 cups cubed fresh rhubarb
½ teaspoon salt
½ to 1 cup chopped walnuts (optional)

Whipped cream
Strawberries for garnish

Preheat oven to 350°F.

To prepare the crust, place 2 cups flour and the powdered sugar into a bowl. Cut in the butter, until the mixture resembles coarse crumbs. Press into the bottom of a 9-by-13-inch cake pan, and bake 15 to 20 minutes, until edges are a little browned.

To prepare the filling, beat the eggs and gradually add the granulated sugar; then beat in ½ cup flour, baking powder, and vanilla. Stir in the rhubarb, salt, and walnuts, if desired. Pour filling into the crust, and bake 30 to 40 minutes, until the top is crisp and golden. Serve with whipped cream and garnish with fresh strawberries.

Simple
Cooked Puddings

Puddings, both the simple, straightforward cooked and thickened creams that soothe and settle and those with subtle blends of flavor that defy analysis—spicy, fragrant mixtures—are an old American tradition. From the beginning of this country's history, puddings have been an important part of family dessert cookery.

These puddings are simple mixtures, based mainly on milk or fruit juices, cooked with cornstarch, flour, tapioca, or rice to thicken them. The ingredients are easily available, mostly on hand at all times, so that a dessert can always be whipped up. The milk in the puddings can be counted into the daily nutritional allocation necessary for good health.

Cooking with cornstarch or flour as thickeners requires a little experience and/or common sense. One of the frequent troubles is that the mixture may break down after cooking because:

1. The mixture may be overcooked.
2. The mixture may be undercooked, leaving some of the uncooked starch in the blend, which causes the breakdown. Gelatinization occurs at approximately 195°F. for both cornstarch and flour.
3. There may be too much cornstarch or flour in the mixture.
4. The mixture may be overbeaten after cooking.
5. There may be too much sugar in the mixture, causing the starch to break down.
6. The presence of an acid (such as lemon juice, fruit juice, or vinegar) may break down a mixture that has thickened while cooking. Precaution: Be sure to thoroughly cook puddings that have these ingredients added. (For stove cooking, boil the mixture vigorously 3 minutes, stirring continuously to avoid scorching. If you have a microwave oven, put the whole mixture into a glass bowl and cook 10 minutes on high, stirring occasionally, so that the edges won't burn. The slightest bit of uncooked mixture in the presence of a fruit acid can cause it to break down.)

Vanilla Cornstarch Pudding

MAKES 4 SERVINGS

Cornstarch puddings are all-time American family favorites. Packaged pudding mixes are simply cornstarch, sugar, salt, and flavoring. When you make your own, not only do you save money, but you have better and fresher flavor.

3 *tablespoons cornstarch*
⅓ *cup sugar*
A dash of salt
¼ *cup cold milk*
2 *cups milk, scalded*
1 *teaspoon vanilla*

In a heavy saucepan or in the top of a metal double boiler, combine the cornstarch, sugar, and salt. Add the cold milk. Add the scalded milk slowly, whisking all the time. Cook, stirring constantly, over low heat or over simmering water until the mixture thickens. Be sure that the mixture reaches 195°F. (use a candy thermometer), so that the cornstarch is completely cooked. Cover and cook an additional 10 minutes. Stir in the vanilla, cover, and cool.

COCONUT PUDDING: Add ½ cup flaked coconut to the milk as you scald it.

BUTTERSCOTCH PUDDING: Omit the granulated sugar. Melt 1 tablespoon butter and add ⅓ cup brown sugar, cook, and stir until sugar melts. Add sugar slowly to the hot, scalded milk, and stir until well blended. Mix cornstarch and salt with the cold milk, and proceed as directed above.

CHOCOLATE PUDDING: Add 2 squares (2 ounces) unsweetened chocolate to the milk as you scald it. Proceed as directed above. Whip ½ cup heavy cream, and fold into the pudding after it has cooled.

Cocoa Cornstarch Pudding

MAKES 4 SERVINGS

¼ *cup dark unsweetened cocoa*
½ *cup sugar*
3 *tablespoons cornstarch*
A dash of salt
2 *cups whole milk (see Note)*
1 *teaspoon vanilla*
Heavy cream

In a heavy-bottomed saucepan or in the top of a double boiler, combine the cocoa, sugar, cornstarch, and salt. Slowly add the milk, stirring well to keep mixture lump-free. (The milk mixes better if it is slightly warmed, but not hot.) Cook over low heat or boiling water until pudding is thickened. In the top of a double boiler, the pudding will not reach a boil very easily, but will reach 200°F. (Check temperature with a candy thermometer.) Cover and cook over low heat for 5 minutes, or until you can no longer taste the cornstarch. Stir until cooled. Add the vanilla. Turn into serving dish, cover with wax paper or plastic wrap, and chill. Serve with cream to pour over it.

NOTE: For a low-calorie pudding, reduce sugar to ¼ cup and use skim milk instead of whole milk; the flavor will not be as rich.

Spanish Cream

MAKES 4 SERVINGS

Spanish cream is an old-fashioned, Sunday-dinner dessert. The difference between Spanish cream and a regular cornstarch pudding is that it has gelatin added to the pudding along with egg instead of cornstarch, and the whites are whipped to lighten the mixture. As the cream cools and sets, it divides into two layers.

2 *cups cold milk*
1 *package (1 tablespoon) unflavored gelatin*
⅓ *cup sugar*
2 *eggs*
½ *teaspoon vanilla*
Fresh berries for garnish (optional)
Slightly sweetened whipped cream for garnish (optional)

In a custard cup or small bowl, mix ¼ cup of the cold milk with the gelatin. Set aside. In heavy saucepan, heat the remaining milk. Add the sugar and stir until sugar is dissolved. Separate the eggs; put the yolks in one small bowl, the whites in another. Whisk a portion of the hot milk into the egg yolks, and then return mixture to saucepan with the rest of the hot milk and sugar. Cook over low heat until the mixture coats the back of a wooden spoon (about 160°F.). Stir in the gelatin mixture until dissolved. Remove from heat. Add the vanilla. Cool. Whisk the egg whites until stiff, and fold them into the pudding. Pour into a bowl or fancy 4-cup mold that has been dipped in cold water, and chill until set, about 2 hours.

Unmold onto a serving plate. Decorate with berries and whipped cream, if desired.

CHOCOLATE SPANISH CREAM: Add 2 squares (2 ounces) unsweetened chocolate to the milk while scalding it. Beat until blended.

COFFEE SPANISH CREAM: Add 2 tablespoons instant coffee powder to the milk while scalding it.

Bavarian Cream

MAKES 6 SERVINGS

Bavarian cream differs from Spanish cream in that it has not only gelatin added to the mixture, but heavy cream as well. It does not separate into two layers as it sets, and the mold is lined with sponge cake or ladyfingers.

1 *cup milk*
2 *egg yolks, lightly beaten*
2 *tablespoons granulated sugar*
1 *package (1 tablespoon) unflavored gelatin*
¼ *cup cold water*
2 *egg whites*
1 *cup heavy cream*
3 *tablespoons powdered sugar*
1 *teaspoon vanilla*
Sponge Cake (see recipe) or ladyfingers

In a heavy saucepan, heat the milk until scalded. Beat the egg yolks with the granulated sugar, and beat in a portion of the hot milk. Return the entire mixture to the saucepan with the rest of the hot milk, and cook over low heat until mixture thickens and coats the back of a wooden spoon (or reaches 160°F.). Mix the gelatin with the cold water and let soften a few minutes. Stir gelatin mixture into the hot mixture. Remove from the heat and let cool. Beat egg whites until stiff. Fold egg whites into the custard. Turn custard into a metal bowl over ice water and stir, scraping from the bottom and sides of the pan, until the mixture begins to set and thicken. Whip the cream until stiff, and fold into the custard. Blend in the powdered sugar and vanilla. Line individual molds or a large mold with strips of Sponge Cake or ladyfingers. Turn custard into the mold and cover. Chill until set.

Tapioca Cream Pudding

MAKES 4 TO 6 SERVINGS

Tapioca is a starch obtained from the cassava root, a tropical American shrub. Tapioca is available in little round balls or ground into a coarse granular form that cooks more quickly and is the easiest to use. Although it is not always mentioned, I like to mix quick-cooking tapioca into the liquid in which it will be cooked and allow it to stand about 15 minutes before cooking. Tapioca thickens a pudding by swelling and becoming transparent. It continues to thicken while cooking. A tapioca-thickened pudding should be stirred while cooking, but overstirring while cooling tends to disrupt the tapioca particles, resulting in a sticky, gelatinous mixture.

1½ *tablespoons quick-cooking or minute tapioca*
2 *cups milk*
⅓ *cup sugar*
2 *egg yolks, lightly beaten*
2 *egg whites*
1 *teaspoon vanilla*

Sprinkle the tapioca over the milk in a heavy saucepan. Let stand 15 minutes to soften. Place over low heat. Stir and heat until mixture just comes to a boil. Add half the sugar to the egg yolks. Pour a small amount of the hot mixture into the yolk mixture. Transfer both mixtures to the top of a double boiler, and cook 5 minutes longer. Cool. Whip the egg whites with the remaining sugar and vanilla until stiff. Fold the egg whites into the pudding. Cover and chill.

Simmered Rice Pudding

MAKES 4 TO 6 SERVINGS

Rice, another thickening agent, is classic to Early American puddings, as well as to the puddings of today. This is a great way to use leftover rice. It can be any kind, short- or long-grain, quick-cooking, converted, brown or white, just as long as it is cooked. This is a stirred custard, with the egg whites whipped and folded into the pudding after cooking.

2 *cups milk*
1 *cup cooked rice*
2 *egg yolks*
½ *cup sugar*
2 *egg whites, stiffly beaten*
1 *teaspoon vanilla*
Cinnamon sugar

In a heavy saucepan, scald the milk; add the rice. In a bowl, beat the egg yolks with the sugar. Add the hot mixture slowly to the egg yolks. Return the entire mixture to the saucepan and cook over low heat, stirring constantly, until thickened. Fold in the egg whites and add the vanilla. Cover and chill, or serve immediately, sprinkled with cinnamon sugar.

Vanilla Rice Cream

MAKES 6 SERVINGS

To fancy up an old-fashioned rice pudding, gelatin and whipped cream are added to this classic. It is a wholesome family dessert and a perfect base for fresh berries in season. It is often served with ice cream toppings such as caramel, butterscotch, or chocolate syrup and chopped nuts.

3 *cups milk*
3 *tablespoons short-grain rice*
1 *package (1 tablespoon) unflavored gelatin*
3 *tablespoons cold water*
1 *tablespoon sugar*
1 *teaspoon vanilla*
1 *cup heavy cream, whipped*

In a heavy saucepan, combine 2 cups milk and rice. Place over low heat and cook until the rice is tender, about 30 minutes. Mix the gelatin with the cold water and let soften a few minutes. In a bowl, combine the gelatin mixture, sugar, and 1 cup milk. Mix into the hot-milk-and-rice mixture. Cool. Add the vanilla, and then fold in the whipped cream. Spoon into dessert dishes and chill.

PINEAPPLE RICE CREAM: Before chilling, add 1 cup thoroughly drained canned crushed pineapple to the rice cream.

Strawberry Flummery

MAKES 4 TO 6 SERVINGS

A flummery is a pudding of milk or fruit juice that is thickened with flour or cornstarch. It was originally made of oatmeal steeped in water. The Shakers were especially attentive to the needs of their elders, and flummeries were included in special diets for the aged. Flummeries are also a favorite dessert in the East and in parts of the Midwest. Cornstarch-thickened puddings have the quality of "setting," and they can be poured into a ring mold or individual molds while still warm to be unmolded later onto a chilled serving platter. Flummeries were often set ring molds.

3 *cups milk*
½ *cup granulated sugar*
⅓ *cup cornstarch*
A *dash of salt*
1 *egg*
1 *teaspoon vanilla*
1 *pint ripe strawberries, hulled*
2 *tablespoons powdered sugar*

In a heavy saucepan, heat the milk to simmering. In a mixing bowl, combine the granulated sugar, cornstarch, and salt. When milk is simmering, add the sugar mixture slowly, whisking to keep it smooth. Cook over low heat, whisking constantly, until the mixture comes to a boil and thickens. Whisk the egg in a small bowl and add a small portion of the hot mixture to it. Return the egg mixture to the saucepan and cook, stirring constantly, 3 to 4 minutes longer; do not boil.

Remove from the heat and stir in the vanilla. If you wish to mold the flummery, turn it immediately into a 6-cup ring mold that has been rinsed and is still wet. Cover and chill. Unmold onto a chilled platter. Or, turn the flummery into a serving bowl and cover with wax paper pressed down onto the surface of the pudding. Chill at least 2 hours.

Before serving, clean the berries and halve them. Place halves in a bowl and sprinkle with powdered sugar. Toss to coat. Arrange strawberries on top of the flummery and serve immediately.

Blueberry Flummery

MAKES 6 SERVINGS

This is the thickened-fruit-juice variety of flummery that is set in a ring mold and served with additional berries and whipped cream.

4 cups blueberries
1 cup water
3 tablespoons cornstarch
¼ teaspoon salt
½ cup sugar
Grated rind and juice of 1 lemon
Fresh or thawed frozen whole blueberries, to serve
Whipped cream

In a saucepan, combine 4 cups blueberries and the water. Bring to a boil and simmer 10 minutes, until blueberries are soft. Purée the berries, then pour through a fine sieve to remove skin and seeds. Measure and add water to equal 2 cups liquid. Cool. Combine the cornstarch, salt, and sugar. Mix the blueberry juice with the lemon rind and lemon juice, and blend juice mixture into the cornstarch mixture. Place over medium-low heat and cook, stirring constantly, until mixture just comes to a boil and is thickened. Pour immediately into wet individual molds or a 3-cup ring mold. Cover and chill.

Unmold onto a chilled platter, fill the center with whole blueberries, and serve with whipped cream.

Blackberry Flummery

MAKES 6 SERVINGS

This version of a flummery is a cooked berry mixture, sweetened and slightly thickened, which has whipped cream folded in after it has cooled.

4 *cups fresh or frozen blackberries*
1 *cup sugar*
1 *tablespoon cornstarch*
¼ *cup water*
1 *cup heavy cream, whipped*

In a saucepan, simmer the berries with the sugar for 15 minutes, stirring occasionally. Mix the cornstarch with water until dissolved, and stir into the hot berry mixture. Cook until thickened. Cool. Fold in the whipped cream and chill until ready to serve.

Pennsylvania Dutch Blackberry Mush

MAKES 6 TO 8 SERVINGS

Desserts for the Pennsylvania Dutch were more likely to be "poverty puddings" from the thrifty Colonial past. This dessert, however, showed promise and turned out to be quite good, with lemon and sugar added to the thickened cooked blackberries.

One 16-ounce package frozen blackberries, or 1 quart fresh blackberries
½ cup water
½ cup sugar
¼ cup all-purpose flour
2 tablespoons lemon juice
Heavy cream

Place the berries in a heavy saucepan. Add the water and cover. Cook over medium heat 15 minutes, or until the blackberries are soft. Put the berries through a strainer to remove the seeds. Mix the sugar and flour, and stir into the blackberry mixture. Return to the heat, bring to a boil, and cook, stirring constantly, until thickened. Add the lemon juice. Pour into individual dessert dishes and chill. Serve with cream to pour over each serving.

Scandinavian Berry Pudding

MAKES 6 TO 8 SERVINGS

While cooks in the East were making flummeries, a very similar kind of pudding was being made by Scandinavians in the Midwest. This is the very best when made with plump, fresh-picked berries. However, that isn't always possible, so the second choice is to make it with the berries you have frozen yourself. If that still isn't possible, buy unsugared berries that have been frozen individually.

6½ cups water
6 cups fresh berries (strawberries, blueberries, raspberries, loganberries, blackberries, huckleberries, or any combination of these)
½ cup sugar
1 cinnamon stick
½ cup cornstarch
Whipped cream

In a large saucepan, combine 6 cups water, the berries, sugar, and cinnamon stick. Bring to a boil and cook 3 minutes. Meanwhile, combine the cornstarch and ½ cup water. Slowly stir the cornstarch mixture into the boiling berry mixture. Cook until thickened and clear, stirring constantly. Reduce heat, cover, and simmer 10 minutes more. Remove from heat and cool, covered. Serve with whipped cream.

Winter Fruit Soup

~

MAKES 8 TO 10 SERVINGS

Drying fruits such as apples, pears, apricots, peaches, plums, or prunes was one of the earliest forms of preserving abundance from the orchard and garden. Today, most of us buy commercially dried fruit. Fruit soup is still a favorite country dessert. Some serve it ladled over creamy rice pudding, and others serve it with plain cream poured over it.

One 8-ounce bag mixed dried fruits
One 8-ounce bag dried apricots
2 quarts water
2 tablespoons quick-cooking tapioca
1 cup sugar
3 cinnamon sticks
Lemon juice to taste
Light cream, half-and-half, or heavy cream

In a large saucepan, combine the mixed fruits, apricots, water, tapioca, sugar, and cinnamon sticks. Bring to a boil, cover, and simmer over low heat 25 to 30 minutes, or until fruits are fork-tender. Taste, and add lemon juice. Serve hot or cold with cream to pour over the soup.

Chilled Chocolate Pudding

MAKES 6 SERVINGS

This is a rich, chocolate-lover's dessert. It is best to divide the pudding into individual custard cups or dessert glasses, leaving enough room at the top for the whipped cream topping. If it is chilled in a large bowl, you need to spoon out individual servings, which are not as pretty.

6 *squares (6 ounces) semisweet chocolate*
1/4 *cup water*
1 *teaspoon vanilla*
3 *eggs, separated*
A dash of salt
1 *cup heavy cream*
3 *tablespoons powdered sugar*
Finely chopped pistachio nuts

Break the chocolate into pieces and place in a heavy saucepan. Add the water and heat over low heat, stirring until the chocolate is melted. Remove from the heat and stir in the vanilla. Beat in the egg yolks, one at a time, beating after each addition. Return to low heat, cook, stirring, for 1 minute. Cool. Beat the egg whites with a dash of salt until stiff. Fold the beaten whites into the chocolate mixture. Turn into 6 individual dessert dishes. Chill. When ready to serve, whip the cream with the powdered sugar. Top the desserts with the whipped cream and sprinkle with chopped pistachio nuts.

Norwegian Cream Pudding

MAKES 6 SERVINGS

This is one of the little-known wonders of the dessert-pudding world, known mainly to Norwegians who offer the recipe that calls for a gallon of heavy cream at a time. No wonder it hasn't spread beyond the Scandinavian-American community! Because of its strange (though completely simple) method of preparation, and the rather unappealing-looking combination of ingredients, I had never tried it. Not until a wonderful cook and friend, Eva Rogness, took me through the procedure step-by-step did I finally understand how *Rommegrot* is prepared and what it tastes like when perfectly done. Start with a really good, rich cream—don't use the ultra-pasteurized variety, which has too low a butterfat content to work. The cream is cooked with flour to make a very thick paste. Under continuous cooking, the butterfat renders out, which you save for serving later. Two cups of rich heavy cream will produce about ½ cup melted butter. The resulting pudding is silky-smooth and is served with the warm melted butter and cinnamon sugar. This is one of the most delicious and simple desserts I have ever tasted!

2 cups rich heavy cream
⅓ cup all-purpose flour
1½ cups milk
A dash of salt
½ cup plus 2 tablespoons sugar
1 tablespoon ground cinnamon

Pour the cream into a very heavy 3- to 4-quart saucepan. Bring to a boil over medium heat. Put flour into a sieve and sprinkle it over the boiling cream, beating with a whisk to keep the mixture smooth. Then use a wooden spoon and cook over low heat for 15 minutes, or until the mixture is very stiff, comes away from the sides of the pan, and is reduced in volume. Continue to cook and stir until the butterfat separates from the paste. Pour off the butterfat into a small serving dish and keep warm. Slowly beat or whisk in the milk, salt, and 2 tablespoons sugar. Bring to a boil, stirring constantly, and beat until smooth and thickened. Pour the pudding through a sieve into a serving bowl. (Or process in blender or food processor until smooth.) Stir together the cinnamon and ½ cup sugar. Serve the pudding hot or at room temperature in dessert bowls, pour the butterfat over it, and sprinkle with the cinnamon sugar.

Kiss Pudding

MAKES 8 SERVINGS

As sweet as a kiss! This old-fashioned fancy pudding is first cooked, then baked with a meringue, and then chilled before serving. "The sweet liquor which settles to the bottom in cooling is to be served as a sauce," according to *The New Buckeye Cookbook.*

4 *cups milk*
1 ¼ *cups sugar*
6 *tablespoons cornstarch*
A *dash of salt*
½ *cup light cream*
4 *eggs, separated*
1 *teaspoon vanilla*
¼ *cup grated or flaked coconut*

Preheat oven to 400°F. Butter a 2-quart soufflé dish or casserole and sprinkle with sugar.

In a saucepan, heat 3½ cups milk to boiling. While the milk heats, mix the remaining milk with ¼ cup sugar, the cornstarch, salt, cream, and egg yolks in a small bowl. Add a small amount of the hot milk to the egg yolk mixture and beat well, then combine the mixture with the rest of the hot milk. Return to the heat and whisk constantly, until mixture just barely comes to a boil. Remove immediately and turn into the prepared dish or casserole.

In a large bowl, beat the egg whites until frothy, then gradually add 1 cup sugar along with the vanilla. Spread the meringue on top of the pudding. Bake 15 minutes, or until lightly browned and puffed; it will look like a soufflé. Remove from the oven and sprinkle with coconut. Chill 3 to 4 hours before serving.

Old-style Baked
and
Steamed Puddings

Hearty steamed and boiled puddings clearly have their roots in British cookery. Steamed puddings are most often associated with the cooking of the East and parts of the Midwest, although a few steamed puddings are part of holiday meals in other parts of the country. Adaptations were made as cooking methods changed. In the 1700s, two forms of ovens developed around the fireplace—the built-in brick oven and a portable reflector or "tin kitchen" that stood on the hearth and caught the heat radiated from the fire. In this latter oven they baked roasts, puddings, pies, and cakes.

Puddings were desserts that could be made even when ingredients were scarce. Poverty pudding, penny pudding, poor man's puddings, and economical puddings were made of very basic ingredients: eggs, flour, and milk, some with a few additional ingredients such as a spoonful of butter, chopped suet, or perhaps a few raisins. Cottage pudding, much like a white cake, is unembellished with expensive ingredients and is found in old cookbooks of the South, Midwest, and West, as well as in those of the East. Batter pudding has about the same ingredients but differs in that the eggs are separated and the whites whipped and folded into the mixture.

In *The New Buckeye Cookbook,* dedicated to "plucky housewives who master their work instead of letting the work master them," there are no less than twenty-seven pages describing different kinds of puddings: Apple, Almond, Batter Apple Pudding, Scottish Pudding, Bachelor's Pudding, Danish Pudding, bread and rice puddings, all recipes given in generalities.

Rice puddings and bread puddings were also economy desserts. Rice pudding—with its roots in northern European tradition—and bread pudding—a way to recycle stale bread—served to stretch expensive ingredients.

Sugar was an expensive ingredient in early Colonial days, and it was molasses that was used to sweeten pies, puddings, cookies, and candies. It wasn't until twenty years after the death of Abraham Lincoln that the sugar bowl replaced the molasses pitcher on American dinner tables. At that time, a process involving a vacuum pan and centrifuge came into use to remove the sugar crystals. This new process lowered the cost of refining, so that the cost of sugar came within the reach of common people.

Early sugarcane processing produced molasses as we know it today, and by continued boiling down of the sugarcane sap, sugar crystals were produced and molasses was the by-product. Today, molasses is not entirely a by-product of sugar refining. It is made with pure sugarcane juices, clarified, reduced, and blended with the dark syrup produced by first- and second-strike centrifugal juices to achieve a consistency of mellowness, flavor, and color. Blackstrap molasses is the inky substance left at the bottom of the barrel after the third and final extraction of sugar crystals. Much blackstrap molasses finds its way into health-food stores; the rest is either distilled into industrial alcohol or made into animal feed. Sorghum molasses is the boiled-down sweet sap from sorghum, the brown corn grown mostly for animal feed.

Slightly more caloric than refined sugar, molasses has 50 calories per tablespoon to sugar's 45. Molasses contains iron, potassium, a little calcium, phosphorus, thiamine, and riboflavin. Blackstrap molasses contains more vitamins and minerals than lighter molasses and 43 calories per tablespoon, but has a tarry and astringent flavor. It cannot be substituted for lighter molasses in cooking.

Original Injun' Puddin'

MAKES 8 SERVINGS

Original Injun' Puddin' is one of the oldest of New England's desserts and is probably the result of the shortage of more refined ingredients. This led to the experimentation with rougher meals and sweeteners—corn, whole meal, maple syrup, and molasses—and resulted in puddings and other sweets that still linger in our repertoire.

5 cups milk
⅔ cup dark molasses
⅓ cup sugar
½ cup yellow cornmeal
¾ teaspoon cinnamon
¾ teaspoon nutmeg
½ teaspoon salt
4 tablespoons butter
Heavy cream

Preheat the oven to 300°F.

In a saucepan, heat 4 cups of the milk with all of the remaining ingredients, except the cream. Cook 20 minutes, until the mixture thickens. Pour into a 1½-quart casserole and add the remaining 1 cup milk. Do not stir. Place in the oven and bake 3 hours without stirring. Serve warm with cream to pour over it.

RHODE ISLAND INDIAN PUDDING: Use white cornmeal instead of yellow in this authentic recipe.

DURGIN PARK INDIAN PUDDING: Add 1 egg and a pinch of baking powder before baking the pudding.

77

New England Indian Pudding

MAKES 6 SERVINGS

Long, slow baking is necessary for the classic Indian pudding to cook and develop its flavor and its texture. The resulting pudding will be soft and may separate. Blackstrap molasses or dark molasses should be used for the most authentic flavor.

¼ cup yellow cornmeal
1 cup cold milk
3 cups milk, scalded
½ cup dark molasses
1 teaspoon salt
¼ cup sugar
1 teaspoon cinnamon
4 tablespoons butter
Heavy cream

Preheat oven to 300°F. Butter a 2-quart baking or soufflé dish.
In a small bowl, mix the cornmeal with ¼ cup of the cold milk. Stir mixture into the scalded milk and cook over low heat for 20 minutes, stirring frequently. Add the molasses, salt, sugar, cinnamon, and butter. Pour into the prepared baking dish and pour the remaining ¾ cup cold milk over the top. Place in the oven and bake 3 hours. Remove from the oven and let stand at least 30 minutes before serving. Serve warm with cream to pour over it.

New England Hasty Pudding

MAKES ABOUT 10 SERVINGS

Hasty pudding of the New England variety is a cornmeal mush. It was often made, chilled, sliced, and fried. It was sometimes shaped in glasses or empty baking-powder tins to make round slices. The slices were floured and fried in butter. An old-time sauce for the pudding was New Orleans molasses. Butter and maple syrup is another favorite topping. Hasty pudding was a favorite supper dish on New England farms, where it was sometimes called "stir-about pudding." It was cooked in a big iron kettle, and as the children waited for the fresh warm milk that was to be poured over it, they would watch it pop and sputter. Sometimes it was poured into a big yellow bowl and served for dessert. Leftover pudding was turned into a loaf pan, then sliced and fried for breakfast.

6 *cups water*
1 *teaspoon salt*
1 *cup yellow cornmeal*

In a 2-quart saucepan, bring the water and salt to a rapid boil. Slowly add the cornmeal, stirring with a whisk to keep the mixture free from lumps. Boil 1 minute. Place over a pan of boiling water and cover. Steam 30 minutes, until the pudding has thickened. Serve hot with molasses, maple syrup, or brown sugar; milk, cream, or butter; and nutmeg or cinnamon.

NOTE: If you have any left over, pour into a buttered loaf pan. Cover and refrigerate. Unmold and cut chilled pudding into slices. Heat about 1 tablespoon butter in a heavy skillet and add the slices; brown on both sides until heated through. Serve with molasses, maple syrup, or brown sugar and more butter.

Old Virginia Hasty Pudding

MAKES 4 SERVINGS

Literally "whipped up in haste," this pudding makes a delicious quick dessert out of the most basic ingredients: eggs, milk, a bit of flour, and a bit of sugar. It must be eaten in haste as well because, like a soufflé, it settles almost immediately as it comes from the oven. We found it delicious served with wine sauce (as the old *Virginia Cookbook* recommends); or you can serve with fresh sliced strawberries and cream.

4 eggs, separated
6 tablespoons sugar
1/3 cup all-purpose flour
1 cup milk
A dash of salt
Wine Sauce (see following recipe) or melted butter

Preheat oven to 350°F. Butter a flat, rimmed, ovenproof or metal platter.

In a large mixing bowl, whisk the egg whites with 4 tablespoons sugar, until stiff and meringuelike. In another bowl, beat the egg yolks with the remaining 2 tablespoons sugar, adding the flour, milk, and salt, keeping the mixture smooth and creamy. Fold the yolk mixture into the whipped whites. Turn out onto the buttered platter and bake 20 minutes, until puffy and golden. Serve immediately with Wine Sauce or melted butter.

Wine Sauce

1 *cup sugar*
¼ *cup boiling water*
¼ *cup butter*
White port or sherry to taste
Nutmeg to taste

In a saucepan, heat the sugar with the boiling water. Add the butter and port or sherry and nutmeg to taste. Stir to combine.

Fluffy Rice
Custard Pudding

MAKES 4 SERVINGS

Simply cooked rice is delicious served with chocolate, butter-scotch, or fruit sauces. Leftover rice baked with egg and milk makes a delicious family dessert. If you separate the eggs, and fold the whites into the pudding before baking, the result is a fluffy, soufflé-like rice pudding.

2 *cups milk*
1 *cup cooked rice*
2 *eggs, separated*
½ *cup sugar*
A dash of salt
½ *teaspoon vanilla*

Preheat oven to 375°F. Butter a 2-quart baking dish.

Combine the milk and rice in a heavy saucepan and heat until the milk is scalded. Beat the egg whites with half the sugar until stiff; set aside. In another bowl (without washing the beaters), beat the egg yolks with the remaining sugar and the salt. Add the hot milk-rice mixture slowly to the yolk mixture. Return to the saucepan and cook over low heat, stirring, just until the custard coats the back of a wooden spoon. Do not overheat or boil, or the mixture will separate. Fold in the egg whites. Add the vanilla. Spoon into the prepared baking dish. Bake 10 to 15 minutes, until the top is lightly browned. Serve warm.

Old Williamsburg Raisin Rice Pudding

MAKES 6 SERVINGS

4 *eggs*
¾ *cup sugar*
2 *cups milk*
1⅓ *cups cooked rice*
1 *teaspoon lemon juice*
2 *teaspoons vanilla*
¾ *cup raisins*
½ *teaspoon cinnamon*
1 *tablespoon butter, melted*
Heavy cream

Preheat oven to 350°F. Butter a 2-quart casserole.

Combine the eggs, sugar, milk, rice, lemon juice, vanilla, raisins, and cinnamon. Pour into the prepared casserole. Place in a larger pan.

Fill outside pan with enough boiling water to come about three-quarters of the way up the sides of the casserole. Bake, uncovered, for 45 minutes, or until the custard is set. Drizzle with the melted butter. Serve with cream to pour over it.

Poor Man's Rice Pudding

MAKES 6 SERVINGS

In Colonial days, sugar was more expensive and less available than molasses, so molasses was considered a "poor man's" sweetener. Molasses adds delicious flavor and amber color to this pudding.

¼ *cup rice*
4 *cups milk*
½ *teaspoon salt*
⅓ *cup molasses*
½ *teaspoon cinnamon*
½ *cup raisins*
1 *tablespoon butter*

Preheat oven to 300°F. Butter a 2-quart casserole or ovenproof pudding bowl.

Combine rice, milk, salt, molasses, and cinnamon. Pour into prepared casserole or pudding bowl. Bake, uncovered, for 3 hours. Stir three times with a fork during the first hour of baking, so that the rice will not settle. After the first hour, stir in the raisins and the butter. Serve warm.

Basic Bread Pudding

MAKES 6 TO 8 SERVINGS

There are many combinations that make an excellent bread pudding. If you prefer a pudding that is sweeter, increase the sugar. You may use different kinds of breads. Brioche, cardamom-flavored Christmas bread, egg breads, rye or whole wheat bread, or plain white bread all work. Increase the bread for a firmer pudding; add it diced or layer it in slices for different effects. Orange peel, lemon peel, rum, flavored liqueurs, raisins, figs, chopped apple, dates, walnuts or other nuts, as well as many different spices and/or chocolate, all make delicious variations to bread pudding. To make it fluffy, separate the eggs and beat the whites, folding them in at the last minute before baking. Here is the basic recipe.

2 *cups dry bread cubes*
4 *tablespoons butter*
4 *cups milk, scalded*
½ *cup sugar*
4 *eggs, lightly beaten*
½ *teaspoon salt*
1 *teaspoon vanilla*

Preheat oven to 325°F. Butter a 2½-quart baking dish.

Add the bread and butter to the scalded milk. Cool. Add the sugar, eggs, salt, and vanilla. Pour into the prepared baking dish. Bake 1 hour until set. Serve plain or with cream to pour over it, with whipped cream, or with Lemon Sauce, Brandy Sauce, Rum Custard Sauce, or Golden Brown Sugar Sauce (see recipes).

Orange and Currant Bread Pudding

MAKES 6 TO 8 SERVINGS

¼ cup *Grand Marnier, or other orange-flavored liqueur*
2 cups *dry brioche bread cubes*
4 tablespoons *butter*
4 cups *milk, scalded*
4 eggs, *separated*
½ cup *sugar*
1 teaspoon *vanilla*
¼ cup *currants*
2 teaspoons *grated orange rind*
Heavy cream or Vanilla Cream Sauce (see recipe)

Preheat oven to 325°F. Butter a 2-quart baking dish.

Pour the Grand Marnier or other orange-flavored liqueur over the bread. Add the soaked bread and the butter to the scalded milk. Cool. Combine the yolks with the sugar and the vanilla, and then mix into the bread mixture, along with the currants and orange rind. Whip the egg whites until stiff. Fold whites into the bread pudding; turn into the prepared baking dish. Bake 1 hour until set. Serve with heavy cream or Vanilla Cream Sauce to pour over individual servings.

New Orleans Bread Pudding with Whiskey Sauce

MAKES ABOUT 8 SERVINGS

This is a bread pudding of the South. New Orleans restaurants offer bread pudding with whiskey sauce. The best is tender and eggy, served in a puddle of a buttery sauce flavored with whiskey.

½ pound stale bread (see Note)
4 cups milk
4 eggs
2 cups sugar
2 tablespoons vanilla
1 cup seedless raisins
2 apples, pared, cored, and sliced
¼ cup butter
Whiskey Sauce (see following recipe)

Preheat oven to 350°F.

Crush bread into milk and mix well. Beat the eggs, and add to the bread and milk, along with the sugar, vanilla, raisins, and apples. Melt the butter and pour into a 2½- to 3-quart shallow casserole dish. Then pour in the pudding mixture. Bake 50 minutes, until the pudding is set. Serve chilled or warm with Whiskey Sauce.

NOTE: Use a homemade-style bread; cardamom-flavored bread makes a delicious bread pudding.

Whiskey Sauce

MAKES ABOUT 1 CUP

½ cup melted butter
1 cup sugar
1 egg
Whiskey to taste

Cream the butter and sugar in a double boiler. Add the egg and stir rapidly so that egg doesn't curdle. When well mixed, allow to cool. Add whiskey to taste.

Whole Wheat
Chocolate Bread Pudding
with Rum Custard Sauce

MAKES 6 SERVINGS

White bread is not the only type used in bread puddings. A deft combination of grainy whole wheat bread, chocolate, rich cream, and eggs proves that country-style desserts need not be monotonous.

1 cup heavy cream
3 ounces (3 squares) semisweet chocolate
6 tablespoons sugar
2 eggs, separated, plus 2 egg whites
¼ cup butter
1 teaspoon vanilla
4 slices homemade-style whole wheat bread, crumbled
Rum Custard Sauce (see following recipe)

Preheat oven to 350°F. Butter a 1-quart soufflé dish and dust with 1 tablespoon sugar.

In a medium saucepan, bring the cream to a simmer. Add the chocolate and stir until the chocolate is melted. Remove from the heat. With an electric mixer, beat in 2 tablespoons sugar and the egg yolks. Add the butter and vanilla and mix until smooth. In a large bowl, combine the bread crumbs and the chocolate mixture. In a separate bowl, beat the egg whites until foamy. Gradually beat in the remaining 4 tablespoons sugar and beat until whites are glossy and stiff. Stir a little of the whites into the chocolate mixture, then fold in the remaining whites until the mixture is marbelized (don't completely mix). Turn into the prepared soufflé dish. Set the filled dish in a larger pan and add enough hot water to the larger pan to come halfway up the sides of the soufflé dish. Bake 45 minutes, or until the pudding is set. Remove from the oven and let stand 10 minutes, then invert onto a serving platter. Serve warm, cut into wedges, with the Rum Custard Sauce.

Rum Custard Sauce

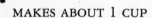

MAKES ABOUT 1 CUP

2 *egg yolks*
3 *tablespoons sugar*
1 *cup half-and-half*
2 *tablespoons dark rum*

In a large bowl, combine the egg yolks and the sugar. Heat the half-and-half to boiling. Gradually whisk a little of the boiling half-and-half into the yolk mixture. Return the entire mixture to the saucepan and cook over low heat, stirring constantly, until the custard is thick enough to coat the back of a wooden spoon, about 10 minutes. Do not boil or the custard may separate. Remove from the heat and pour through a wire strainer into a serving bowl. Add the rum. Cover while the custard cools to prevent a skin from forming on top.

Amana Village
Plain Chocolate Bread Pudding

MAKES 4 SERVINGS

The Amana Society dates back to 1714. To escape persecution, the sect moved to make its new home in America, first in New York and later settling in the area that is now Iowa, along the Iowa River. Of German origin, the Amanas have always enjoyed good substantial food. Their well-rounded meals included desserts of many varieties, but bread pudding was a favorite. This pudding separates into a rich, chocolatey layer on top and a light-colored chocolate custard below. It is best served while still warm.

1 tablespoon butter
1 square (1 ounce) unsweetened chocolate
2 eggs, separated
½ cup sugar
2 cups milk, scalded
1 cup stale (not dry) bread crumbs

Preheat oven to 350°F. Butter a 1½-quart soufflé dish and dust with sugar.

Place the butter and chocolate in a small bowl and set over hot water, stirring occasionally until melted. In a large bowl, whip the egg whites until stiff, and set aside. In another bowl, beat the yolks with the sugar, and add the melted chocolate and butter. Add the milk and the bread crumbs to the yolk mixture. Fold in the beaten whites. Pour into the prepared dish and bake 25 to 30 minutes, until the pudding is set.

Blueberry Bread-and-Butter Pudding

MAKES 6 SERVINGS

This is a bread pudding in which the bread is left in whole slices and the fruit is layered between. The result tastes like blueberry pie.

8 *thin slices white bread*
¼ *cup butter, at room temperature*
4 *cups fresh or frozen unsugared blueberries*
1 *cup sugar*
1 *cup heavy cream, whipped*

Preheat oven to 350°F. Butter a 1½-quart glass loaf pan.

Trim crusts from bread. Butter each slice. Put blueberries and sugar into a saucepan. Simmer 15 minutes, stirring occasionally. Fit 2 slices of buttered bread in the bottom of the prepared pan. If necessary, cut slices to fit. Top with berries. Alternate layers of the berries and buttered bread, ending with a layer of the bread, until all is used. Cover and bake 15 minutes. Chill 4 hours or overnight.

Before serving, unmold onto a serving plate. Spread with whipped cream and cut into slices.

Mormon Bachelor's Pudding

MAKES 6 SERVINGS

The followers of Brigham Young, the Mormons, came to Utah from many countries of the world. Their food was a "melting pot" cuisine, which they adapted to the available ingredients of the area. Simply prepared and heavily loaded with apples and raisins, this steamed pudding was a favorite.

1 egg
2 tablespoons butter, melted
A dash of nutmeg
1 teaspoon grated lemon rind
2 large apples, pared, cored, and chopped (about 2 cups)
2 cups soft bread crumbs
1 cup raisins or currants
½ cup sugar
Golden Brown Sugar Sauce (see following recipe)

Butter a 1-quart steamed-pudding mold. Fit a deep pot with a rack (canning jar rings work well) and add water until it just reaches the top of the rack. Bring water to a boil.

In a large bowl, beat the egg with the butter, nutmeg, and lemon rind until well blended. Add the apples, bread crumbs, raisins, and sugar. Turn this dry, crumbly mixture into the prepared pudding mold. Cover tightly and place on the rack in the pot with the boiling water (water should not touch the mold). Steam for 2 hours, adding more boiling water to the pot as necessary. Unmold and serve hot with Golden Brown Sugar Sauce.

Golden Brown Sugar Sauce

MAKES 3 CUPS

This sauce can be made ahead and refrigerated. It is delicious served over slices of chocolate cake or over your other favorite steamed puddings.

2 eggs, separated
½ cup brown sugar
½ cup heavy cream
1 teaspoon vanilla

In a medium bowl, beat the egg whites until foamy; gradually beat in half the brown sugar, and beat until mixture holds firm but rounded peaks. In another bowl, beat the egg yolks with the remaining sugar until light and fluffy. In a third bowl, whip the cream until stiff. Fold all three mixtures together, and flavor with the vanilla. Chill until ready to serve.

Oregon Huckleberry Buckle

MAKES 6 SERVINGS

Huckleberries or whortleberries, which are dark blue and smooth, are often confused with blueberries. The good news is that blueberries can be substituted for huckleberries, which grow in the Northwest and are rarely available in other parts of the country.

THE BERRY LAYER

¼ *cup butter*
½ *cup sugar*
1 *egg, beaten*
1 *cup all-purpose flour*
1½ *teaspoons baking powder*
⅛ *teaspoon salt*
⅓ *cup milk*
1 *teaspoon vanilla*
2 *cups fresh huckleberries or blueberries or thawed frozen blueberries*

THE CRUMB TOPPING

½ *cup sugar*
¼ *cup butter*
⅓ *cup all-purpose flour*
½ *teaspoon cinnamon*

Whipped cream

Preheat oven to 375°F. Butter and flour a 9-inch pie pan.
In a large mixing bowl, cream ¼ cup butter and ½ cup sugar. Add the egg and beat well. Combine the dry ingredients and add to the butter mixture alternately with the milk and vanilla. Pour into the prepared pan. Pour berries over the top of the batter.

93

To prepare the crumb topping, blend all of the ingredients together until crumbly. Sprinkle over the berries. Bake 45 minutes. Serve warm with whipped cream.

Old-fashioned Chocolate Rum Cottage Pudding

MAKES 10 TO 12 SERVINGS

½ cup butter

1 teaspoon vanilla

1¼ cups granulated sugar

2 squares (2 ounces) unsweetened chocolate, melted

2 eggs

2 cups cake flour (see Note)

½ teaspoon salt

2 teaspoons baking powder

1 cup milk

6 tablespoons dark rum

1 cup heavy cream

3 tablespoons powdered sugar

Chocolate Rum Sauce (see following recipe)

Preheat oven to 350°F. Butter and flour a 9½-inch angel food tube pan.

In a large bowl, cream the butter. Add the vanilla and beat in the granulated sugar, chocolate, and eggs, until mixture is light. Combine the flour with the salt and baking powder. Add dry ingredients alternately with the milk to the creamed mixture. Turn into the prepared pan and bake 35 to 45 minutes, or until the cake tests done.

Remove from the pan and cool. Invert onto a deep serving platter and drizzle with 4 tablespoons of dark rum.

Whip the cream until stiff. Add the powdered sugar and the remaining rum. Fill the center of the cake with the whipped cream, allowing it to pile up on top of the cake. Pour Chocolate Rum Sauce around the cake.

NOTE: To measure the cake flour, sift into a bowl and spoon into a dry-measure cup. Level with the straight edge of a knife.

Chocolate Rum Sauce

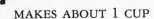

MAKES ABOUT 1 CUP

2 *squares (2 ounces) unsweetened chocolate*
1 *tablespoon butter*
½ *cup boiling water*
1 *cup sugar*
A *pinch of salt*
2 *tablespoons dark rum*

In a heavy saucepan or in the top of a double boiler, melt the chocolate with the butter. Stir in the water, sugar, and salt. Bring to a boil. Remove from the heat and add the rum.

Baked Carrot Pudding

MAKES 6 TO 8 SERVINGS

The American country cook's tradition of using ingredients at hand started with the use of cornmeal instead of flour in Indian pudding. Pumpkin, another native American fruit, became a dessert ingredient, so it was not unthinkable to utilize other vegetables in sweet mixtures. Carrots were being used as an ingredient in carrot pudding in the early 1900s, and this pudding was the forerunner of today's carrot cake, which has become a standard.

½ cup butter
½ cup tightly packed brown sugar
1 egg
1 cup grated raw carrots
2 teaspoons grated lemon rind
½ cup raisins
1 cup currants
1¼ cups all-purpose flour
1 teaspoon baking powder
½ teaspoon salt
½ teaspoon nutmeg
½ teaspoon cinnamon
½ teaspoon baking soda
1 tablespoon hot water
Whipped cream, heavy cream, Vanilla Cream Sauce (see recipe), or
  caramel sauce

Preheat oven to 350°F. Butter a 6- to 8-cup tube-type mold or eight individual fancy molds.

Cream the butter with the brown sugar. Add the egg and beat well. Add all of the remaining ingredients except the cream or sauce and mix to combine. Pour mixture into the mold or molds and bake

96

1 to 1½ hours for the tube-type mold, or about 45 minutes for the small molds. Invert onto a serving platter or individual plates and serve with whipped cream, heavy cream, Vanilla Cream Sauce, or caramel sauce.

Denver Fudge Pudding

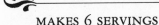

MAKES 6 SERVINGS

This has a cakelike top and a fudgy pudding on the bottom. It is best served the day it is made, while the top is still moist.

1¼ *cups granulated sugar*
1 *cup all-purpose flour*
2 *teaspoons baking powder*
A dash of salt
7 *tablespoons dark unsweetened cocoa*
¼ *cup butter*
½ *cup milk*
1 *teaspoon vanilla*
½ *cup brown sugar*
1½ *cups cold water or cold coffee*
Whipped cream or ice cream (optional)

Preheat oven to 350°F. Butter a 9-by-9-inch baking dish.

In a bowl, combine ¾ cup granulated sugar, the flour, baking powder, salt, and 3 tablespoons cocoa. Melt the butter and add it along with the milk and vanilla to the dry ingredients. Mix until just blended. Pour into the prepared baking dish.

Scatter over the top of the pudding, without first mixing, the brown sugar, ½ cup granulated sugar, and 4 tablespoons cocoa. Pour the cold water or coffee over the pudding. Bake 40 minutes. Let stand at room temperature until cool but not chilled. Serve with or without whipped cream or ice cream.

Cinnamon
Wild Rice Pudding

MAKES 8 TO 10 SERVINGS

Wild rice, another all-American grain, was introduced to us by the Indians. It is indigenous to the northern part of our country, along the Canadian border. Wild rice, which is not really a rice at all, but a grass that grows in lakes and marshy areas, is harvested in the late summer. In the areas where wild rice is harvested, it is an important part of all meals. Served simply cooked with a topping of maple syrup (also a product of the north), wild blueberries, and cream, it is a delicious dessert or breakfast dish. Settlers in the area quickly learned that wild rice is delicious served many ways, and that when baked into a pudding with raisins, maple syrup, and cinnamon, it made still another variation to classic rice pudding.

¾ cup golden or dark raisins
½ cup maple syrup
2 eggs
½ teaspoon cinnamon
¼ teaspoon nutmeg
1 teaspoon vanilla
2 cups cooked wild rice (see Note)
2 cups hot half-and-half
Cinnamon sugar

Preheat oven to 350°F.

Combine raisins, maple syrup, eggs, cinnamon, nutmeg, vanilla, rice, and half-and-half. Turn into a 1½-quart casserole. Sprinkle with cinnamon sugar. Bake 1 hour, or until pudding is set. Serve warm or chilled.

NOTE: To make 2 cups wild rice, measure ⅔ cup uncooked rice. Rinse in hot tap water three times to remove dust. Put rice in a saucepan. Add 2 cups water and bring to a boil, stir, cover, and simmer 35 to 45 minutes, or until the rice is tender. Drain off any extra liquid that has not been absorbed.

Indiana Persimmon Pudding

MAKES 12 SERVINGS

It takes about 10 Indiana persimmons to make 1 cup pulp. Wash the persimmons and remove the caps and black tips. Quarter and place in a food processor with the steel blade in place; process until puréed. Indiana persimmons have a more intense flavor than the large California variety and are best for a pudding; however, it takes only 2 California persimmons to make 1 cup pulp, which can be used if the other variety is not available.

⅓ cup butter

2 cups persimmon pulp (see headnote above)

2 cups sugar

2 eggs, beaten

1¾ cups all-purpose flour

2 teaspoons baking powder

1 cup buttermilk

1 cup half-and-half or light cream

1 teaspoon baking soda

½ teaspoon ground cinnamon

Sweetened whipped cream

Preheat oven to 325°F.

While preparing the pudding, put the butter into a 9-by-13-by-2-inch baking pan and place in the oven as it preheats, to melt the butter. Brush melted butter all over the pan (retain 4 tablespoons melted butter for use in pudding).

In a large mixing bowl, combine the persimmon pulp with the sugar and eggs. Combine the flour and baking powder. Mix the buttermilk, half-and-half, and baking soda. Add the liquid ingredients alternately with the flour mixture to the persimmon pulp, mixing until the batter is smooth. Pour 4 tablespoons of the melted butter into the batter along with the cinnamon, and mix. Turn batter into the butter-coated pan and bake 55 minutes to 1 hour, or until set. The pudding will be dark, with a heavy and moist consistency, a little more dense than pumpkin pie. Serve with slightly sweetened whipped cream.

Carrot Pudding with Butt'ry Sauce

MAKES 8 SERVINGS

Because of their sweet taste and smooth texture, carrots, though neither fruit nor berry, have been used as an ingredient in desserts.

Sometime between the early Colonial and frontier days, all kinds of desserts made with carrots as an ingredient had emerged. Carrot puddings and cakes do not appear in old historical cookbooks, but they do appear in *all* collections of "favorite old recipes" from the early 1900s and late 1800s, with notations such as "I always make this for Thanksgiving Dinner." Steamed, this is served with a buttery brown-sugar sauce or a lemon-flavored sauce.

1 *cup all-purpose flour*
1 *teaspoon baking soda*
1 *teaspoon cinnamon*
1 *teaspoon nutmeg*
1 *teaspoon allspice*
½ *teaspoon ground cloves*
½ *teaspoon salt*
1 *cup fine dry bread crumbs*
1 *cup tightly packed light or dark brown sugar*
1 *cup finely shredded carrots*
1 *cup shredded raw potato*
1 *cup ground seedless raisins*
1 *cup chopped walnuts*
1 *cup chopped or ground suet*
1 *tablespoon dark molasses*
2 *eggs, lightly beaten*
Butt'ry Sauce (see following recipe) or Lemon Sauce (see
    recipe)

In a large bowl, combine the ingredients in the order given except for the molasses, eggs, and sauce. Blend the molasses and eggs together, then stir into the mixture. Butter a 2-quart steaming mold or pudding mold. Turn mixture into the mold. Cover top of mold with wax paper and cover with a square of folded muslin. Tie with twine to fasten. If the mold has its own cover, simply cover with wax paper, then with the cover of the mold. Or, turn into 8 individual molds, about 6 ounces each. Molds should be filled two-thirds full. Place onto rack in deep steamer, kettle, or roaster. Add boiling water to pan, up to the level of the rack. Cover kettle and maintain a simmer, adding water if necessary. Steam large molds for 3 hours, or until a skewer inserted through the center comes out clean; or steam individual molds for 1½ hours. Remove pudding from molds and serve hot. Or, wrap and freeze; rewarm by steaming to serving temperature (or rewarm in microwave oven, being careful not to overheat the pudding). Serve with Butt'ry Sauce or Lemon Sauce.

Butt'ry Sauce

MAKES 3 CUPS

½ cup butter
1 cup tightly packed light or dark brown sugar
1 egg
1 tablespoon white wine vinegar
A dash of nutmeg
1 teaspoon vanilla
1 cup heavy cream, whipped

In the top of a double boiler, cream the butter with the brown sugar. Add the egg and vinegar and beat until very light and fluffy. Add the nutmeg. Place over boiling water and cook, stirring constantly, for 10 minutes, or until thickened. Add the vanilla. Chill. Just before serving, fold in the whipped cream.

Lemon Sauce

MAKES 3 CUPS

½ cup fresh lemon juice
1¾ cups water
1 cup tightly packed light or dark brown sugar
¼ cup granulated sugar
¼ cup butter
⅛ teaspoon salt
2 tablespoons cornstarch

In a saucepan, combine the lemon juice, 1½ cups water, sugars, butter, and salt. Bring to a boil over medium-high heat and cook 2 minutes, stirring constantly. Mix the cornstarch and ¼ cup water together until smooth. Stir into the boiling mixture and cook, stirring constantly, until smooth and thickened. Serve hot.

Colonial Plum Pudding with Brandy Sauce

MAKES 12 TO 16 SERVINGS

Clearly, plum puddings point back to a British heritage. This was an American Colonial pudding as well, served traditionally for dessert during the Christmas holidays. Plum pudding is best when made a few weeks ahead of the holidays, so that it can be wrapped and aged like fruitcake. It's important to use bread crumbs from a good quality bakery bread or a homemade bread. Before serving, the pudding should be steamed again to warm to serving temperature. It is served in thin slices. If desired, it may be served with Hard Sauce instead of the Brandy Sauce.

¾ *cup dark seedless raisins*
¾ *cup golden raisins*
¾ *cup currants*
½ *cup mixed candied peels*
½ *cup chopped almonds*
1 *small tart apple, pared, cored, and grated*
½ *teaspoon grated lemon peel*
1 *cup chopped beef suet*
½ *cup all-purpose flour*
⅔ *cup tightly packed light or dark brown sugar*
1¼ *cups bread crumbs*
½ *teaspoon ground cloves*
½ *teaspoon allspice*
½ *teaspoon cinnamon*
½ *teaspoon nutmeg*
¼ *teaspoon salt*
2 *eggs*
2 *tablespoons brandy*
1 *tablespoon lemon juice*
Brandy for aging (optional)
Brandy Sauce (see following recipe) or Hard Sauce (see recipe)

In a large bowl, combine the raisins, currants, candied peels, almonds, apple, and lemon peel. In another large bowl, combine the suet with the flour; blend in the sugar, bread crumbs, spices, and salt. Blend flour mixture into the fruit mixture. Beat the eggs, add 2 tablespoons brandy and the lemon juice, then blend into the fruit-flour mixture, until evenly combined. (At this point, the mixture may be held overnight.)

Grease a 1-quart pudding mold or pudding bowl. Turn pudding

mixture into the bowl. The bowl should be two-thirds full. Cover top with wax paper, overlapping the edge of the bowl by 2 inches or so. Cover with a folded square of muslin. Tie on wax paper and muslin with kitchen twine. Place into deep kettle or roasting pan on rack. Add water to the pan, up to the level of the rack or about 1 inch. Cover and steam 4 hours, keeping the water at a simmer and adding water to prevent the pan from boiling dry.

Remove bowl from steamer and cool. Store pudding in the bowl; or remove from bowl, drizzle with brandy, if desired, wrap in wax paper and foil, and store in a cool place for 3 to 4 weeks. Before serving, place pudding into the bowl or onto a plate and steam 30 minutes on a rack over water in deep pot or roasting pan. Cut in slices and serve with Brandy Sauce or Hard Sauce.

Brandy Sauce

MAKES ABOUT 2 CUPS

1 ½ *cups heavy cream*
2 *tablespoons brandy or dark rum*
1 *tablespoon superfine sugar*

Whip cream until soft peaks form. Blend in the brandy or rum and sugar.

Hard Sauce

MAKES ABOUT 6 SERVINGS

Hard sauce really means a "hard sauce," in that it is simply a stiff mixture of powdered sugar, butter, and flavorings, which can be sliced or rolled out and cut with a fancy cookie cutter to make individual servings.

½ *cup butter*
1½ *tablespoons brandy or sherry*
1 *teaspoon vanilla*
1⅔ *cups packed powdered sugar*

Cream the butter until soft. Add the brandy and vanilla, then blend in the powdered sugar, until the mixture is fairly stiff and smooth. Press into a shallow mold, or shape into a roll and wrap in plastic. Chill until firm. Slice, or cut into fancy shapes with a cookie cutter.

Pear Walnut Pudding

MAKES 8 SERVINGS

This pudding is something like a very moist cake and is delicious served warm out of the oven with a topping of whipped cream.

2 *eggs*
1 *cup sugar*
⅔ *cup sifted all-purpose flour*
¼ *teaspoon salt*
2½ *teaspoons baking powder*
2 *cups peeled and cored chopped fresh pears*
1 *cup chopped walnuts*
2 *teaspoons lemon juice*
½ *cup flaked coconut*
Whipped cream (optional)

Preheat oven to 350°F. Butter a 9-inch-square baking dish.

Beat the eggs, and gradually add the sugar, beating until fluffy. Sift the flour with the salt and baking powder into the egg mixture. Blend well. Fold in the pears, nuts, and lemon juice. Pour mixture into the prepared baking dish. Sprinkle coconut over the top. Bake 30 minutes, or until top is golden. Serve warm or cold, cut into squares and topped with whipped cream, if desired.

Pastries, Pancakes, Baked Dumplings, and Fried Doughs

From the diversity of the American ethnic patchwork come stuffed baked pastries; puffy, deep-fried fritters; deftly handled doughs, batters, and crusts.

Some seem to exemplify the melting-pot tradition of American cookery. Roly-poly, for instance, takes a baking-powder biscuit dough, not unlike that of English scones or Southern biscuits, and encloses fruit or jam within it. It's baked in a syrup, something like a dumpling. This is truly an American invention, designed to make use of available fruit. Similar in principle is strudel, which has its roots in Central European—German, Viennese, Hungarian, and Bohemian—cooking. The Pennsylvania Dutch make *apfelstrudel,* but the technique of stretching dough to egg-membrane thinness is typical of many ethnic American cuisines.

Even though Greeks immigrated in relatively smaller numbers, they, too, have left their stamp on the American culinary scene. With the introduction of Greek restaurants, crunchy, honey-and-nut-filled baklava became a favorite American dessert. Bohemians and Czechs make a similar, delicately stretched, nut-filled strudel-like pastry for special occasions called *potica*. Country cooks, with nimble fingers, time, and patience, to this day create all of these pastries to celebrate holidays and special occasions.

Midwestern Czech and Slav cooks have added their everyday specialties, too. *Kolaches* are so popular that supermarket bakeries in the middle and northern Midwest produce these flaky pastries, filled with fruit, berries, cream cheese, nuts, or poppy seeds, in quantities.

The *empanadas* of Southwest cookery come basically from a Spanish background, and they are yet another way to enclose fruit in a crusty filling. Sometimes they are deep-fried, and sometimes they are baked to golden crispness. Typical of many foods basic to a culture, the variety that exists is about as great as the number of cooks making *empanadas*. They might be filled with chopped raisins or dates or yams and pineapple or apples or dried fruits.

Puffy pancakes, *pannequaiques,* such as Dutch Apple Pancakes, are natural to all dairy-producing European countries, as well as to America. Butter, flour, eggs, and milk are combined in still another proportion and subjected to a high oven temperature to make a glorious, spectacular, delicate, and buttery shell for fruit that is either fresh, or sautéed as the pancake cooks. Puffy, deep-fried *beignets* are rectangular doughnuts served fresh and hot around the clock at French Market coffeehouses in New Orleans.

The Dutch introduced *oylkoeks* (oily cakes) or doughnuts to the New World, described by Diedrich Knickerbocker as "a large dish of balls of sweetened dough fried in hog's fat." Other desserts were fried as well. To be on the safe side, lest anybody go away from the table hungry, the Pennsylvania Dutch offered fruit fritters in addition to a baked pudding, pies, and cakes. Today such heavy desserts might be served with a beverage at nonmeal times, such as coffee and doughnuts after the ski club meeting.

Choux paste, baked into cream puffs and eclairs, have long been American dessert favorites. A similar dessert is a Danish Puff (not known in Denmark), which looks something like a flat cream puff. It is served as a dessert with coffee by Scandinavian-Americans. The base is a layer of flaky pastry, topped with cream puff paste, and, after baking, it is drizzled with an almond-flavored icing and sprinkled with toasted almonds.

Yeast-raised Doughnuts

MAKES 24 DOUGHNUTS

Across the country, but especially in small towns, you're likely to find the locals enjoying "dunkers" and coffee in the morning. "Dunkers" to some mean yeast-raised doughnuts such as these, but to others they may be Cake Doughnuts as in the recipe on p. 112. Either variety may be dusted with powdered sugar, cinnamon sugar, or glazed with a variety of frostings.

1 *package active dry yeast*
¼ *cup warm water (105°F. to 115°F.)*
¼ *cup sugar*
1 *teaspoon salt*
½ *teaspoon nutmeg*
1 *cup milk, scalded and cooled to lukewarm*
1 *egg*
¼ *cup butter, melted*
3 *to* 3½ *cups all-purpose flour*
Hot oil for frying
Powdered sugar, cinnamon sugar, or Powdered Sugar Glaze (see
   following recipe)

In a large mixing bowl, dissolve the yeast in the warm water. Add the sugar and let stand 5 minutes, until the mixture becomes foamy. Add the salt, nutmeg, milk, egg, butter, and 2 cups of flour. Beat by hand until smooth, or use electric mixer and beat at low speed for 3 minutes until satiny. Stir in the remaining flour to form a stiff dough. Cover and let rise in a warm place until doubled, about 1 to 1¼ hours.

Dust work surface with flour. Turn dough out of bowl onto the surface. With floured hands, pat dough out until it's smooth and an even thickness. With rolling pin, roll out to ½-inch thickness. Cut with floured doughnut cutter and place on a flour-dusted cookie sheet in a warm place until light and doubled in size, about 45 minutes.

In a skillet or large saucepan, heat 2 to 3 inches oil to 375°F. Lift doughnuts into the oil. Fry about 1 minute on each side or until golden brown. Drain on paper towels. While still warm, dust with sugar or dip in glaze.

LONG JOHNS: Roll dough out to make a ½-inch-thick square. Cut into 1½-by-4-inch rectangles. Let rise and fry as directed for doughnuts. Frost with one of the suggested glazes.

BISMARKS: Roll dough to ½ inch thick and cut with a 2- or 3-inch cookie cutter (no hole in the center). Let rise and fry as directed for doughnuts. Fit a pastry bag or cake decorating tube with a metal tip with a ¼-inch opening. Fill bag or tube with strawberry or raspberry jelly. Make a hole in the edge of the warm fried bismark with the tip and force the jelly into the center of the bismark; you will be able to squeeze about 1 tablespoon jelly into each. Dust with powdered sugar or frost with vanilla-flavored Powdered Sugar Glaze.

Powdered Sugar Glaze

MAKES ABOUT 1½ CUPS

There are nine different taste variations in this basic recipe. By using water, milk, *or* coffee with vanilla, lemon juice, *or* maple extract, you can experiment to find your favorite.

2 *cups powdered sugar*
1 *teaspoon vanilla or lemon juice, or* ½ *teaspoon maple extract*
2 *tablespoons butter, melted*
3 *to* 4 *tablespoons water, milk, or coffee*

In a mixing bowl, blend the powdered sugar with flavoring, butter, and liquid. Mix until smooth.

CHOCOLATE GLAZE: Add 2 ounces melted chocolate.

HONEY GLAZE: Add 2 tablespoons warm honey; omit vanilla and use water (not milk or coffee) as the liquid.

Cake Doughnuts

MAKES 15 DOUGHNUTS

2¼ *cups all-purpose flour*
½ *cup sugar*
1½ *teaspoons baking powder*
½ *teaspoon baking soda*
¼ *teaspoon salt*
¼ *teaspoon nutmeg*
½ *cup buttermilk*
2 *tablespoons vegetable oil*
½ *teaspoon vanilla*
1 *egg, slightly beaten*
Hot oil for frying
Powdered sugar, cinnamon sugar, or Powdered Sugar Glaze (see
recipe) (optional)

In a large mixing bowl, blend the flour, sugar, baking powder, baking soda, salt, and nutmeg. In a measuring cup, blend the buttermilk, vegetable oil, vanilla, and egg. Stir liquid ingredients

into the dry ingredients, just until dry ingredients are moistened.
Heat 2 to 3 inches oil in a skillet or saucepan to 375°F.

Dust work surface with flour and turn dough out onto it. Knead
lightly until dough is no longer sticky. Roll dough out to about ½-
inch thickness. Cut with floured doughnut cutter. With a pancake
turner, transfer doughnuts into the oil and fry 1 minute on each side,
until golden brown. Drain on paper towels. Dust while warm with
powdered or cinnamon sugar and glaze if desired.

Apple Roly-poly

MAKES 6 SERVINGS

This old-fashioned farm-style dessert is made with rich biscuit
dough filled with apples and baked in a spicy cinnamon syrup. It is best
served warm with cream.

1¾ cups sugar
1½ cups water
2 teaspoons ground cinnamon
2 cups all-purpose flour
2 teaspoons baking powder
½ teaspoon salt
½ cup butter, firm
1 egg
Milk
1 tablespoon butter, at room temperature
3 cups pared, cored, and chopped tart apples
Heavy cream or whipped cream

Preheat oven to 400°F. Butter a 9-by-13-inch baking pan or shallow casserole with sides.

In a saucepan, combine 1 ½ cups sugar, the water, and cinnamon. Bring to a boil and simmer 5 minutes. Pour into the prepared baking pan, reserving ½ cup of the syrup.

In a large bowl, or in the work bowl of a food processor, combine the flour, ¼ cup sugar, baking powder, and salt. Cut ½ cup butter into thin slices and drop into the flour mixture. Process using on / off bursts, or cut the butter into the flour until blended into the mixture. Beat the egg in a measuring cup and add enough milk to make ⅔ cup. Add egg and milk to the dry ingredients all at once, and stir until the dough holds together. Knead 10 to 12 strokes on a floured surface. Roll out dough to make a 12-inch square.

Spread dough with 1 tablespoon soft butter and cover with the apples. Roll up, as for a jelly roll. Cut into 12 slices and place on the syrup in the pan.

Bake 30 minutes. Spoon the reserved syrup over the rolls and bake 10 to 15 minutes longer, or until bubbly and browned. Serve warm with plain or whipped cream.

Shaker
Rosy Apple Dumplings

MAKES 4 SERVINGS

The special flavor in these dumplings comes from the addition of rosewater, an ingredient that this herb-loving community made themselves. From *The Shaker Cookbook* by Caroline B. Piercy: "To make Shaker Rosewater, when roses, red or damask ones preferred, are at their best, pluck off the petals from fresh blooms. Do not use fallen petals or faded blooms. To every peck of petals use a quart of fresh spring water. Put this in a cold still over a very low fire and distill slowly. Distill it a second time. Bottle the rosewater and cork loosely and let stand 3 days. Then fasten the cork down tightly and let age before using."

4 *medium tart apples*
1 *single-crust 9-inch pie shell (p. 187 or 188)*
½ *cup sugar*
2 *tablespoons heavy cream*
1 *tablespoon rosewater (see Note), or 1 teaspoon grated lemon rind*
½ *cup hot maple syrup*
Hard Sauce (see recipe)

Preheat oven to 450°F. Butter a 9-inch-square baking dish.

Pare and core the apples. Divide pastry into 4 parts and roll each out to make a circle about 8 inches in diameter, or large enough to wrap an apple. Place an apple in the middle of a pastry square. Blend the sugar, cream, and rosewater or lemon rind. Fill the center of each apple with one-quarter of the mixture. Wrap the apple in the pastry, moistening the edges with water and pressing to seal. Pierce pastry on top with a fork. Place in the baking dish and bake 15 minutes at 450°F; reduce heat to 350°F and bake 10 minutes more. Baste with the maple syrup. Bake another 10 to 15 minutes. Serve with Hard Sauce.

NOTE: Commercial rosewater can be obtained at pharmacies. Be sure to ask for the food-flavoring rosewater, not the type used for hand lotion. Rosewater may also be found in the gourmet section of well-stocked markets.

Stina's Michigan Apple-and-Rhubarb Dumplings

MAKES 6 SERVINGS

This recipe is from *Stina,* by Herman Smith. It is a nostalgic story about a Michigan farm family of the late 1880s, and of Stina, a superb cook. This is a springtime dessert, made with fresh, juicy rhubarb and apples that have been "wintered."

1 *cup pared, diced apples*
1 *cup cubed fresh pink rhubarb (cut into ½-inch pieces)*
½ *cup sugar*
1 *double-crust 9-inch pie shell (p. 187 or 188)*
Heavy cream, Vanilla Cream Sauce (see recipe), or softly whipped cream

Preheat oven to 350°F.

In a bowl, combine the apples and rhubarb with the sugar. Roll out the pastry to about ¼-inch thickness; cut into six 6-inch squares. Put ⅓ cup of the fruit mixture onto the center of each pastry square. Moisten the edges with cold water and fold the sides up over filling; pinch to seal. With a fork, pierce a vent to prevent bursting. Place on an ungreased cookie sheet and bake 25 to 30 minutes, or until golden. Serve with cream, Vanilla Cream Sauce, or softly whipped cream.

Pennsylvania Dutch Apfelstrudel

MAKES 10 TO 12 SERVINGS

Fruit-enclosed pastries are natural to the Pennsylvania Dutch. *Apfelstrudel* in its original form is made with a thinly stretched dough filled with a mixture of apples, sugar, and spices. Raisins, nuts, chopped candied citron, or cherries are sometimes added to the strudel. To stretch the strudel dough, it is helpful to have at least two extra sets of hands (invite your friends to a "strudel stretch").

THE PASTRY

3 *cups all-purpose flour*
2 *eggs*
½ *teaspoon salt*
3 *tablespoons oil*
¾ *cup warm water*
½ *cup plus* 1 *tablespoon melted butter*
Toasted bread crumbs or cinnamon sugar

THE APPLE FILLING

10 *large tart apples, pared, cored, and sliced*
2 *tablespoons lemon juice*
1 *cup sugar*
2 *teaspoons cinnamon*
Nutmeg

To prepare pastry, put flour into a large bowl and make a well in the center. Combine the eggs, salt, oil, and water. Whip mixture with a fork until blended, and pour into the well of flour. Stir until a soft dough forms. Pick up the dough with one hand and slap it into the bowl or onto a breadboard about 100 times, or until it becomes very elastic and is no longer wet and sticky but leaves the board and your hands clean. The dough is very sticky in the beginning, but as you work with it, it becomes less sticky. Let dough rest for 5 to 10 minutes.

Cover a table with a clean tablecloth or sheet (a round table about 5 feet in diameter is ideal). Dust lightly with flour. Dust the ball of dough with flour, and place it in the center of the cloth. Roll out the dough with a rolling pin to make a circle about 20 inches in diameter.

Starting with one person stretching the dough, reach under the dough with palms up. Turn hands sideways making fists of your hands, and very slowly rotate fists outward under the dough to stretch it. When it is about 24 inches in diameter, set dough back onto the cloth.

At this point, it is helpful to have several sets of hands working. Very carefully, hands under the dough with palms up and fingers straight out (not curved upward), stretch the dough evenly and very slowly from the center outward. Keep pulling evenly in all directions until it is tissue-thin and almost transparent. It should be about as thin as the membrane of an egg. The dough should be 4 to 5 feet in diameter. A thick edge will remain; cut it away with a knife and save it for making noodles.

Preheat oven to 400°F.

Brush dough all over with ½ cup melted butter and sprinkle with toasted bread crumbs or cinnamon sugar.

To make the filling, put the apple slices in a mixing bowl. Sprinkle with the lemon juice, sugar, cinnamon, and a dash of nutmeg. Toss lightly.

Sprinkle filling over two-thirds of the dough, leaving one-third free (this will be the end of the roll). Fold the two sides perpendicular to the free end about 4 or 5 inches over the filling, to hold it in the ends when the strudel is rolled.

Starting with the filled end, gently lift the cloth to roll the strudel, rolling toward the empty end. Place the roll on a buttered cookie sheet, bending it into a horseshoe or wreath shape. Brush it with about 1 tablespoon melted butter, and bake 35 to 45 minutes, or until golden brown.

CHERRY FILLING: Combine two 16-ounce cans drained, pitted sweet cherries with ½ cup sugar, 1 cup raisins, 1 cup finely chopped toasted almonds, 1 teaspoon grated lemon peel, and 1 teaspoon cinnamon. Mix well.

POPPY-SEED AND ALMOND FILLING: Simmer 1 cup poppy seeds in ½ cup milk until milk is completely absorbed, about 30 minutes. Whirl 1 cup blanched almonds in a blender or food processor until fine. Add the finely pulverized almonds to the poppy seeds, and mix in ½ cup honey, ½ cup sour cream, ½ cup sugar, 1 cup raisins, 2 teaspoons grated lemon peel, and 1 teaspoon cinnamon.

Apple Strudel Squares

MAKES 16 SERVINGS

The ever-present apple has brought out the apple cookery and bakery of the cooks of every country that has settled in the United States. Some classics have evolved over the years into desserts that are a bit easier to make than the original. This is a strudel that is made with a flaky pastry that lines a jelly-roll pan, with a filling not unlike the classic apple pie.

THE PASTRY

3 cups all-purpose flour
1 teaspoon salt
1 cup lard, chilled
½ cup water
1 egg
1 tablespoon cider vinegar

THE FILLING

3 *pounds (about* 11 *or* 12 *medium to large) tart cooking apples*
2 *cups granulated sugar*
6 *tablespoons all-purpose flour*
2 *teaspoons cinnamon*
¼ *teaspoon salt*
½ *cup chopped pecans*
¼ *cup butter*

THE GLAZE

2 *tablespoons butter, melted*
1 *cup powdered sugar*
½ *teaspoon vanilla*
Milk

Preheat oven to 375°F.

Mix 3 cups flour with 1 teaspoon salt in a large bowl. Cut in the lard until it is about the size of peas. Combine the water, egg, and vinegar. Add to the flour mixture and mix with fork until the dough holds together in a ball. Divide the dough in half.

Roll out half the dough and fit onto an ungreased 11-by-17-inch jelly-roll pan.

Pare, core, and slice the apples, and arrange over the crust in the pan. Combine the granulated sugar, 6 tablespoons flour, cinnamon, and ¼ teaspoon salt. Sprinkle mixture over the apples. Sprinkle with the nuts. Dot with butter. Roll out the remaining dough. Place over the top of the apples. Seal the edges. Make several slits on top, and bake 1 hour, or until golden.

To prepare the glaze, combine the melted butter, the powdered sugar, vanilla, and enough milk to make a thin glaze. Drizzle over the warm pastry.

Southwestern Fruit Empanadas

MAKES 24 EMPANADAS

Fresh fruits dry naturally in the hot, dry atmosphere of the American Southwest. *Empanadas* are a Spanish-American classic, little turnovers that may be filled with spicy bits of meat and served as an appetizer. In this version, however, a filling of cooked dried fruit turns them into a delicious dessert.

1 ½ *cups all-purpose flour*
1 *teaspoon baking powder*
½ *teaspoon salt*
½ *cup lard or vegetable shortening, chilled*
Ice water
1 *cup minced cooked dried fruit (see Note)*
½ *cup sugar*
½ *teaspoon cinnamon*
⅛ *teaspoon ground cloves*

Preheat oven to 425°F.

In a large mixing bowl, combine flour with baking powder and salt. Cut in lard or shortening, until mixture resembles coarse crumbs. Add just enough ice water to make a dough that will hold together in a ball. Working with part of the dough at a time, roll out to ⅛-inch thickness. Cut into 3-inch rounds.

Combine fruit, sugar, cinnamon, and cloves. Place fruit on one half of the circles of dough. Fold circle in half, moisten edges with water, and press together to seal. Pinch ends between thumb and forefinger, shaping the *empanada* into a crescent. Place on an ungreased cookie sheet, and bake 12 to 15 minutes, or until golden.

NOTE: Any fruits or combination of dried fruits may be used, such as dried apricots, prunes, apples, peaches, or raisins. Simmer in boiling water to cover, with no sugar added, until tender, about 15 to 20 minutes. Drain and mince.

Kolaches

MAKES 18 KOLACHES

The coffee break on a Midwestern farm often is accompanied by this Bohemian pastry, which may have a filling of poppy seeds, cream cheese, berries, or fruit and is served warm from the oven, dribbled with a thin powdered-sugar frosting.

THE PASTRY

One 8-ounce package cream cheese
1 cup butter, at room temperature
2 cups all-purpose flour

THE POPPY-SEED FILLING

½ cup poppy seeds, ground
⅓ cup sour cream or sweet cream
1 tablespoon butter
1 tablespoon honey
¼ cup chopped almonds
1 teaspoon grated lemon rind
1 tablespoon candied orange peel
¼ cup golden raisins
2 tablespoons sugar
1 tablespoon cornstarch
2 tablespoons red currant jelly

FINISHING THE KOLACHES

1 *egg, beaten with* 2 *tablespoons milk*
2 *tablespoons granulated sugar*
1 *cup powdered sugar*
2 *tablespoons hot water or coffee*
¼ *teaspoon vanilla*

In a bowl, cut the cream cheese into the butter and flour until the mixture forms a stiff pastry. Chill 3 hours or overnight.

To make the poppy-seed filling, combine all the ingredients in a 2-quart saucepan. Stir over medium heat until mixture comes to a boil. Boil 1 minute. Cool.

Preheat oven to 400°F.

Roll dough out to ⅛-inch thickness, and cut into squares. Divide filling between the squares. Lift two opposite corners up over the filling to make a packet, with the other two ends open. Press to seal. Place on a lightly greased cookie sheet. Brush with egg-and-milk mixture and sprinkle with granulated sugar. Repeat until all of the *kolaches* have been filled. Bake 10 to 13 minutes, until golden.

Combine the powdered sugar, water or coffee, and vanilla. Drizzle over the warm *kolaches*.

APPLE FILLING: Pare, core, and slice 4 medium tart apples. Heat ¼ cup butter in a frying pan and add apples. Sauté over medium heat until tender-crisp, about 5 minutes. Sprinkle with ½ cup sugar and cool. Add ½ teaspoon cinnamon.

Dutch Apple Pancakes

MAKES 4 TO 5 SERVINGS

Billowy, puffy baked pancakes make a wonderful dessert for brunch or supper. Serve a light first course, such as a vegetable soup or salad.

6 *tablespoons butter*
1 *cup all-purpose flour*
1 *cup milk*
5 *eggs*
1 *tablespoon granulated sugar*
½ *teaspoon salt*
3 *Granny Smith or Golden Delicious apples, pared, cored, and sliced*
Powdered sugar

Preheat oven to 425°F.

Place a heavy 12-inch skillet over medium heat and add 4 tablespoons butter. In a bowl, combine the flour, milk, eggs, granulated sugar, and salt. Pour into the heated skillet and place in the preheated oven. Bake 20 to 25 minutes, or until puffed and browned.

While the pancake bakes, add remaining 2 tablespoons butter to a frying pan. Add the apples and sauté over medium heat for 15 to 20 minutes, until tender. Sprinkle pancake with powdered sugar and serve topped with the sautéed apples.

New Orleans Beignets

MAKES ABOUT 4 DOZEN DOUGHNUTS

These are the favorite deep-fried doughnuts served at the Café du Munde near the New Orleans French Market. These should be served with espresso or café au lait.

2 *tablespoons vegetable shortening*
¼ *cup granulated sugar*
¼ *teaspoon salt*
½ *cup boiling water*
½ *cup undiluted evaporated milk*
1 *package active dry yeast*
¼ *cup warm water (105°F. to 115°F.)*
1 *egg*
3¾ *cups all-purpose flour*
Hot oil for deep frying
Powdered sugar

In a large mixing bowl, blend the shortening with the granulated sugar, salt, and boiling water. Add the milk and cool to lukewarm. Dissolve the yeast in the warm water, and add the sugar mixture to the yeast mixture. Stir in the egg and 3 cups flour. Beat until very smooth. Stir in enough of the remaining flour to make a soft dough. Place in a greased bowl, turn to grease the top of the dough. Cover and refrigerate 2 to 4 hours.

Roll chilled dough, a small portion at a time, to ¼-inch thickness; cut into 2-inch squares. Do not allow to rise before frying. Fry in oil heated to 370°F. to 375°F. Brown on one side for 2 minutes; turn and brown the other side 1 minute. Drain. Dust with powdered sugar and serve hot.

Dutch Fruit Fritters

MAKES ABOUT 18 FRITTERS

Apples are the fruit used most often, but bananas, peaches, or other fruits that are in season can be made into fritters.

Corn or peanut oil for frying
1 cup all-purpose flour
1 teaspoon baking powder
1/2 teaspoon salt
1/4 teaspoon nutmeg
2 tablespoons granulated sugar
2 eggs
1/3 cup milk
Sliced apples, bananas, and/or peaches
Powdered sugar

Begin heating oil to 375°F.
In a mixing bowl, combine the flour, baking powder, salt, nutmeg, and granulated sugar. Add eggs and milk. Beat with whisk until smooth. Dip fruit into batter and drop into hot oil. Fry about 3 minutes, turning once during that time, until golden. Drain, and sprinkle with powdered sugar. Serve hot.

Spudnuts

MAKES 18 DOUGHNUTS

Doughnuts with potato in the yeast batter have been very popular throughout the Midwest and the East. The Pennsylvania Dutch claim them as *oylkoeks;* in northern New England they could be yeast-raised or cake doughnuts, but are called potato doughnuts. At the Minnesota State Fair forty years ago, spudnuts were at the height of popularity.

1 *package active dry yeast*
¼ *cup warm water (105°F. to 115°F.)*
¾ *cup milk, scalded and cooled to lukewarm*
¼ *cup granulated sugar*
1 *teaspoon salt*
½ *teaspoon nutmeg or cinnamon*
¼ *cup butter, melted*
1 *egg*
¾ *cup mashed potatoes*
3 *to 3½ cups all-purpose flour*
Hot oil for frying
Powdered sugar or Honey Glaze (see following recipe)

In a large bowl, dissolve the yeast in the warm water. Add the milk, granulated sugar, salt, nutmeg or cinnamon, butter, egg, and mashed potatoes. Add 1½ cups flour and beat with an electric mixer until dough is very smooth. Stir in enough of the remaining flour to make a stiff dough. Cover and let rise in a warm place until light and doubled in size, about 1 hour.

On a floured surface, knead the dough a few times to remove air bubbles. Roll out to ½-inch thickness. Cut with a floured doughnut cutter. Cover and let rise in a warm place until light and doubled in size, about 45 minutes. Heat oil to 375°F. Fry doughnuts in the oil 1 minute on each side, or until deep golden brown. Drain on paper towels. Dust with powdered sugar, or dip into Honey Glaze. To dip, hold hot spudnut with a fork, dip one side, invert and place on wax paper or on a rack over wax paper, and cool until glaze is set.

Honey Glaze

MAKES ABOUT 1 CUP

½ cup honey
1¼ to 1½ cups powdered sugar

In a saucepan, heat honey to boiling. Add 1 cup powdered sugar and stir until smooth. Add enough additional sugar to make a thin, lump-free glaze. Keep warm while glazing the Spudnuts.

Danish Puff

MAKES 16 TO 20 SLICES

When coffee and dessert is to be the menu, Scandinavian-Americans often serve this pastry.

THE PASTRY BASE

½ cup butter, sliced
1 cup all-purpose flour
2 to 4 tablespoons water

THE PUFF TOPPING

1 cup water
½ cup butter
1 cup all-purpose flour
3 eggs

THE ICING

1 *cup powdered sugar*
1 *tablespoon butter, at room temperature*
½ *teaspoon almond extract*
2 *to 3 tablespoons milk*

GARNISH

Toasted sliced almonds

Preheat oven to 350°F.

In a large mixing bowl or food processor with the steel blade in place, combine ½ cup butter and 1 cup flour. Process, or with pastry blender, mix the butter into the flour, until the butter is about the size of peas. Add in enough water to make a stiff dough. Shape into a ball. Divide the dough into 2 parts. On ungreased cookie sheet, pat or roll out the dough to make 2 strips 12 inches by 3 inches.

In a 2-quart saucepan, bring 1 cup water and ½ cup butter to a boil. Remove from the heat, and pour in 1 cup flour. Beat with a wooden spoon until dough forms a ball that comes away from the sides of the pan. Beat in the eggs, one at a time, until thoroughly incorporated.

Spread half of the cooked paste over each strip on the cookie sheet. Bake 45 to 55 minutes, or until golden and puffy.

Meanwhile, blend the powdered sugar with the soft butter, almond extract, and enough milk to make an icing that can be spread. Spread cooled puff strips with the icing, and sprinkle with the nuts.

Cream Puffs

MAKES 6 PUFFS

Cream puffs stem back to French choux paste as much as our all-American apple pie stems back to its early English counterpart. American cooks take liberties with the filling for cream puffs, filling them with vanilla pudding, fruit, ice cream, or whipped cream instead of fancy pastry creams.

½ cup water
½ teaspoon granulated sugar
⅛ teaspoon salt
¼ cup butter
½ cup all-purpose flour
2 eggs
3 cups whipped cream, ice cream, vanilla pudding, or fruit for filling
Whipped cream for topping
Powdered sugar

Preheat oven to 400°F.

In saucepan, combine the water, granulated sugar, salt, and butter. Slowly bring to a boil, stirring to melt the butter. When mixture is at a rapid boil, stir in the flour all at once. Stir over heat for 30 seconds; remove from the heat and beat until smooth and thick, so that paste comes together in a ball. Beat in the eggs, one at a time, until paste is smooth and shiny. Allow to cool 15 minutes.

On lightly greased cookie sheet, divide paste into 6 portions, making ball-like rounds of dough about 3 inches apart. Bake 35 to 45 minutes, until puffs are golden and lightweight. Split puffs while hot to keep crisp.

Just before serving, fill each puff with about ½ cup of your choice of filling. Top with whipped cream and dust with powdered sugar.

Eclairs

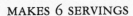

MAKES 6 SERVINGS

Eclairs are simply cream puff paste shaped into long, narrow strips and baked. They are usually frosted with a chocolate icing.

1 *recipe cream puff paste (see preceding recipe)*
1 *cup heavy cream, whipped, or Vanilla Filling (see following recipe)*
6 *ounces chocolate chips*

Preheat oven to 400°F.

Prepare cream puff paste as directed. Fit a pastry bag with a ½- or 1-inch-diameter tip and fill bag with the paste. On a greased cookie sheet, press dough out to make 1-by-4-inch strips. Bake 35 to 45 minutes, or until golden. Split while hot to let steam escape.

Just before serving, fill with whipped cream or Vanilla Filling. Place chocolate chips in a metal bowl over a pan of hot water. Stir until completely melted. Frost eclairs with glaze.

Vanilla Filling

MAKES ABOUT 2½ CUPS

1 *tablespoon butter*
⅓ *cup sugar*
A *dash of salt*
¼ *cup all-purpose flour*
1 *cup milk*
1 *cup heavy cream*
2 *eggs*
1 *teaspoon vanilla*

In a saucepan, blend butter, sugar, salt, and flour. Scald the milk and beat gradually into the flour mixture. Cook over low heat, stirring vigorously, until mixture is very thick. In a bowl, beat the heavy cream with the eggs. Stir hot cooked mixture into the egg mixture; return mixture to pan and cook again until thick, but do not boil. Add the vanilla. Cool. This makes a very thick paste for filling cream puffs or eclairs.

Baklava

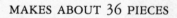

MAKES ABOUT 36 PIECES

Between 1820 and 1920 some 360,000 Greeks immigrated to the United States, bringing the Greek restaurant to these shores. Greeks also became candy-kitchen operators, displaying taffy pulling in candy-shop windows, the exhaust fans blowing out the enticing sweet smells into streets. Among the most famous of Greek sweets, not a candy but a near confection, is baklava, made with layers of thin strudel pastry, honey, and ground nuts.

1 package (1 pound) phyllo leaves

THE FILLING

4 cups almonds or walnuts
3/4 cup sugar
1 teaspoon ground cloves
1 teaspoon cinnamon
Grated peel of 1 lemon
1 cup butter, melted
36 whole cloves

THE SYRUP

1/2 cup sugar
1/2 cup water
1 1/2 cups honey

Thaw frozen phyllo leaves in refrigerator. Preheat oven to 300°F.

Spread almonds or walnuts on cookie sheet and toast for 10 minutes. Place nuts in food processor with steel blade. Process until the nuts are pulverized. Mix in 3/4 cup sugar, ground cloves, cinnamon, and lemon rind. With a pastry brush, spread some of the melted butter in the bottom of a 9-by-13-inch baking pan.

Unroll the phyllo and cover with a sheet of wax paper and a damp cloth to prevent its drying out while assembling the baklava.

Arrange 1 sheet of phyllo dough over the bottom of the baking pan, letting it hang over the edges of the pan an inch or two. Brush with melted butter and top with a sheet of dough. Brush that sheet and repeat until you have layered 8 sheets in the pan.

Brush the top sheet with melted butter, and sprinkle about one-quarter of the nut mixture over it. Fold over the top sheet of the overlapping sides, enclosing the nut layer. Leave the other 7 sheets hanging over the edge of the pan for now.

Reserve 5 sheets of the phyllo dough for the top layer. The rest of the sheets will be divided into 3 layers, which will be alternated with 3 more layers of the nut mixture. With these 3 layers of phyllo, cut or tear all but the top sheet of each to fit the size of the pan. Remember to brush each individual sheet with melted butter and to fold the top (larger) sheet of each layer in to enclose the nut layers. Pieces of phyllo left over from trimming other sheets to fit should also be buttered and layered in with the phyllo layer.

Proceed, alternating the 3 phyllo and nut layers.

Preheat oven to 250°F.

Fold the overhanging 7 sheets of dough (from the bottom layer) over the top. Add the last 5 sheets of phyllo (all cut to fit the pan) as the top layer, brushing each with melted butter. Cut diagonally across the pan as deep as the first nut layer, making diamonds about 1 inch wide and 1 ¼ inches long. Stick a whole clove in the center of each diamond. Bake for 2 hours.

While baklava bakes, combine ½ cup sugar and the water, and simmer 10 minutes, stirring. Add the honey and cool. When baklava has finished baking, cut through diagonal pieces completely with a sharp knife. Pour the honey syrup over the hot baklava. Let cool for a while before serving (although very edible earlier, it is easier to cut after cooling 3 to 4 hours).

Potica

MAKES TWO 9-INCH LOAVES

The Bohemian-Slovenian population of Minnesota's Iron Range considers this specialty an essential part of any family celebration, be it Christmas, Easter, a wedding, anniversary, birthday, or funeral. *Potica* (po-teet-sa) is thinly stretched yeast dough filled with ground walnuts and cooked with honey and milk. The technique for stretching the dough to paper-thinness is much the same as for strudel (see pages 117–19).

THE DOUGH

1 *package active dry yeast*

¼ *cup warm water (105°F. to 115°F.)*

½ *cup milk, scalded and cooled to 105°F. to 115°F.*

⅓ *cup sugar*

1 *teaspoon salt*

½ *cup butter, at room temperature*

2 *eggs*

4 *cups all-purpose flour*

THE FILLING

3 *cups pulverized walnuts*

¾ *cup undiluted evaporated milk*

¾ *cup sugar*

⅓ *cup honey*

½ *teaspoon vanilla*

To prepare the dough, dissolve the yeast in the warm water in a large bowl. Let stand 5 minutes until foamy. Add the milk, ⅓ cup sugar, and salt. Stir in the butter, eggs, and half of the flour. Beat until smooth. Add the remaining flour and mix until a soft dough is formed. Knead about 10 minutes by hand or about 5 minutes with dough hook on heavy-duty mixer. Place in lightly oiled bowl and turn to coat entire surface with oil. Cover and let rise until doubled in bulk, about 1 hour.

While dough rises, combine the walnuts, evaporated milk, and ¾ cup sugar in saucepan. Stir in the honey. Bring to a boil, stirring constantly, and cook 1 minute. Remove from heat and add the vanilla. Cover and let cool to about 100°F.

Cover a table with a flannel-lined plastic tablecloth (with a smooth surface). Grease two 9-by-5-inch loaf pans. Without punching dough down, dump it out onto the center of the plastic tablecloth. Pat dough down first, then roll out with rolling pin as thinly and evenly as possible. Then, carefully stretch into a rectangle about 20 inches by 70 inches. Dough should be so thin that you can see through it. Trim off thick edges. (Shape scraps into a loaf and bake for bread.) Spread filling over dough to within ½ inch of edges. Turn about 2 inches of the long edges over the filling and, starting at a narrow end, roll up tightly to make 1 compact roll. Cut into 2 equal-sized loaves and place into prepared pans. Let rise in a warm place until doubled, about 1 hour.

Preheat oven to 350°F. Bake loaves until golden, about 45 minutes. Remove from pans and let cool on racks. Serve cut in thin slices.

Cream Waffles

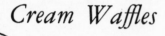

MAKES 4 TO 6 SERVINGS

Waffles have been an American dessert, brunch dish, and supper standby. They were introduced in the 1800s by the Dutch, and a waffle iron carved with a bride's initials and wedding date was a customary wedding gift. The Scandinavians make heart-shaped waffles and serve them with fresh berries or jam. Belgian waffles, baked in the deep-gridded irons, are a favorite dessert. Serve the waffles here with butter and honey or maple syrup, or with whipped cream and berries.

5 eggs
½ cup sugar
½ teaspoon salt
1 cup all-purpose flour
1 cup sour cream
¼ cup butter, melted

In the large bowl of an electric mixer, beat the eggs and sugar on high speed until mixture forms ribbons when beaters are lifted from the bowl, about 10 minutes. Beat in the salt. Sprinkle the flour over the surface of the batter and, with a rubber spatula, fold in the flour. Fold in the sour cream and butter. Let mixture stand 10 minutes. Heat a waffle iron, pour on batter, and bake waffles until crisp and light brown.

Old-time Icebox Desserts and Cakes

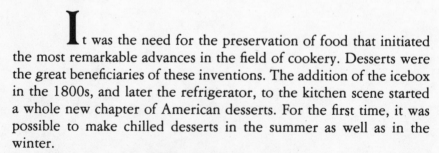

It was the need for the preservation of food that initiated the most remarkable advances in the field of cookery. Desserts were the great beneficiaries of these inventions. The addition of the icebox in the 1800s, and later the refrigerator, to the kitchen scene started a whole new chapter of American desserts. For the first time, it was possible to make chilled desserts in the summer as well as in the winter.

The icebox was the first refrigerator and it usually sat with its drip pan under it on the back porch, so that the iceman could fill it without coming into the house. In northern rural areas, one of the jobs of early spring was to cut huge quantities of ice from frozen ponds, lakes, and rivers into blocks and store them on the north side of the house under a deep cover of sawdust.

About the same time, railroads began carrying foods cooled by ice, transporting fresh fruits, vegetables, and dairy products to places far from their origin. Ice, too, was shipped from the north to the south, making it an important commodity.

Iceboxes changed very little in design from the 1800s until about 1910. Electric refrigerators came into being shortly thereafter. In 1927, a cookbook written for the exclusive few who could afford this $900 addition to the kitchen was published by the General Electric Company. It was written by Miss Alice Bradley, principal of Miss Farmer's School of Cookery and cooking editor of *Woman's Home Companion.* In her enthusiastic endorsement of electric refrigeration she wrote: "To many people electric refrigeration is still such a novelty that they scarcely realize the range of its possibilities. It is almost like having an Aladdin's lamp and not knowing the right way to rub it."

The book goes on to give recipes for plain and fancy ice blocks, frozen salads, ices, sherbets, and frozen fruits, as well as frozen delicacies to "tempt the invalid." In explaining the mysteries of electric refrigeration, the book says that it need not be near an outside door, nor placed for the convenience of the iceman. All that is necessary is a handy electric outlet into which it can be plugged.

By the 1940s the price had come down to an affordable level, and refrigerators were considered indispensable in every home. Freezers were not common, though, until after World War II. At this point, foods that were once only for the rich were attainable by common people.

Apart from the mechanical aid of refrigeration, new ingredients provided incentive for cooks to create new and delightful desserts. The need for the preservation of milk led to another invention in the mid-1800s. That was when Gail Borden developed and patented sweetened condensed milk and used his new product to feed both Northern and Southern troops in the Civil War. After watching the Shakers use a vacuum method to preserve fruits, Borden developed a similar method to remove the water from milk. He added sugar as a preservative. Sales were slow, but once the Civil War broke out there was such a demand for the milk that he licensed other manufacturers to produce it. After the war, he adopted the American bald eagle as the symbol for the milk to signify the original product.

Sweetened condensed milk was originally used to feed armies and babies. In the early 1900s, it was used as a creamer and sweetener for coffee, tea, and cocoa. It was quickly adopted in the South as a convenient form of both milk and sugar for making a great variety of ice creams. The California Mission cooks, short of fresh milk and sugar as well, used it for making a creamy and smooth caramel flan. During World War II, when sugar was rationed, it was used in a variety of desserts and sweets.

Hazelnut Icebox Pudding

MAKES 6 TO 8 SERVINGS

The American hazel shrub grows wild in most parts of the United States, although it prefers a cool climate. The nuts of the hazel shrub are enclosed in a prickly husk, which when dried can be removed and the nuts taken out. Filberts are the commercial counterpart. They are larger than wild hazelnuts, but the flavor is about the same. Although this recipe calls for hazelnuts, in reality, commercial filberts are a more practical and available ingredient.

1 *package unflavored gelatin*
¼ *cup cold water*
1 *cup milk*
4 *egg yolks*
¼ *cup sugar*
A pinch of salt
¾ *cup hazelnuts or filberts, toasted and pulverized*
2 *tablespoons dark rum*
1 *cup heavy cream*
Toasted whole hazelnuts or filberts for garnish (optional)

In a small bowl, sprinkle gelatin over cold water to soften. Combine milk, egg yolks, sugar, and salt in a heavy saucepan. Cook, stirring, over low heat until mixture will coat a wooden spoon. Stir in gelatin. Chill until partially set. Fold in the ground nuts and rum. Whip the cream until stiff, and fold into the mixture. Turn into a 1½-quart mold, glass bowl, or 6 individual dishes. Chill 2 to 4 hours, until set. Serve garnished with toasted nuts, if desired.

Cabinet Pudding

MAKES 6 SERVINGS

This is a deluxe pudding sometimes called "diplomate" pudding, which resembles both a Bavarian cream and a Russe.

1 *cup half-and-half or light cream*
2 *tablespoons sugar*
4 *egg yolks*
¼ *teaspoon salt*
1 *package (1 tablespoon) unflavored gelatin*
2 *tablespoons cold water*
⅓ *cup heavy cream*
1 *teaspoon vanilla*
2 *tablespoons chopped mixed candied fruits*
⅓ *cup diced firm sponge cake, ladyfingers, or macaroons*
Red currant jelly
Candied fruits and whipped cream for garnish

Scald the half-and-half or light cream with the sugar. Whisk the egg yolks in a bowl with the salt. Whisk a portion of the scalded cream into the yolks and, when blended, add the egg mixture into the remaining hot cream. Cook over low heat for 2 to 3 minutes longer; do not boil. The custard should coat the back of a wooden spoon when finished.

In a small bowl, soften the gelatin in the cold water. Add the gelatin to the custard. Cool. Stir in the heavy cream, vanilla, candied fruits, and diced cake or ladyfingers. Brush a 1-quart mold generously with the jelly, and turn the mixture into the mold. Cover and chill about 2 to 4 hours, until set.

Unmold onto a serving platter and garnish or decorate with additional candied fruits and plain whipped cream.

Maple Charlotte

MAKES 6 TO 8 SERVINGS

Even though we generally think of Vermont in connection with maple syrup, it is made in most northern states where maple trees flourish.

1 *package (1 tablespoon) unflavored gelatin*
¼ *cup cold water*
¾ *cup hot maple syrup*
2 *cups heavy cream*
Ladyfingers or sponge cake slices

In a small bowl, soften the gelatin in the cold water. Pour in the hot maple syrup and stir until the gelatin dissolves. Place over a bowl of ice water and stir until mixture begins to thicken. Whip the cream until stiff, and fold into the maple mixture. Line individual molds (use six 1-cup molds or eight ⅔- or ¾-cup molds) or a

6-cup mold with ladyfingers or sponge cake slices. Fill molds or mold with the maple mixture. Chill several hours, until set. Unmold onto serving platter.

Lemon Icebox Cake

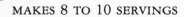

MAKES 8 TO 10 SERVINGS

When the family purchased a new Westinghouse electric refrigerator in the 1940s, the book that came with it included this recipe. It was about that time when the sleek, rounded refrigerators started to be indispensable in the modern American kitchen. Cooking contests also promoted the use of the sweetened condensed milk invented 100 years before. The combination of these two innovations resulted in a recipe that can be found today in some version or other in most Junior League and church-organization recipe collections.

2 cups vanilla wafer crumbs
½ cup melted butter
6 eggs, separated
½ teaspoon cream of tartar
½ cup sugar
¼ teaspoon salt
½ cup fresh lemon juice
Grated rind of 1 lemon
One 14-ounce can sweetened condensed milk

Preheat oven to 350°F.
Combine the wafer crumbs with the butter and firmly pat into the

bottom of a 9- or 10-inch springform pan. Bake 15 minutes, or until crust is lightly browned.

Meanwhile, in a large bowl, beat the egg whites until foamy. Add the cream of tartar. Add the sugar gradually, and beat until a stiff, shiny meringue is formed. Set aside. Without washing the beaters, in another bowl, beat the egg yolks until thick and fluffy. Add salt, lemon juice, and lemon rind. Slowly beat in the condensed milk, and beat until lemon-colored and semi-thick. Fold about one-third of the meringue into the lemon mixture. Pour into the baked crust. Spread the remaining meringue evenly over the filling, spreading it to touch the edges of the pan all around. Bake 20 minutes, until top is lightly browned. Cool, then cover and chill at least 24 hours, or until cake is set. Remove rim of pan before serving.

Icebox Pumpkin Cream Roll

MAKES 8 TO 10 SERVINGS

It must have been a wonderland—all the new and interesting produce that the Indians had to offer the settlers in the New World. Pumpkin was called "pompion" by the English settlers, and was new to Europeans. The Indians had made up many imaginative ways to use the produce from their fields. Pumpkin Pie (see recipe) lingers as the most famous American classic. But European cooks quickly adapted pumpkin, corn, and squashes to many other interesting desserts, and main dishes as well. This pumpkin roll includes cooked puréed pumpkin, spices, and lots of eggs to make a spicy cake that can be rolled up with a filling that has pumpkin in it, too.

THE CAKE

6 *eggs, separated*
½ *cup granulated sugar*
½ *cup cooked puréed pumpkin*
1 *teaspoon mixed pumpkin pie spice*
⅓ *cup all-purpose flour*
½ *teaspoon baking powder*
¼ *teaspoon salt*

THE FILLING

1 *cup heavy cream*
¼ *cup powdered sugar*
½ *cup cooked puréed pumpkin*
½ *teaspoon mixed pumpkin pie spice*
1 *cup chopped toasted pecans*
1 *teaspoon vanilla*

Preheat oven to 350°F. Line a 10½-by-15½-inch jelly-roll pan with parchment or wax paper, and grease the paper well.

To prepare the pumpkin roll, beat the egg yolks and granulated sugar until light and thick. Blend in ½ cup pumpkin purée, 1 teaspoon pumpkin spice, flour, and baking powder. Beat egg whites with salt, until firm peaks form. Fold whites into yolk mixture. Pour batter into the prepared pan. Bake 15 minutes, until cake bounces back when touched in the center. Turn out onto wax paper that has been sprinkled with powdered sugar. Immediately peel off top paper and carefully roll up cake, making the roll lengthwise. Cool.

Meanwhile prepare filling. Whip the cream until stiff, beating in ¼ cup powdered sugar. Blend in ½ cup pumpkin purée, ½ teaspoon pumpkin spice, pecans, and vanilla. Unroll cooled cake. Spread with the filling, and roll it up again. Chill 2 to 4 hours. When ready to serve, sprinkle with additional powdered sugar.

Coffee Mallow

MAKES 6 SERVINGS

Older than sweetened condensed milk is another ingredient often used in refrigerated desserts: marshmallows. If Cleopatra would have had graham crackers and squares of chocolate, she could have provided the marshmallows to sandwich her s'mores. Marshmallows are a food as old as the pyramids. The ancient Egyptians were the first to prepare marshmallows, using the root of the mallow plant and sugar, which they believed to have medicinal qualities.

The mallow tree was introduced to America and was planted along the coasts of New England and New York, in Michigan and Arkansas. Though the transplantation was specifically for the purpose of utilizing its sticky root, it was so expensive to process the genuine mallow root that the formula for marshmallows changed. It was replaced in 1870 by a gum arabic and egg white combination. Further changes to produce a more tender, less grainy, lighter, better-looking, better-tasting, and better-keeping product evolved. The name remains the same, but today's jet-puffed marshmallows find themselves at the ends of sticks over a campfire or melted into confections or dessert mixtures, rather than in a medicine cabinet.

16 *marshmallows, quartered, or 2 cups miniature marshmallows*
½ *cup hot coffee*
1 *cup heavy cream*
1 *teaspoon vanilla*

Combine the marshmallows and coffee in a metal bowl. Place over hot water and heat until the marshmallows are melted. Remove from water and stir until cooled. With electric mixer, beat until fluffy. Whip the cream until stiff, and fold into the mixture. Add the vanilla. Pour into dessert glasses and chill 2 to 4 hours, until set.

Calliope Coffee

MAKES 6 SERVINGS

Simple coffee-flavored gelatins such as this were considered quite elegant desserts at the turn of the century. This is a dessert that was served on a showboat that traveled from the head of the Allegheny River down the Ohio to the Mississippi. The calliope was the musical steam whistle, perched on top of excursion boats, that was played on a keyboard to announce the arrival of the steamships.

1 *package (1 tablespoon) unflavored gelatin*
¼ cup strong, cold coffee
1½ cups strong, hot coffee, preferably espresso
2 tablespoons sugar
Sweetened whipped cream

Soften the gelatin in the cold coffee. Stir in the hot coffee and sugar, until gelatin and sugar are dissolved. Allow to cool. Pour into 6 small, individual molds and refrigerate 2 to 4 hours, until set. Unmold onto individual serving plates. To serve, top with sweetened whipped cream.

Chocolate Mocha Icebox Pudding

MAKES 6 SERVINGS

2 squares (2 ounces) unsweetened chocolate
¾ cup hot coffee
1 package (1 tablespoon) unflavored gelatin
¼ cup cold water
3 eggs, separated
⅓ cup sugar
1 small sponge cake, angel food cake, or pound cake (see Note)
1 cup heavy cream
2 tablespoons powdered sugar
1 teaspoon vanilla

Melt the chocolate with the coffee in a bowl over hot water. Soften the gelatin in the cold water, and add to the melted chocolate mixture. Stir this mixture into the egg yolks.

In a large mixing bowl, whip the egg whites until stiff, beating in the sugar until the mixture is stiff and meringuelike. Pour the chocolate mixture over the whites, and fold until blended. Cut cake into ½-inch cubes, and fold into the mixture. Spoon mixture into a 6-cup mold and chill several hours or overnight.

Unmold onto serving platter. Whip cream until stiff, and add the powdered sugar and vanilla. Decorate the mold with the whipped cream squeezed through a pastry bag with a fancy tip.

NOTE: Preferably, use one of the cakes in this book—see pp. 250–54.

Chocolate Rum Russe

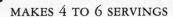

MAKES 4 TO 6 SERVINGS

The old *Fannie Farmer Cookbook* suggests that this may be chilled in individual sherbet glasses, as well as being made in a large mold. The mold is chilled, turned out on a plate, then decorated with ladyfingers or slices of jelly roll.

1 *package (1 tablespoon) unflavored gelatin*
¼ *cup cold water*
½ *cup hot milk*
⅓ *cup powdered sugar*
3 *tablespoons dark rum*
1 *square (1 ounce) unsweetened chocolate, grated*
1 *cup heavy cream*
6 *ladyfingers or slices of jelly roll for garnish*

Soften the gelatin in the cold water. Add to the hot milk and stir until dissolved. Turn into a mixing bowl and add the sugar and rum. Place bowl over a pan of ice water and stir until mixture begins to thicken. Beat until fluffy. Fold in the grated chocolate. Whip the cream, and fold into the pudding. Pour into 4 to 6 individual molds (depending on size) or 1-quart mold. Chill 2 to 4 hours, until set. Turn out onto a serving platter and garnish with ladyfingers or slices of jelly roll.

Old-fashioned Chocolate Icebox Cake

MAKES 6 SERVINGS

This recipe was especially prepared for the owners of new General Electric Refrigerators in 1927.

32 *ladyfingers (1 inch wide)*
4 *eggs, separated*
A *dash of salt*
2 *squares (2 ounces) semisweet chocolate*
2 *tablespoons powdered sugar*
2 *tablespoons water*
Whipped cream

Line a 4-by-8-inch loaf pan with plastic wrap. Make a layer of ladyfingers with the flat side up in the bottom of the pan, covering the entire bottom evenly.

Whip the egg whites with a dash of salt, until stiff. Set aside. Combine the chocolate, sugar, and water in the top of a double boiler. When the chocolate is melted, add the egg yolks and beat with an electric mixer (no need to wash beaters after whipping the whites), beating at high speed, until mixture is light and fluffy. Fold the egg whites into the chocolate mixture. Turn half the mixture into the pan lined with the ladyfingers. Top with another layer of ladyfingers. Cover with remaining chocolate mixture and still another layer of ladyfingers.

Cover and chill 24 hours, until set. Unmold onto serving platter and decorate with whipped cream.

Nesselrode Pudding

MAKES 6 SERVINGS

Nesselrode pudding is named for Count K. R. Nesselrode, a Russian diplomat who lived from 1780 to 1862. There have been many versions popular in our country. The mixture usually includes dried fruits, puréed chestnuts, and cream. In the 1800s, a great variety of intricately fancy pudding molds were used to freeze the pudding into elaborate shapes. It was generally included as a dessert during the holiday season, as is plum pudding.

½ *cup currants*
¼ *cup raisins*
½ *cup dark rum*
4 *egg yolks*
1 *cup sugar*
2 *cups light cream*
One 8-ounce can chestnut purée (approximately)
1 *teaspoon vanilla*
1 *cup heavy cream*
1 *teaspoon vegetable oil*
Sweetened whipped cream
1 *candied chestnut (optional)*

Soak currants and raisins in rum at least 15 minutes. Beat the egg yolks until foamy, then beat in ⅔ cup sugar. Continue beating until the yolks are thick and form a ribbon when the beaters are lifted.

Heat the light cream in a small saucepan, until bubbles form around edge of the pan. Slowly beat the hot cream into the egg yolk mixture, and return to pan. Cook, stirring, until mixture thickens and coats back of a spoon. Do not boil. Remove from the heat and add the chestnut purée, rum with fruits, and vanilla. Chill about 30 minutes.

Whip the heavy cream until stiff. Add the remaining ⅓ cup sugar and whip until cream forms firm peaks. Fold into the chilled Nesselrode mixture.

Brush a 1½-quart fancy dessert mold with the oil and drain any excess. Fill the mold with the Nesselrode mixture, cover, and freeze at least 6 hours.

To unmold, run a knife around the inside edge of the mold. Dip the bottom in hot water and wipe dry. Place serving plate on top of the mold and invert to unmold. Rap once or twice to dislodge pudding, if necessary. Garnish with lightly sweetened whipped cream squeezed through a pastry bag with a star tip. Top with a candied chestnut, if desired.

Baked Alaska

MAKES 8 SERVINGS

The idea of baking ice cream in meringue was around long before Alaska was part of the United States. An American-born scientist, Benjamin Thompson, who later became Count Rumford in England, claimed his "omelette surprise" was the by-product of research in 1804 into the resistance of stiffly beaten egg whites to heat. The idea of "baked ice" spread, and there were many variations on it. At one time the dessert was known as Alaska-Florida, and later as Baked Alaska. Every source quotes a different recipe, which is basically made of a sponge cake base (at least 1 inch thick), a brick of ice cream on top of the cake, and a thick coating of meringue covering the cake and ice cream. This concoction can be kept in the freezer until serving time or baked immediately in a 500°F. oven until the meringue is tinged with gold. It does not take much imagination to know that there are lots of variations possible on the theme—chocolate cake with chocolate ice cream, white cake with strawberry ice cream, spice cake with butter pecan ice cream, and so forth.

1 *layer Country Pound Cake or Sponge Cake (see recipes),* 1 *inch thick*

A 1-*quart brick of ice cream*

4 *egg whites*

A dash of salt

1 *cup sugar*

Cover a breadboard or a thick plank with a piece of foil. Place the layer of cake on top of the foil. Top with the brick of ice cream. The cake should be large enough to extend at least ½ inch beyond the ice cream all around. Place in the freezer while you prepare the meringue.

In a large bowl, whisk the egg whites and salt until they hold soft peaks. Add the sugar, 1 tablespoon at a time, while whisking or beating at high speed, until the meringue is very stiff and stands in firm peaks. Cover the ice cream and the edge of the cake completely with the meringue. Keep frozen until ready to serve.

Preheat oven to 500°F. Place cake in the oven for 3 to 5 minutes, or until edges of the meringue are tinged with gold. Serve immediately cut into wedges or slices.

Ice Creams, Sherbets, and Ices

It is surprising to discover that what sometimes seems to be a rather modern food is really an ancient one. An example is ice cream. What seems even more incredible is that the early Americans were willing to go through a lot of trouble to make this frozen delicacy out of rather simple ingredients. In the South, ice creams were more popular than in the North, where it would have been much easier to accomplish making ice cream for a larger portion of the year. But then, ice was a saleable commodity for Northerners, and perhaps considered too valuable to "waste" on such things as ice cream making. A bit of the same philosophy as the shoemaker's children not having shoes.

The history of ice cream, however, is much longer than that of our country. It is believed to be a Chinese invention of about three thousand years ago. It was brought to Europe by Marco Polo, and a

Sicilian introduced it to France in the mid-1600s. It was the wealthy of America who first enjoyed ice cream. It is recorded that in 1758, in Virginia, a hailstorm provided a supply of ice, which Governor Fauquier used to cool wine and freeze cream. George Washington, in 1784, purchased an ice cream machine for one pound, thirteen shillings, and four pence. Although George Washington made ice cream, it was Dolley Madison who popularized it. Ice cream was often served at elaborate dinners; at Madison's Second Inaugural Ball in 1813, the climactic moment was marked by the serving of ice cream. The cream came from the presidential dairy at Montpelier, and strawberries were from the garden.

Italy contributed tutti-frutti, spumoni, and biscuit tortoni to the variety of ice creams on the American table. Although we may think that the love of chocolate is truly American, it was the Swiss and Dutch who brought chocolate to America, where it became one of the classic ice cream flavors.

Ice cream was first made in a "pot freezer," in which the ingredients were beaten by hand and then shaken up and down in a pan of ice and salt until frozen. In 1846, Nancy Johnson invented the hand-cranked ice cream freezer. In 1851, Jacob Fussell, a milk dealer in Baltimore, set up the first large wholesale ice cream business. In 1874, the ice cream soda was introduced at the semicentennial of the Franklin Institute in Philadelphia. The ice cream cone originated at the St. Louis World's Fair in 1904. The ice cream sundae, originally an ice cream soda without soda, came into being to skirt a law prohibiting the sale of "stimulating beverages" on Sunday.

With the availability of electric refrigerators, making ice cream was much easier. Cooks everywhere created recipes for water ices and frappés that would seem sophisticated today. Milk sherbets, fruit creams, mousses, parfaits, and ice creams all expanded the repertoire of the well-informed cook.

Ices are made of sweetened fruit juices diluted with water; a sherbet is made with milk, cream, and/or egg whites, not necessarily just water. Ice creams are smoothest when made with a high percentage of cream, but are also the richest and most caloric. Inventive cooks over the decades in the last 150 years have experimented with different methods of making ice cream smooth without the high fat content. Gelatin, eggs, and fruit pectin, as well as a cornstarch-thickened base, work to smooth out the cream. They do, however, add their own flavor to the mixture, which purists would not accept.

One ingredient that has been used since the turn of the century to make exceptionally smooth ice cream is sweetened condensed milk. The extra milk solids, with the higher fat content and sugar, are what make it work. After the Civil War, sweetened condensed milk became widely available. Because the South had such an avid taste for ice cream, and sweetened condensed milk was so convenient and made a very smooth and rich ice cream, it came into extensive use there, where they created a wide variety of ice cream flavors.

Fruit Jelly Ice

The simplest of the frozen desserts, fruit ices are the forerunners of ice cream itself. Fruit ices are a mixture of fruit juice, sugar, and water that when frozen with agitation, as in a mechanical or hand-cranked ice cream freezer, creates a smooth, fruit-flavored ice. The old *White House Cookbook* (1887) gives four recipes for ices. In a rather matter-of-fact suggestion, the book says that when fruit jellies are used, they should first be heated gently with water to melt them sufficiently. "Other flavors may be made in this manner, varying the flavoring to taste."

Homemade or good-quality store-bought fruit jelly
Water
Lemon juice to taste

Blend the jelly with an equal amount of water, whisking until smooth. Add lemon juice to taste. Turn into a hand-cranked or mechanical ice cream freezer and freeze according to the manufacturer's directions. Flavors that work well are raspberry, plum, grape, strawberry, apple, pineapple, and cranberry.

Lime Sherbet

MAKES ABOUT 1 QUART

Egg white enhances the smooth texture of this low-calorie sherbet. It can be made in any kind of ice cream freezer, as well as in a freezer tray. The whipped egg white is added *after* the mixture is partially frozen, regardless of the freezing method. For lemon sherbet, substitute lemon juice; and for orange sherbet, add orange juice and grated orange rind, if desired.

3 cups water
1½ cups sugar
⅔ cup fresh lime juice
A dash of green food coloring (optional)
1 egg white

In a 2-quart saucepan, combine the water and sugar and boil 5 minutes. Cool. Add lime juice and a dash of green food coloring, if desired. Turn into a hand-cranked or mechanical freezer, or into freezer trays. Freeze until slushy. Beat the egg white until soft peaks form and add to the partially frozen sherbet. Continue freezing until firm.

If using freezer trays, beat the egg white and the slush together in a bowl until fluffy, then return to the freezer trays. Freeze again until slushy, and remove and whip again in a bowl. Return to trays and freeze until firm.

Orange Cream Sherbet

MAKES ABOUT 1 QUART

This is close to an ice cream, even though it is called a sherbet. The mixture may curdle when combined, but it smooths out after freezing.

½ *cup sugar*
1 *cup fresh or frozen concentrated orange juice*
1 *cup milk*
1 *cup heavy cream*

Combine all of the ingredients. Place into a hand-cranked or mechanical ice cream freezer and freeze according to the manufacturer's directions.

Strawberry Milk Sherbet

MAKES ABOUT 1 PINT

By the 1920s, unflavored gelatin was in use and it was added to ice creams and sherbets to smooth the texture, as in this recipe.

1 *pint strawberries, cleaned and hulled*
½ *cup sugar*
A few grains of salt
1½ *teaspoons unflavored gelatin*
2 *tablespoons cold water*
1½ *cups milk*

In a large bowl, crush the strawberries with the sugar and salt. Cover and let stand for 2 hours.

Soak the gelatin in the cold water. Scald the milk and add the gelatin to the hot milk. Cool. Press the strawberries through a coarse sieve, and blend with the milk. Turn into a freezer tray and place in the freezer. When the mixture is partially frozen, stir it toward the front to thoroughly mix the frozen and liquid portions. Return to the freezer and continue to stir and mix every 15 to 20 minutes. When mixture is firm, turn into a large bowl and beat with a rotary beater until very smooth. Return mixture to tray and place in the freezer until ready to serve. Or, if using a mechanical or hand-cranked freezer, follow the manufacturer's directions.

Lemon Cream Sherbet

MAKES ABOUT 1 QUART

A combination of sour cream and gelatin makes this sherbet rich and smooth.

⅓ *cup sugar*
⅓ *cup light corn syrup*
⅓ *cup freshly squeezed lemon juice*
1½ *cups milk*
½ *cup sour cream*
A few grains of salt
2 *teaspoons unflavored gelatin*
2 *tablespoons cold water*

In a mixing bowl, combine the sugar, corn syrup, and lemon juice. Heat milk and sour cream to scalding and add the salt. Soften the gelatin in cold water, then add to the hot milk and stir until dissolved. Cool completely, then add the lemon juice mixture. Turn into a freezer tray and freeze 1 hour. Remove from the freezer, turn into a bowl, and beat with a rotary beater until very light. Place mixture in the tray and return to freezer until frozen. Or freeze in a hand-cranked freezer according to the manufacturer's directions.

Vanilla Custard Ice Cream

MAKES 1½ QUARTS

A smooth, creamy product is the desired end result of the ice cream maker. Although some may object to thickening an ice cream mixture with cornstarch, it will smooth out the texture. It is important to cook the cornstarch completely to eliminate the flavor of uncooked starch. Ice cream tastes the best when it is not solidly frozen and rock-hard, as it can be after being stored in a deep freeze. Be sure to remove it from the freezer 20 to 30 minutes before serving for the best flavor and texture.

2 *cups milk*
1 *tablespoon cornstarch*
¾ *cup sugar*
2 *egg yolks, or 1 egg, lightly beaten*
¼ *teaspoon salt*
2 *cups heavy cream*
1 *tablespoon vanilla*

Pour 1 ½ cups milk into a saucepan and heat to simmering. Mix the remaining ½ cup milk with the cornstarch and sugar. Stir part of the scalded milk into the sugar mixture until smooth, then return to the saucepan with the remaining milk. Cook, stirring constantly, until the custard is thick enough to coat the back of a wooden spoon. Stir the yolks or whole egg in a bowl. Add a small portion of the hot mixture to the yolks, and whisk until smooth. Whisk the egg mixture back into the hot milk. Cook, stirring, for 2 minutes. Cool. Add the salt, heavy cream, and vanilla. Chill.

Freeze in a mechanical or hand-cranked freezer using the manufacturer's directions. Or put in freezer trays and place in the freezer. When mixture is slushy, remove from freezer and beat until smooth. Return mixture to trays and place in freezer until solid, about 4 to 6 hours.

CHOCOLATE ICE CREAM: Add 2 to 6 ounces (squares) unsweetened chocolate to the custard while it is cooking. Increase sugar to 1 cup.

COFFEE ICE CREAM: Add 1 tablespoon instant coffee to the custard while it is cooking.

LEMON-GINGER ICE CREAM: Add 1 tablespoon grated lemon rind and ½ cup chopped crystallized ginger to the chilled custard before freezing.

PISTACHIO ICE CREAM: Add 1 teaspoon almond extract, ½ cup chopped pistachio nuts, and a few drops of green food coloring to the custard before freezing.

TOASTED-ALMOND FUDGE ICE CREAM: Toast 1 cup chopped almonds. In a saucepan, combine 2 squares (2 ounces) semisweet chocolate and ½ cup heavy cream and cook over low heat until chocolate is melted. Add 1 cup sugar, a few grains of salt, and 2 tablespoons butter, stirring while cooking, until this is a smooth sauce. When ice cream is almost completely frozen, add the almonds to the ice cream along with 1 cup of the fudge sauce; continue freezing until firm.

Southern-Style Ice Cream

MAKES ABOUT 1½ QUARTS

This smooth and creamy ice cream is so simple to prepare because it is based on the use of sweetened condensed milk. With not much effort, one can produce a wide variety of popular flavors.

One 14-ounce can sweetened condensed milk
2 egg yolks, beaten
2 teaspoons vanilla
¼ cup whole milk
2 cups heavy cream

In a mixing bowl, combine the sweetened condensed milk, egg yolks, vanilla, and whole milk. Stir in the heavy cream. Turn into a hand-cranked or mechanical ice cream maker and freeze according to the manufacturer's directions. Or, whip the cream and fold into the mixture. Pour into a 1-quart metal pan and freeze 6 hours, or until firm.

BUTTER PECAN ICE CREAM: Melt 2 tablespoons butter, and stir in ¼ cup chopped pecans. Add 1 teaspoon maple flavoring and the buttered pecans to the basic ice cream mixture before freezing.

STRAWBERRY ICE CREAM: Thaw one 10-ounce package frozen strawberries in syrup. Place in a food processor or blender and process or blend until smooth. Omit eggs, vanilla, and whole milk. Add strawberries to the sweetened condensed milk and heavy cream, and freeze as described above.

RASPBERRY ICE CREAM: Thaw one 1-pound package frozen unsugared raspberries. Turn into a food processor or blender and process or blend until smooth. Omit eggs, vanilla, and whole milk from basic mixture. Add raspberries to the sweetened condensed milk and heavy cream, and freeze as described above.

CHOCOLATE FUDGE ICE CREAM: Omit egg yolks, vanilla, and whole milk, and add ¾ cup chocolate fudge ice cream topping to the mixture before freezing.

Philadelphia Vanilla Ice Cream

MAKES 1½ QUARTS

Philadelphia ice cream contains only cream, sugar, and flavoring. It goes back to the 1800s, when Mrs. Lincon, writing in *The American Kitchen,* explained that Philadelphia ice cream is the ice cream made without eggs. Scalding the cream intensifies the flavor of both the cream and the vanilla. Use a hand-cranked ice cream maker or the new ice cream machines for the best results.

1 *quart half-and-half or light cream*
¾ *to* 1 *cup sugar*
A few grains of salt
1½ *tablespoons vanilla*

Scald the half-and-half or light cream. Add the sugar and salt. Cool. Add the vanilla. Chill, then transfer to the ice cream maker and freeze according to the manufacturer's directions. If desired, prepare one of the following variations.

CHOCOLATE CHIP ICE CREAM: Add 1 cup (6 ounces) miniature chocolate chips to the cooled mixture, or coarsely chop an 8-ounce milk chocolate bar and add to the cream before cranking and freezing.

PEPPERMINT CHIP ICE CREAM: Add 1 cup chopped peppermint stick candy when ice cream is about half frozen.

RUM-RAISIN-NUT ICE CREAM: Soak ½ cup raisins in ½ cup rum for 30 minutes. When the ice cream is finished, add the raisins and rum and continue cranking until they are mixed in and the ice cream has refrozen. Blend in ⅓ cup chopped toasted walnuts with a spoon or spatula.

Coconut Ice Cream

MAKES ABOUT 1 QUART

The only way to get true coconut flavor in ice cream is to use a fresh whole coconut. The extra effort is worth it!

1 *medium coconut, with liquid*
2 *cups milk, scalded*
3 *egg yolks*
¾ *cup sugar*
A *pinch of salt*
2 *cups heavy cream*

With hammer and screwdriver or nail, tap holes in the 3 eyes of the coconut, drain out the liquid, and reserve it. Split the coconut and pry out the meat. In a food processor with the shredding blade in place, shred the coconut meat. Place shredded coconut in a bowl and pour hot milk over it. Marinate 1 hour, then drain through fine cloth over a bowl. Squeeze out all the milk. There should be about 1 ½ cups coconut milk. Mix with the liquid from the coconut.

Beat the egg yolks and sugar in a bowl, until thick and lemon-colored. Add salt. Bring coconut milk to a boil and stir a small part of it into the egg mixture. Add the egg mixture to the pan with the coconut milk over low heat and stir until thickened. Do not boil. Cool.

Whip the cream until soft peaks form, and combine with the coconut-egg mixture. Freeze in a mechanical or hand-cranked freezer according to the manufacturer's directions.

Tutti-frutti Ice Cream

MAKES ABOUT 1½ QUARTS

The old *White House Cookbook* (1887) records a great variety of ices and ice creams, and these frozen desserts were most impressive for state dinners. Fruit creams and raspberry, black cherry, strawberry, and the classic chocolate and vanilla ice creams are given, but an ice cream that used fruits preserved especially for this purpose was a favorite. Tutti-frutti ice cream was often molded in a fancy ice cream mold, a red food coloring swirled throughout for a marbelized effect.

4 *cups heavy cream*

1 *cup sugar*

2 *eggs*

1 *tablespoon vanilla*

½ *pound mixed candied fruits, such as pineapple, cherries, peaches, apricots, plums, cut into small dice (about 1 cup)*

In a 3-quart saucepan, whisk together the cream, sugar, and eggs. Place over medium heat and cook, stirring constantly, to just below the boiling point. Do not boil or the mixture may curdle. Remove from the heat, cover, and cool. Add the vanilla. Turn into a hand-cranked or mechanical freezer and freeze according to the manufacturer's directions. When almost entirely frozen, stir in the fruits until evenly blended into the ice cream mixture; finish freezing.

Colonial Molasses Pecan Ice Cream

MAKES 2 QUARTS

This is a very fluffy mixture to begin with, and when kept in a deep freeze, will still retain a scoopable texture. Molasses adds a caramel, rather than a bitter, flavor to this old Colonial favorite.

¾ *cup chopped pecans*

¼ *cup butter*

6 *eggs, separated*

1 *cup superfine sugar*

⅔ *cup light or dark molasses*

½ *teaspoon vanilla*

2 *cups heavy cream*

Preheat oven to 300°F. Place the pecans and butter on a cookie sheet and bake 10 minutes. On the cookie sheet, stir the nuts and butter together to mix; return to oven for another 10 to 20 minutes, until toasted. Remove from oven and let cool.

In the large bowl of an electric mixer, beat the egg whites until frothy. Beat in the superfine sugar, a little at a time, until the mixture holds stiff peaks. Beat in the egg yolks, 1 at a time, the molasses, and vanilla. In another bowl, whip the cream until it holds soft peaks. Fold the whipped cream into the egg mixture. Pour into a shallow, 3-quart metal dish and freeze until mushy. Stir in the pecans. Freeze until just firm. Or, turn unwhipped cream into the mixture and freeze in a mechanical ice cream freezer, according to the manufacturer's directions.

Old-fashioned Burnt-Sugar Ice Cream

MAKES 2 QUARTS

This is one of the oldest and simplest of the flavored ice creams. Basically, only two ingredients are used, sugar and cream. The sugar is melted to a caramelized bittersweetness and dissolved into the cream. For the smoothest results, use a hand-cranked or mechanical ice cream freezer.

2 *cups sugar*
1 *quart heavy cream*
1 *quart half-and-half*

In a heavy cast-iron frying pan, stir the sugar over medium to low heat, until the sugar melts and becomes a deep amber color. Turn heat down to the lowest possible setting and pour in 2 cups heavy cream. Cook and stir until the sugar is dissolved into the cream. Pour into a bowl. Add the remaining 2 cups heavy cream and the half-and-half. Turn into a hand-cranked ice cream freezer and freeze according to the manufacturer's directions.

Country Dairy Desserts: Custards, Soufflés, and Creams

In 1611 the first dairy cows arrived on American shores, brought by the Jamestown colonists. That was the beginning of what was to be a nationwide industrial giant. Milk and dairy products, of course, were at first the most abundant in the East. Milk that once was so scarce became so plentiful that John Cotton remarked, "Milk and ministers were the only things cheap in New England" (from *The American Heritage Cookbook*).

It took almost two hundred years for cows to reach California. Helen Evans Brown, writing in her *West Coast Cookbook,* quoted Dame Shirley, who wrote in the early to mid-1800s from the gold fields: "No milk, no eggs, no nothing"—which, one could think, meant "no desserts" as well. Dairy products and even sugar were very expensive when they first became available in the state in the late 1800s. As dairy products became more abundant, California began a love affair with desserts, and cookbooks were devoted to little more than desserts.

Meanwhile, in the East and Midwest, sprawling dairy farms were producing milk in great quantities. Delicate custards ranged from the wholesome "family" desserts to impressively flavored, rich, creamy finales for fancy meals.

Eggs, too, were scarce in the West, and they cost a dollar apiece if you could get them at all! In the Midwest, South, and East, the chicken was a staple farm bird, and eggs were always in supply in the country kitchens there. Custards were standard, and a smooth stirred custard topped with poached fluffs of egg whites whipped into meringue created a favorite dairy-farm dessert known as "floating islands."

Crisply aproned and hair retained in a dustcap, early cooks knew the basic rules for cooking. For instance, the rule for a baked custard is: 8 eggs to a quart of milk (or 2 eggs per cup of milk). To get by during times when fewer eggs were available (the chickens molt and stop laying eggs in the middle of the winter), 6 eggs per quart of milk and a tablespoon of flour were used to make a custard. Duck eggs, because they were larger, were recommended for an extra-rich custard, and you could get by with fewer of them.

Hints from the *White House Cookbook* (1887) revealed a basic belief that the flavor of butterfat makes desserts delicious. The book suggests adding a "lump of butter" to the custard, or to use cream instead of milk, or to double the quantity of eggs, omitting all the whites. A note also added something that is still true: The flavor of the custard is improved if the milk is boiled and cooled first. In the early kitchen, custard mixtures may have been cooked on top of the stove or they were steamed.

Colonists were quick to adapt available ingredients to old cooking methods. To flavor a baked custard with maple sugar made a pleasant dessert. To add puréed pumpkin to a basic custard mixture, was still another creative idea. To whip the egg whites and fold them into the basic custard mixture created a soufflé-like custard. Beating both the egg yolks and whites separately and folding them together made an especially light and inexpensive dessert.

Baked Country Custard

MAKES 8 SERVINGS

Old, historic cookbooks give rather general directions for custards, such as this one published in 1879 in *Housekeeping in Old Virginia:* "For Baked Custard. Seven eggs; one quart milk; three tablespoonfuls sugar. Flavor to taste."

7 *eggs*
4 *cups milk, scalded and cooled*
½ *cup sugar*
1 *tablespoon all-purpose flour*
1 *teaspoon vanilla*
Nutmeg
Maple syrup

Preheat oven to 325°F. Butter a 1½-quart baking dish. Fit it into a larger dish into which you will pour boiling water. Heat some water to a boil in a kettle.

Beat the eggs in a bowl. Blend in the milk, sugar, flour, and vanilla. Pour into the baking dish. Sprinkle with nutmeg. Pour boiling water into the larger dish to come about 1 inch up the sides of the dish holding the custard. Bake, uncovered, 30 minutes, or until the custard is set. Do not overbake or the custard may separate. Serve warm or chilled with maple syrup to pour over individual servings.

Cup Custards

MAKES 4 SERVINGS

Custards baked in individual cups require a shorter baking time. Chilled, they are delicious served with sliced fresh strawberries.

2 cups milk or half-and-half
4 tablespoons sugar
A dash of salt
2 eggs
1 teaspoon vanilla
Nutmeg

Preheat oven to 325°F. Place 4 custard cups in a shallow baking pan. Heat some water to a boil in a kettle.

In a saucepan, heat the milk or half-and-half to the scalding point, and stir in the sugar and salt. Beat the eggs in a bowl and slowly whisk in the hot milk. Add the vanilla. Pour through a fine-meshed wire strainer into the custard cups, and sprinkle with nutmeg. Place pan with filled custard cups in the oven. Pour boiling water into the baking pan to about half full. Bake 20 minutes, or until custards are set. Insert a silver knife off center in one of the custards; if it comes out clean, the custards are done. Do not overbake or the custards will be watery.

Cream Custards

MAKES 4 TO 6 SERVINGS

On a Midwestern dairy farm these were called "cream custards," designating just that—they were made with cream.

2 *cups heavy cream*
3 *tablespoons sugar*
A *dash of salt*
4 *egg yolks*
1 *teaspoon vanilla*

Preheat oven to 325°F. Place 4 custard cups or 6 tiny heatproof pots de crème or demitasse cups in a pan. Heat some water to a boil in a kettle.

In a saucepan, combine the cream, sugar, and salt. Bring to a simmer, stirring. In a bowl, whisk the egg yolks until mixed. Slowly whisk in the hot cream until blended but not frothy. Stir in the vanilla. Pour through a fine-meshed wire strainer into the cups or pots de crème. Place pan with cups in oven, and fill pan halfway with boiling water. Bake custard 25 to 30 minutes, or just until set. To check, tap the sides of the cups with a spoon. When custards are done they will have a jellylike shake. Or insert a thin knife into one of the custards and if it comes out just barely clean, it is ready. Do not overbake or the custards will separate. Remove pan from oven and set custards aside to cool on a rack.

Old Salem Custard Soufflé

MAKES 6 SERVINGS

Not quite a custard, yet not quite a soufflé, this is a puffy, eggy, delicate dessert that should be served at once with sweetened whipped cream and a sprinkling of maple sugar.

2 *tablespoons butter*
2 *tablespoons all-purpose flour*
1 *cup milk*
4 *eggs, separated*
3 *tablespoons sugar*
1 *teaspoon vanilla*
¼ *teaspoon almond extract*
A dash of salt
Sweetened whipped cream
Maple sugar or grated sweet chocolate

Preheat oven to 350°F. Butter a 1½-quart baking dish or soufflé dish.

In a saucepan, heat the butter and blend in the flour. Gradually whisk in the milk and cook, whisking, until thickened and smooth. In a bowl, whisk the egg yolks with the sugar, vanilla, almond extract, and salt, and slowly whisk in the hot mixture. Return mixture to the saucepan and cook 1 minute, until thickened (mixture should not boil). Remove from the heat. In a large bowl, beat the egg whites until stiff. Fold whites into the thickened sauce. Turn into the prepared baking pan and bake 40 to 45 minutes, or until set. Serve at once with sweetened whipped cream and a sprinkling of maple sugar or grated sweet chocolate.

Maple Custard

MAKES 4 SERVINGS

The Indians of North America were tapping maple trees and using the sap long before the white settlers arrived. They taught the pioneers to make the syrup and sugar, because cane sugar was prohibitively expensive, if not unavailable. This is not a small project; it takes 30 to 50 gallons of the sap from the sugar maple to produce 1 gallon of syrup. It is made in North America only in New England and along the Great Lakes, where the majority of the trees grow. "Minute pudding," a simple dish made with a quart of milk and thickened with ¾ cup flour and a bit of salt, was served with maple syrup. Maple Custard is another more appealing, simple dessert that is sweetened with maple syrup.

3 eggs, beaten
½ cup maple syrup
2 cups milk
A dash of salt

Preheat oven to 350°F.
In a bowl, blend the eggs, syrup, milk, and salt. Pour into 4 custard cups. Set the cups in a pan. Add hot water to about 1 inch depth. Bake 20 to 30 minutes, or until a knife inserted in the center comes out clean. Serve warm or chilled.

Pumpkin Custard

MAKES 6 SERVINGS

Another "gift" of the American Indian to our classic desserts is the use of the big yellow squash—the pumpkin. Pumpkin that is cooked and puréed and blended with a basic custard mixture and spices is the forerunner of pumpkin pie.

2 *cups milk or half-and-half*
1 *teaspoon butter*
3 *eggs, beaten*
½ *cup tightly packed light brown sugar*
½ *teaspoon salt*
½ *teaspoon cinnamon*
½ *teaspoon nutmeg*
1 *cup cooked, puréed pumpkin*

Preheat oven to 350°F.

Scald the milk or half-and-half and add the butter, eggs, sugar, salt, cinnamon, nutmeg, and pumpkin. Pour into a shallow 1-quart baking dish or into 6 custard cups. Set filled baking dish or cups into a larger pan with hot water to about 1 inch depth. Bake 35 to 40 minutes, or until a knife inserted in the center comes out clean. Serve warm or chilled.

Baked Honey Custard

MAKES 6 SERVINGS

Sugar was perennially a scarce, therefore expensive, item on the American frontier and many families substituted "tree-sweetenin', bee-sweetenin', and molasses." European settlers introduced honeybees into the New World, and they soon became indispensable, as the honey was used in all kinds of desserts.

2 *cups milk*
1/4 *cup honey*
3 *eggs*
1/4 *teaspoon salt*
A dash of nutmeg

Preheat oven to 375°F. Heat some water to a boil in a kettle.

In a small saucepan, scald the milk and stir in the honey. In a bowl, beat the eggs and salt together, then slowly beat in the hot milk, a little at a time. Pour mixture through a fine-meshed strainer into 6 custard cups, and sprinkle with nutmeg. Set custard cups in a large pan and fill pan with boiling water to about 1/2 inch of the top rim of the custard cups. Bake 20 to 25 minutes, until a knife inserted in the center comes out clean. Do not overcook or the custards will become watery. Remove cups from water immediately, cover, and chill.

California Burnt-Almond Cream

MAKES 6 SERVINGS

Speaking Californian, this is "Aamand Cream" (*a* as in *apple,* not as in *car).* California is known for producing almonds, and brandy, too.

½ *cup chopped almonds*
2 *cups heavy cream*
6 *tablespoons brown sugar*
⅛ *teaspoon salt*
7 *egg yolks*
1 *tablespoon California brandy*
Brown sugar for glaze

Place the almonds in a heavy skillet over low heat. Stir and toast until pale golden brown. Set aside. Have ready a shallow, heatproof earthernware or glass dish for setting and serving the cream.

In a saucepan, combine the heavy cream with the brown sugar and salt. Heat to a simmer. In a bowl, beat the egg yolks; whisk in the hot cream and the brandy. Place the bowl over boiling water, or transfer mixture to the top of a double boiler, and cook, stirring, until thickened. It should be smooth and about the thickness of cream sauce. Stir in the toasted almonds. Turn into the serving dish. Cover and chill at least 12 hours.

About 1 hour before serving, sift additional brown sugar over the top of the custard in a thin, even layer. It should be about ¼ inch thick. Preheat the broiler and place the dish under the broiler, about 4 inches from source of heat, until the sugar melts and just begins to brown. Chill, uncovered, until ready to serve. The melted sugar will harden to a thin, icelike glaze that has to be cracked with a sharp rap of a spoon. Spoon some of the glaze with the custard into each serving dish.

Mission Flan

MAKES 6 SERVINGS

The California missions spearheaded much of the good cooking done in the West. When sweetened condensed milk became available in the late 1800s, the missionaries of Spanish descent combined caramel custard with it to make this superb dessert.

½ *cup sugar*
4 *eggs*
One 14-ounce can sweetened condensed milk
1 *cup water*
1 *teaspoon vanilla, rum, or brandy*

Preheat oven to 350°F. Have ready a shallow 1-quart casserole or pie pan. Heat some water to a boil in a kettle.

Pour the sugar into a cast-iron skillet and stir over low heat until the sugar melts and caramelizes. Pour the molten sugar into the pie pan, coating the bottom and sides evenly. Allow sugar to cool while you prepare the custard.

In a bowl, beat the eggs and add the milk, water, and your choice of flavoring. Pour into the prepared dish and set in a larger pan containing 1 inch of boiling water. Bake 1 hour, or until set. Loosen flan with a spatula and turn out onto a deep serving dish. Chill, and serve with the sauce that accumulates around the flan spooned over it.

Shaker Floating Islands

MAKES 6 SERVINGS

Plenty of rich milk and nest-fresh eggs characterized the food of the Shaker Kitchen Sisters, who labored to "please God in preparing the viands entrusted to their hands." This is a favorite old recipe. Rosewater can be purchased in pharmacies, specialty food stores, and, sometimes, in the mix department of a well-stocked liquor store.

1 *tablespoon cornstarch*
4 *cups milk*
5 *eggs, separated*
½ *cup plus* 3 *tablespoons sugar*
½ *teaspoon rosewater or vanilla*
⅛ *teaspoon salt*

In a small dish, mix the cornstarch with a small amount of the cold milk. Heat the remaining milk to a simmer. In a bowl, whisk the cornstarch mixture with the egg yolks, and slowly beat in ½ cup sugar. Slowly whisk in the hot milk, keeping the mixture smooth. Return mixture to the saucepan and cook over low heat, stirring constantly, for 3 minutes, or until mixture thickens but does not quite come to a boil. Add the rosewater or vanilla. Pour into a serving dish.

In a large pot, bring about 2 quarts of water to a boil. In a large mixing bowl, whisk the egg whites until frothy. Add the salt and continue beating, adding the remaining 3 tablespoons sugar, until whites are smooth and stiff. Drop egg-size spoonfuls of the whites into the boiling water and cook 2 minutes. Remove whites, drain, and place on top of the custard. These are the "islands." Chill before serving.

Angel Parfait Cream

MAKES ENOUGH FOR 20 SERVINGS

This was a favorite dessert at state dinners, which is understandable because it is an easy recipe, providing you have a number of parfait glasses on hand to make enough desserts for a large party. Alternate layers of cream with ice cream or sherbet in the parfait glasses.

1 *cup sugar*
¼ *cup water*
2 *egg whites*
A *pinch of salt*
2 *teaspoons vanilla or flavored liqueur to taste*
2 *cups heavy cream, whipped*
4 *quarts ice cream in your choice of flavor*

In a heavy 2-quart saucepan, combine sugar and water. Place a candy thermometer in the syrup and boil to 230°F. to 234°F. In the large bowl of an electric mixer, beat the egg whites and salt until foamy, then beat until stiff. Slowly pour the syrup into the egg whites, continuing to beat until thick and meringuelike. Cool. Add vanilla or liqueur. Fold in the whipped cream. Alternate layers of cream with ice cream in the parfait glasses.

CRÈME DE MENTHE PARFAITS: Flavor the cream with crème de menthe to taste. Alternate layers of cream with lime sherbet and vanilla ice cream.

CHOCOLATE ALMOND-CRUNCH PARFAITS: Flavor the cream with crème de cacao. Alternate layers of cream with almond brittle or almond crunch ice cream; top with shaved chocolate.

STRAWBERRY-STRIPE PARFAITS: Flavor the cream with vanilla, and alternate layers with strawberry ice cream.

Shaker Dessert Omelet

MAKES 4 SERVINGS

The Shakers were very successful orchardists, and they believed in the importance of apples in the diet. Combining apples with sweet fresh butter and fresh eggs, the Shakers made this wholesome dessert and served it with a cider sauce made from homemade cider.

4 *large tart apples, pared, cored, and chopped*
Cider
½ *cup sugar*
½ *teaspoon nutmeg*
Cider Sauce (see following recipe)
4 *eggs, well beaten*
1 *tablespoon butter*

In large saucepan, cook the apples in cider to cover, until soft. Strain and reserve the juices for the sauce. Press apples through a sieve to purée. Combine with the sugar and nutmeg. Cool.

Prepare the Cider Sauce.

Preheat oven to 250°F. When apples are completely cooled, beat in the eggs. Spread butter evenly over the bottom and sides of a shallow 1-quart baking dish. Pour mixture into the dish. Bake 20 minutes. Serve warm with Cider Sauce.

Cider Sauce

MAKES 1½ CUPS

Reserved juices from cooking apples (about 1 cup)
1 cup cider
1 tablespoon butter
1 tablespoon all-purpose flour
2 tablespoons sugar

Combine reserved juices with the cider. Place juices and cider in a large saucepan over high heat and boil to reduce to 1½ cups. In a small saucepan, melt the butter and add the flour and sugar. Slowly beat in the hot juices and boil 5 minutes, until thickened. Serve hot.

Omelet Soufflé

MAKES 4 SERVINGS

This must be served immediately as it comes out of the oven. You can, however, prepare it for baking and hold it at room temperature for up to 1 hour. Place it in the preheated oven 12 minutes before you plan to serve dessert.

6 eggs, separated
½ cup sugar
½ teaspoon vanilla extract
A pinch of salt
Powdered sugar
Grated chocolate

Preheat oven to 375°F. Butter and dust with sugar a shallow 1-quart baking dish.

Beat the egg whites until frothy, then beat with half the sugar until stiff and meringuelike. In another bowl, without washing the beaters, beat the egg yolks with the remaining sugar, vanilla, and salt, until light and lemon-colored. Fold the whites and yolks together. Turn mixture into the buttered dish and bake 10 to 12 minutes, until golden. Serve immediately with powdered sugar and grated chocolate to sprinkle over individual servings.

Rhubarb Soufflé

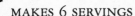

MAKES 6 SERVINGS

Pie plant, as rhubarb is known, is a native of Asia and a member of the buckwheat family of plants, though it grows profusely almost everywhere in the Americas. Because it needs a lot of fertilizer, the most natural place for rhubarb to grow well is when it is used as a shrub around barns and outbuildings. The stalks are eaten; the leaves are poisonous. Most commonly, the stalks were cooked into a sauce that was served with vanilla custard or over rice pudding, or with heavy cream poured over it.

1½ *pounds fresh rhubarb, cut into ½-inch pieces*
1 *cup sugar*
3 *tablespoons butter*
4 *tablespoons all-purpose flour*
3 *eggs, separated*
2 *egg whites*
¼ *teaspoon salt*
Sweetened whipped cream or Vanilla Cream Sauce (see recipe)

183

Combine the rhubarb and just enough water to cover the bottom of a saucepan. Simmer until rhubarb is tender, about 15 minutes. Measure, and return 3 cups of the stewed rhubarb to the saucepan (refrigerate the remaining rhubarb, if any, for another use). Add the sugar, butter, and flour and bring to a boil, stirring, until thickened. Blend in the egg yolks. Cook 1 minute longer. Do not boil. Remove from heat.

Preheat oven to 375°F. Butter and dust with sugar a 1½-quart baking dish or soufflé dish.

Whip the 5 egg whites and salt until stiff. Fold the rhubarb mixture into the egg whites. Turn mixture into the baking dish and place in a larger pan of hot water. Bake 30 minutes, or until soufflé is set, puffed, and delicately browned on top. Serve hot with sweetened whipped cream or Vanilla Cream Sauce.

All-American Pies

For some Americans, it isn't dessert unless it comes in a crust. Pie has traditionally been America's favorite dessert. Even though we are led to believe that New England invented the pie, crust-enclosed fruit pastry can be traced back to the peasant cookery of almost every European country.

The slope-sided pie pan, as we know it, is truly American. It was designed with economy in mind, to literally cut corners and stretch ingredients. Americans preferred to bake shallow pies.

The simple mixture of shortening, flour, and water, of which pastry is made, originated with the Greeks during their Golden Age. The Romans carried home recipes for pastry as a prize of victory when they conquered Greece. Because "all roads led to Rome," the idea of pastry spread throughout Europe, and with the immigrants to America.

For all practical purposes, American pies start with apple. Beyond that, anything is just a variation on a theme. But in collecting apple pie recipes, one finds some subtle and some not so subtle differences. The type of apple, of course, still depends on the area in which you live—especially when making pies in the fall, when the orchards are heavy with fruit. Later in the year, the same apple types are available to all, but they've been kept in refrigeration for months and so will be less juicy and less flavorful.

Not only are apple varieties a little different from one part of the country to another, local favorites give a special character to apple pies. Discounting the standard brands of frozen pies in the supermarkets, American apple pies offer variety. This variety is due to different preferences in the crust, the spices, the thickening agent, the design of the top crust, and ingredients besides apples that are used in the filling.

"Apple pie without cheese is like a kiss without a squeeze," said the Reverend Henry Ward Beecher. Wisconsin took the Reverend Beecher literally and passed a law that is still on the books that requires eating establishments to have available Wisconsin Cheddar cheese for every piece of apple pie. The law doesn't state whether you are charged extra for it, but a customer can demand a slice of cheese.

For the Pennsylvania Dutch, pies perform special services, such as poor man's pies or *flitche,* which make use of anything handy and satisfy the children while the major business of pie making goes on. Amish half-moon pies or preaching pies do not drip because they are stuffed with dried apples, but they keep children quiet during long Sunday services. *Rosina boi* or raisin pie, made with raisins, are called "funeral pies," because they are served to fortify mourners after a funeral.

The Pennsylvania Dutch bake pies by the dozens and store them in the pierced-tin "pie cupboards." Safe in these ventilated cabinets, they are always available. They eat "stack pies" at barn raisings. These are simply six or eight different pies, stacked on top of each other. They cut wedges down through the whole stack and help themselves to a stack of all kinds of pie. It saves trying to make up one's mind about which variety to choose!

Deep-dish pies, somewhat resembling cobblers, have always been practical everyday desserts. They were developed by farm women to salvage fruit that might otherwise be wasted when the orchard yields a bumper crop.

When pioneers traveled inland, their cherished pie recipes went with them. New types of pies were invented as new ingredients required improvisation. Pecan pies, cream pies, and pies made with a variety of fruits and vegetables kept the idea of pie from becoming static. Tender baked pastry was used to cradle fresh berries and fruits made beautiful with a shiny glaze. Old favorites evolved into new creations like chiffon pie. Chiffon pies were originally served in a restaurant in Iowa. They retain many of the characteristics of cream pies and "fluff" pies, but gelatin was added to transform the old pies into spectacular refrigerated creations.

Pies have the advantage of being portable desserts. As a result, they were carried to potlucks, picnics, family reunions, and festivals. Pie-eating contests were organized at county fairs. Pie auctions were fund-raising events at one-room schoolhouses. Pie-baking contests challenged young homemakers to bake the best pie in the region.

Buttery Pastry for Pies

MAKES PASTRY FOR 1 DOUBLE-CRUST PIE,
OR 2 SINGLE-CRUST PIE SHELLS

Use this old-fashioned classic pastry for any of the pies in this chapter. If you need only a single pie crust, make this double batch anyway and freeze the remainder sealed in a Ziploc bag.

1½ cups all-purpose flour
4 tablespoons lard, chilled
2 tablespoons butter, chilled
⅛ teaspoon salt
3 tablespoons ice water

In the large bowl of an electric mixer or in the work bowl of a food processor with the steel blade in place, combine the flour, lard, butter, and salt. Process on/off with processor, or blend just until shortening is in pieces about the size of peas. Sprinkle ice water over mixture and toss to blend. Press together to make a ball. Knead dough once or twice to blend.

For a double-crust pie, on a lightly floured board, roll out half the crust to fit the pie pan. Fit crust into pan. Add filling. Roll out the second half of the crust and place over filling. Moisten with water the top edge of the bottom crust. Trim both the top and bottom to within ½ inch of the edge of the pan. Fold both top and bottom crusts under and crimp edges with fingers or with a fork.

For two single-crust pie shells, divide the dough into two balls. On a lightly floured board, roll out each ball to fit a 9-inch pie pan. Place in pan and trim the excess pastry to within ½ inch of the rim of the pie. Fold under and crimp edges with fingers or with a fork.

For a prebaked pie shell, preheat oven to 400°F. Line a pie pan or tart shell with enough pastry for 1 crust. Cut a piece of foil large enough to line the inside of the pastry. Press the foil down firmly inside the pie shell, and fill the foil with uncooked beans or uncooked rice. Bake 15 to 20 minutes, until the edge of the crust is golden brown. Remove from the oven, cool, and remove weights and foil from the crust. (For a *partially* baked pie shell, bake 10 to 15 minutes, or until edges are just *beginning* to brown.)

No-Fail Lemon Pastry

MAKES PASTRY FOR 1 DOUBLE-CRUST PIE,
OR 2 SINGLE-CRUST PIE SHELLS

The use of lemon and egg in this pastry is an old-fashioned "trick" for making a flaky pastry. Use this pastry for any of the pies in this chapter that call for a single or double crust.

1 ½ *cups all-purpose flour, stirred before measuring*
½ *teaspoon salt*
½ *cup plus 1 tablespoon butter, chilled, or ½ cup lard, chilled*
1 *egg, lightly beaten*
2 *teaspoons lemon juice*
3 *to 4 tablespoons ice water*

Combine the flour and salt in large mixing bowl. Cut in the butter or lard, using a pastry blender, two knives, or a pastry fork, until the fat is the size of dry peas. In a small bowl, whisk together the egg, lemon juice, and 3 tablespoons ice water. Drizzle the liquid mixture over the crumbly mixture. With a fork or spatula, mix until the pastry holds together in a ball, adding more ice water if necessary. Turn out onto a lightly floured board. Knead one or twice, lightly, to shape the dough into a ball. Wrap in foil or plastic wrap and refrigerate 30 minutes before rolling out; see instructions in previous recipe for rolling out.

WHOLE WHEAT PASTRY: Substitute ¾ cup whole wheat flour for ¾ cup all-purpose flour in the recipe.

Easy Pastry
with an Electric Mixer
or Food Processor

MAKES PASTRY FOR 1 DOUBLE-CRUST PIE,
OR 1 SINGLE-CRUST PIE SHELL

By using a food processor to cut the shortening into the flour, it is possible to prepare pie pastry very quickly. Be careful not to over-process the mixture, or you will have a cookie dough—tender but not flaky.

SINGLE CRUST

¼ *cup vegetable shortening*
¾ *cup all-purpose flour*
½ *teaspoon salt*
2 *tablespoons cold water*

DOUBLE CRUST

½ *cup vegetable shortening*
1½ *cups all-purpose flour*
1 *teaspoon salt*
¼ *cup cold water*

Combine shortening, flour, and salt in the bowl of an electric mixer. Blend at low speed about 30 seconds, or until fat is in pea-size pieces. Or combine the ingredients in the work bowl of a food processor with the steel blade in place. Process using on/off bursts, until fat is in pea-size pieces. Add all the water at one time and mix about 15 seconds with the electric mixer, or with 8 to 10 pulses of the food processor, until dough clings together. Shape into a ball; it should feel smooth and moist, not wet. Chill until ready to roll out. To roll out, follow instructions on p. 188.

Hot-Water Pastry

MAKES TWO 9- OR 10-INCH PIE SHELLS,
OR 1 DOUBLE-CRUST PIE

This is a more generous recipe, which allows for more edge-trimming, crimping, or filling a larger pie pan if needed.

2 cups all-purpose flour
½ teaspoon baking powder
1 teaspoon salt
⅓ cup boiling water
⅔ cup vegetable shortening

In a large mixing bowl, combine the flour, baking powder, and salt. In another bowl, combine the boiling water and shortening and mix with a fork until creamy. Add flour mixture to water and shortening and mix until a dough forms. Chill 30 minutes to 1 hour before rolling out (see instructions, p. 188).

Old-fashioned Country-Style Apple Pie

MAKES ONE 9-INCH PIE

Those who make apple pies often don't even need to follow a recipe, but this is how to make a basic apple pie. A few variations follow.

Pastry for 1 double-crust 9-inch pie (see recipes)
¾ to 1 cup sugar (less for sweeter apples, more for tart)
2 to 3 tablespoons all-purpose flour (less for drier apples, more for juicy ones)
½ to 1 teaspoon cinnamon to taste
⅛ teaspoon nutmeg (optional)
¼ teaspoon salt
6 to 7 cups thinly sliced, pared apples (2 to 2½ pounds)
2 tablespoons butter

Prepare the pastry, roll out half of it, and line a 9-inch pie pan. Preheat oven to 425°F.

In a large bowl, combine the sugar, flour, cinnamon, nutmeg, if desired, and salt. Fold in the apples and mix until evenly coated. Heap the apples in the pastry-lined pan and pat down firmly. Dot with butter. Roll out top crust and fit over the apples. Cut vent holes and flute the edges. Bake 50 minutes to 1 hour, or until the crust is browned and apples are tender.

DUTCH APPLE PIE: Cut large vents in the top crust and omit the butter. Five to 10 minutes before baking time is up, remove pie from the oven and pour ½ cup heavy cream into the pie through the vents. Return pie to oven and finish baking.

CANDY APPLE PIE: Omit cinnamon and nutmeg and add 3 tablespoons red cinnamon candies to the sugar. Make a lattice-style top crust.

APPLE-RAISIN PIE: Add ½ cup seedless golden or dark raisins to the apples.

STREUSEL APPLE PIE: Omit top crust and butter. Top the pie with a mixture of ¼ cup brown sugar, ½ cup all-purpose flour, and ¼ cup butter, blended to make coarse crumbs.

APPLE-PECAN PIE: Add ¼ cup chopped pecans to the apple mixture.

WISCONSIN APPLE PIE: Lay 4 thin slices (4 ounces) sharp Wisconsin Cheddar cheese on top of the apples after dotting them with the butter. Cover with top crust and bake as directed.

Mush-Apple Pie

MAKES ONE 9-INCH PIE

Samuel Clemens (Mark Twain) in his eccentricity often ate just Mush-Apple Pie and milk for all meals. There were those who worried about his health and nutritional well-being; however, some folks today should eat so well! With hardly anything but applesauce in the crust, the name is understood.

10 *medium tart apples*
1 *cup water*
1 *cup sugar*
Pastry for 1 double-crust 9-inch pie (see recipes)
Whipped cream

Pare, core, and slice the apples. Place in a 3-quart saucepan and add the water. Cover and cook over low heat 15 minutes, stirring occasionally, until the apples are soft. Add the sugar and continue to simmer 30 minutes over low heat, stirring occasionally, until liquid is cooked away. Be careful not to scorch the apples. Stir until the apples are mushy. Cool.

Preheat oven to 450°F. Line a 9-inch pie pan with half of the rolled-out pastry. Pour in the cooled applesauce and cover with the remaining crust. Cut to make vents in top crust. Moisten edges with water and press to seal. Bake 20 minutes, reduce heat to 350°F, and bake 25 minutes more, until the crust is browned. Serve warm with whipped cream.

Rhubarb-Strawberry Pie

MAKES ONE 9-INCH PIE

Not only do the flavors of rhubarb and strawberry enhance each other, they happen to be in season at the same time. The strawberries lend rhubarb a mellow sweetness, and rhubarb adds its own tang to the pie. For those who buy strawberries and have rhubarb in their garden, the economical advantage is obvious.

Pastry for 1 double-crust 9-inch pie (see recipes)
1 pint fresh strawberries, cleaned, hulled, and sliced
2 cups sliced raw rhubarb
¾ cup tightly packed light brown sugar
½ cup granulated sugar
2 tablespoons all-purpose flour
2 tablespoons butter
1 egg white, lightly beaten
Granulated sugar
Whipped cream or heavy cream

Prepare the pie crust and use half of it to line a 9-inch pie pan. Preheat oven to 425°F.

In a bowl, combine the strawberries, rhubarb, brown sugar, granulated sugar, and flour. Pile the fruit in the pastry-lined pie pan and level off. Dot with butter. Lay the top crust over the fruit. Seal and flute the edges. Cut vents in the top. Brush crust with beaten egg white and sprinkle with sugar. Bake 40 to 50 minutes, until golden. Serve warm or cooled to room temperature with whipped cream or cream to pour over pieces of the pie.

Wild Blueberry or Huckleberry Pie

MAKES ONE 9-INCH PIE

Wild or "low bush" blueberries grow profusely in the northern areas of the United States. In Maine, wild blueberry producers help along the self-propagating little blueberries with fertilization, weeding, and general tending. In Minnesota, low bush berries grow in the rocky northern wilderness and are accessible and available only to those who know where they are. Blueberry picking is more of a sport than a necessity for food. Every August foragers—local people, families, old ladies with their heads protected with scarves, canoe-trippers, and backpackers—fill pail after pail with the little blueberries. In 1918, vast areas of northern Minnesota were burned by a forest fire, killing all the weeds and vegetation, and for many years after that blueberry patches were so abundant that old-timers will tell of the berries they "milked" into pails.

Because huckleberries are similar in tartness and flavor to blueberries, they can be used interchangeably. Mark Twain, a lover of pies, loved huckleberry pie, and when he was depressed, it was reported that he would eat a half a pie with a quart of milk every morning.

Pastry for 1 double-crust 9-inch pie (see recipes)
4 cups wild blueberries or huckleberries
¾ cup sugar
3 tablespoons all-purpose flour
½ teaspoon cinnamon
1 tablespoon butter

Preheat oven to 375°F.

Roll out half the pastry and line a 9-inch pie pan. In a large bowl, gently combine the berries with the sugar, flour, and cinnamon. Turn mixture into the crust-lined pan. Dot with butter. Roll out top crust and cover the berries. Moisten edges with water, and crimp to seal. Bake until crust is golden brown, about 45 to 55 minutes.

Cranberry Pie

MAKES ONE 9-INCH PIE

Early Colonial cooks used molasses for sweetening this pie.

Pastry for 1 double-crust 9-inch pie (see recipes)
4 cups fresh cranberries, washed and halved
1¾ cups tightly packed light brown sugar
3 tablespoons all-purpose flour
½ teaspoon cinnamon
2 tablespoons butter
Whipped cream or ice cream

Preheat oven to 375°F.

Roll out half the crust to line a 9-inch pie pan. In a bowl, gently combine the cranberries, brown sugar, flour, and cinnamon. Turn mixture into the pastry-lined pan. Dot with butter. Roll out top crust and cut into ½-inch strips. Arrange in a lattice pattern on top of the cranberry filling. Moisten edges with water, trim off strips, and crimp edges to seal. Bake 45 to 55 minutes, until filling is bubbly and crust is golden. Cool before serving. Serve with whipped cream or ice cream.

Honey Rhubarb Pie

MAKES ONE 9-INCH PIE

If the rhubarb is not the pink variety, cooks add a few drops of red food coloring to the rhubarb mixture.

Pastry for 1 double-crust 9-inch pie (see recipes)
4 cups cubed fresh rhubarb (cut into ½-inch pieces)
1 cup sugar
6 tablespoons all-purpose flour
¼ teaspoon salt
2 teaspoons grated lemon rind
Red food coloring (optional)
⅓ cup honey
2 tablespoons butter

Preheat oven to 400°F.

Roll out half the pastry and line a 9-inch pie pan. In a large bowl, combine the rhubarb, sugar, flour, salt, and lemon rind. Turn mixture into the pastry-lined pie pan. Drizzle with the honey (if using red food coloring, mix with the honey before drizzling over the rhubarb). Dot with the butter. Roll out top crust, moisten edges with water, and crimp to seal. Cut vents in the crust. Bake for 50 minutes to 1 hour, until golden.

Fresh Red Cherry Pie

MAKES ONE 9-INCH PIE

George Washington chopped down the famous cherry tree, and February, his birthday month, has become the month of cherry pies. But the best cherry pies are not baked in February when all that is available are the canned or frozen varieties. The best are made in the summer when cherries are ripe. Also, the best pies are made with tart, red cherries rather than the sweeter, more bland black cherries that are excellent eaten out of hand.

Pastry for 1 double-crust 9-inch pie (see recipes)
4 cups fresh tart cherries, pitted
1⅓ cups sugar
⅓ cup all-purpose flour
A dash of salt
3 to 4 drops almond extract (optional)
2 tablespoons butter
Milk
Sugar

Preheat oven to 425°F.

Line a 9-inch pie pan with half of the pastry. In a bowl, gently blend together the cherries, 1⅓ cups sugar, flour, salt, and almond extract, if desired. Turn mixture into the pastry-lined pan, and dot with butter. Roll out the top crust and cut into ½-inch strips. Arrange strips in a lattice pattern over the cherries. Moisten edges with water, trim, and crimp to seal. Brush top of lattice strips with milk, and sprinkle with sugar. Bake 35 to 40 minutes, until golden.

NOTE: When fresh cherries are not available, drain two 16-ounce cans pitted red cherries very well. Add a dash of nutmeg to the mixture.

Cow Lake Township Funeral Pie

MAKES ONE 9-INCH PIE

Pies were baked for special occasions by the Southerners, as well as by the Pennsylvania Dutch. Raisin pie or *rosina boi* came to be known as "funeral pie" in Pennsylvania. Also in Arkansas, this version of raisin pie, flavored with a touch of bourbon whiskey, was baked to console mourners and satisfy their hunger. It was served after the funeral, along with other nourishment.

1 ½ *cups raisins*
3 *tablespoons bourbon*
1 ½ *cups water*
1 *egg*
1 ½ *cups sugar*
1 *tablespoon grated orange rind*
⅓ *cup all-purpose flour*
¼ *cup lemon juice*
A dash of salt
1 *unbaked 9-inch pie shell (see recipes)*

Preheat oven to 350°F.
In a heavy saucepan, combine the raisins, bourbon, and water. In a medium-size bowl, beat the egg, and add the sugar, orange rind, flour, lemon juice, and salt. Mix egg mixture into the raisins. Bring to a boil, stirring constantly, and cook until thickened. Cool. Pour filling into the pie shell, and bake for 25 minutes.

Sugar Pie

MAKES ONE 9-INCH PIE

A meal without pie seemed unthinkable to the early Shakers.
When the apple bins were empty in the spring they made sugar pie
out of the ingredients that were available—butter, sugar, cream. Sugar
pies were made in the South, too, except there they used vanilla
instead of rosewater, the favorite Shaker flavoring. In New England,
the pie was made with maple sugar and called maple sugar pie. In
Indiana, a similar pie, made minus the eggs and butter and using
vanilla as a flavoring, was called Hoosier cream pie. This is a sweet
and rich pie; you will want to serve just a thin wedge. It is excellent
with fresh strawberries on the side.

1 *unbaked 9-inch pie shell (see recipes)*
1 *unbeaten egg white*
½ *cup butter, at room temperature*
1 *cup light or dark brown sugar or maple sugar*
1 *tablespoon all-purpose flour*
1 *cup heavy cream*
3 *eggs*
½ *teaspoon rosewater or vanilla*
⅛ *teaspoon nutmeg*

Brush the pie shell with the egg white and allow to stand until
dry, about 30 minutes.
Preheat oven to 450°F.
Spread one-third of the butter evenly over the bottom of the pie
shell. Sprinkle with one-third of the sugar. Repeat the layers until all
the butter and sugar are used, then sprinkle the last layer with flour.
Mix the cream with the 3 eggs and rosewater or vanilla, and pour over
the ingredients in the pie shell. Dust with nutmeg. Bake at 450°F. for
10 minutes. Reduce heat to 350°F and bake 25 to 30 minutes more,
until the top is lightly browned and set. Cool and chill completely
before serving.

Country Kitchen Custard Pie

MAKES ONE 9-INCH PIE

Simple and nutritionally sensible, you don't need to apologize for having dessert if it is custard pie. If you prebake the crust, it won't end up soggy. Some country cooks, not satisfied with anything but the crispiest crust, will bake the crust and filling separately, then slip the baked custard into the baked crust.

1 *unbaked 9-inch pie shell (see recipes)*
3 *eggs*
½ *cup sugar*
2½ *cups milk*
A dash of salt
1 *teaspoon vanilla*
A dash of nutmeg

Preheat oven to 450°F.

Line the pastry in the pie pan with aluminum foil and weight it down with uncooked beans or rice or with pie weights. Bake 15 minutes. Remove the weights and foil and cool.

In a bowl, beat the eggs and sugar. Heat the milk to scalding. Whip the hot milk into the eggs and sugar; add the salt and vanilla. Pour through a fine-meshed wire strainer into the baked pie shell, and top with nutmeg. Reduce heat to 350°F. and bake 25 to 35 minutes, or until custard is set and knife dipped just off center comes out clean.

Original Pumpkin Pie

MAKES ONE 9-INCH PIE

Our favorite Thanksgiving pie, pumpkin pie is really just a variation on the custard-pie theme. A correctly made pumpkin pie must be deep, delicate, with light pastry, a little "trembly" as it comes from the oven, yet delicately browned on top. For a smooth but not so rich pie, modern cooks often use evaporated milk in place of the heavy cream.

2 cups cooked, puréed pumpkin, or one 16-ounce can pumpkin
⅔ cup tightly packed brown sugar
2 teaspoons cinnamon
½ teaspoon ginger
¼ teaspoon salt
1 cup heavy cream
3 eggs, well beaten
1 unbaked 9-inch pie shell (see recipes)
Whipped cream

Preheat oven to 350°F.

In a bowl, blend together the pumpkin, brown sugar, cinnamon, ginger, salt, cream, and eggs. Pour mixture into the pie shell. Bake 40 to 50 minutes, or until pie is set. (It should "tremble" when tapped on the side.) Remove from the oven and cool on a rack. Serve with whipped cream.

Creole Sweet Potato Pie

MAKES ONE 9-INCH PIE

In the South, sweet potatoes were used more often than pumpkin in a pie. The pie is similar in texture to a pumpkin pie. The flavor addition of bourbon is classic, but you can leave it out if you choose.

½ cup sugar
1 teaspoon cinnamon
½ teaspoon allspice
½ teaspoon nutmeg
½ teaspoon salt
One 23-ounce can sweet potatoes, mashed (about 1½ cups)
2 eggs, lightly beaten
½ cup light cream or half-and-half
2 tablespoons melted butter
¼ cup bourbon (optional)
1 unbaked 9-inch pie shell (see recipes)
Pecan halves
Lightly sweetened whipped cream

Preheat oven to 400°F.

In large mixing bowl, combine the sugar, cinnamon, allspice, nutmeg, salt, sweet potatoes, and eggs, beating until blended. Stir in the cream, butter, and bourbon, if desired. Turn mixture into the pie shell. Arrange pecan halves around the edge. Bake 40 minutes, or until a knife inserted in the center comes out clean. Serve warm or cooled to room temperature, topped with whipped cream.

Florida Key Lime Pie

MAKES ONE 9-INCH PIE

It is difficult to find a real Key lime in Florida today. The "real Key lime" was the lime of Key West; Key lime juice from Florida is available in bottles in many specialty food stores. The tree itself is not native to Florida and, according to Raymond Sokolov, in his *Fading Feast,* it is a citrus tree that originated in Malaysia or eastern India. How and when the seeds were transported to the New World is pure conjecture, but the limes spread across the West Indies to Mexico and to the Florida Keys. The truth is that when you order a Key lime pie today in a restaurant, you are not getting the real thing. At any rate, this is a recipe that has been used for generations in Florida and is made with sweetened condensed milk, the convenience milk that gained wide use during and after the Civil War.

3 eggs, separated
½ cup Key lime juice, including the pulp, or the juice and pulp of
   any available limes
¼ teaspoon grated lime rind
One 14-ounce can sweetened condensed milk
1 baked 9-inch pie shell (see recipes)
Whipped cream for garnish

Preheat oven to 350°F.
In the large bowl of an electric mixer, beat the egg yolks until light and lemon-colored. Combine the lime juice, rind, and condensed milk, and beat into the egg yolks. Whip the egg whites until stiff, and fold into the lime mixture until marbled, not completely mixed. Pour filling into the pie shell. Bake 20 to 30 minutes, until filling is just set. Chill. Before serving, garnish with whipped cream.

White House Molasses Pie

MAKES ONE 9-INCH PIE

Abraham Lincoln had such a craving for molasses that while he was President he had a standing order for molasses pie at William Taussig's New York Excelsior Steam Cracker Bakery in Washington. The original recipe in the *White House Cookbook* reads like this: "Two teacupfuls of molasses; one of sugar, three eggs, one tablespoonful of melted butter, one lemon, nutmeg; beat and bake in pastry."

½ cup light or dark molasses
½ cup dark corn syrup
½ cup tightly packed light or dark brown sugar
3 eggs
2 tablespoons butter, melted
Juice and rind of 1 lemon
½ teaspoon nutmeg
1 unbaked 9-inch pie shell (see recipes)

Preheat oven to 400°F.
Combine the molasses, corn syrup, sugar, eggs, butter, lemon juice and rind, and nutmeg. Pour filling into the pie shell. Bake 25 to 30 minutes, or until pie is set.

Pennsylvania Dutch Shoofly Pie

MAKES ONE 9-INCH PIE

The Pennsylvania Dutch claim they can make pies out of *anything.* Among them are crumb pies, oatmeal pies, and a concoction that inspired a song—shoofly pie. Shoofly pies were made out of crumbs and molasses, and there are many explanations for the name. One is that the filling is so sweet one must shoo away the flies before one can eat the pie. Another is that flies are partial to molasses and have to be chased away while one is making the pie.

Shoofly pies are breakfast pastries, usually served with morning coffee. They have the consistency of a spongy spice cake baked in a rich, flaky pastry. A good Pennsylvania Dutch cook loves a challenge and can prepare a pie from a minimum of ingredients.

1 ½ *cups all-purpose flour*
½ *cup sugar*
½ *teaspoon cinnamon*
¼ *teaspoon ginger*
¼ *teaspoon nutmeg*
⅛ *teaspoon salt*
¼ *cup butter*
½ *teaspoon baking soda*
½ *cup light or dark molasses*
¾ *cup boiling water*
1 *unbaked 9-inch pie shell (see recipes)*

Preheat oven to 375°F.

In a bowl or in the work bowl of a food processor with the steel blade in place, combine the flour, sugar, cinnamon, ginger, nutmeg, and salt. Cut in the butter until the mixture resembles coarse crumbs. In a mixing bowl, combine the baking soda and molasses, and stir in the boiling water. Add 1 ½ cups of the crumbs to the molasses mixture and stir well. Pour filling into the pie shell. Sprinkle top with the remaining crumbs. Bake 30 to 35 minutes, or until pie is set.

American Cream Pie

MAKES ONE 9-INCH PIE

The original Early American cream pie was really a simple butter-cake with a cream or cooked-custard filling. In the late 1800s, cream pie with a baked pastry crust began to be popular. Bananas were imported from the West Indies and were incorporated into the cream pie. Coconut and chocolate are two further variations on the theme. Graham-cracker-crumb crust, because it is so easy to prepare, has become a popular base for cream pies.

3 cups light cream or milk
⅔ cup sugar
¼ teaspoon salt
3 tablespoons cornstarch
3 egg yolks
1 tablespoon butter
1½ teaspoons vanilla
1 baked 9-inch pie shell (see recipes) or graham-cracker-crumb pie crust
Whipped Cream Topping (see following recipe)

In a saucepan, heat to a simmer 2 cups of the cream or milk over medium to low heat. In a bowl, combine the sugar, salt, cornstarch, and remaining 1 cup cream or milk. Stir mixture into the hot cream and cook, stirring, until thickened, about 5 minutes. Whisk the egg yolks in a bowl and whisk a small portion of the cooked mixture into the yolks. Add the egg yolk mixture to the rest of the cooked mixture in the pan and cook 1 minute longer, or until thickened. Add the butter and vanilla. Cool, covered. Pour filling into the pie shell. Chill. Top with Whipped Cream Topping.

BANANA CREAM PIE: Slice 4 firm but ripe bananas. Layer the bananas with the chilled cream filling. Top with Whipped Cream Topping.

COCONUT CREAM PIE: Fold ¾ cup flaked coconut into the cooled cream filling. Top with Whipped Cream Topping.

Whipped Cream Topping

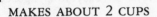

MAKES ABOUT 2 CUPS

1 *teaspoon unflavored gelatin*
1 *tablespoon water*
1 *cup heavy cream*
2 *tablespoons powdered sugar*
½ *teaspoon vanilla*

In a small bowl, soften the gelatin in the water. Place over hot water and heat until gelatin dissolves. Blend gelatin with cream, then whip until stiff. Add the powdered sugar and vanilla.

Lemon Meringue Pie

MAKES ONE 9-INCH PIE

The perfect lemon meringue pie is buttercup yellow, tart-sweet, with a white, gold-tipped meringue. The cornstarch thickening needs to be cooked completely so that it will not break down. Cornstarch gives a beautiful translucent quality to the filling, whereas a thickening of all-purpose flour is more opaque.

2 *cups sugar*
1½ *cups plus* ⅓ *cup water*
¾ *teaspoon salt*
½ *cup cornstarch*
4 *eggs, separated*
½ *cup freshly squeezed lemon juice*
3 *tablespoons butter*
Grated rind of 1 lemon
1 *baked 9-inch pie shell (see recipes)*

In a saucepan, heat 1½ cups sugar with 1½ cups water and ½ teaspoon salt to a boil. Mix the cornstarch with ⅓ cup water until smooth, and add gradually to the boiling mixture, stirring constantly. Cook until thick and clear, about 2 minutes. Remove from the heat. In a medium-size bowl, blend the egg yolks and lemon juice. Stir in a small portion of the hot mixture, then return the entire mixture to the saucepan and bring to just a boil. Remove from the heat. Stir in the butter and lemon rind. Cover and cool to lukewarm.

Preheat oven to 325°F. In a clean bowl, free of any grease, whisk the egg whites with ¼ teaspoon salt until frothy. Gradually add the remaining ½ cup sugar, beating until glossy peaks are formed. Stir 2 rounded tablespoons of the meringue into the lukewarm filling. Pour the filling into the pie shell. Top with the meringue, spreading it over the filling evenly to the edge of the crust. Bake about 15 minutes, or until lightly browned. Chill at least 1 hour before serving; pie will cut into more perfect wedges when chilled.

Old Arkansas Vinegar Pie

MAKES ONE 9-INCH PIE

Surprisingly, this unusual pie tastes a lot like lemon meringue pie.

2 *cups boiling water*
¼ *cup Arkansas apple cider vinegar*
A dash of salt
1 *teaspoon lemon juice*
1 *cup plus 3 tablespoons sugar*
3 *tablespoons all-purpose flour*
3 *egg yolks, lightly beaten*
1 *baked 9-inch pie shell (see recipes)*
3 *egg whites*

In a heavy saucepan, combine the boiling water, vinegar, salt, and lemon juice. Mix 1 cup sugar with the flour, and stir into the vinegar mixture. Cook, stirring constantly, over medium heat until thickened. Stir a small amount of the thickened mixture into the egg yolks, then combine the yolk mixture with the rest of the thickened mixture. Bring to just a boil, stirring constantly. Remove from the heat. Pour filling into the pie shell.

Preheat oven to 450°F.

In the large bowl of an electric mixer, whip the egg whites until foamy, then beat in the remaining 3 tablespoons sugar; beat until stiff. Spread the meringue over the filling in the pie shell. Bake 10 minutes; reduce heat to 300°F. and bake another 15 minutes.

Old Williamsburg Golden Pecan Pie

MAKES ONE 9-INCH PIE

Thomas Jefferson loved pecans and planted hundreds of pecan trees. He was generous in giving nuts to his friends. In 1775, George Washington planted pecan trees at Mount Vernon. Three of the trees are still growing on the banks of the Potomac. This version of our classic pecan pie is made with light corn syrup, which produces a nutty, buttery-tasting pie.

4 eggs
¾ cup sugar
½ teaspoon salt
1½ cups light corn syrup
1 tablespoon butter, melted
1 teaspoon vanilla
1 cup pecan halves
1 unbaked 9-inch pie shell (see recipes)

Preheat oven to 400°F.

In a large bowl, beat the eggs with sugar, salt, syrup, butter, and vanilla. Spread pecan halves on the bottom of the pie shell. Pour in filling. Place pie in oven, reduce heat to 350°F., and bake 40 to 50 minutes, or until pie is set in the center. Cool before serving.

Quaker Town Crumb Pie

MAKES ONE 10-INCH PIE

Pennsylvania Dutch cooks consider themselves master pie bakers. That, they are! They can make a delicious pie even though there's not much in the larder but the basics, and hardly even that. The most authentic pie is made with a lard crust. The large, 10-inch pie pan is important because of the amount of filling and the necessary depth of the pie. You will need to use more than half the recipe for Buttery Pastry for Pies (page 187) or No-Fail Lemon Pastry (page 188). If you choose to prepare the Hot-Water Pastry (page 190), half of the recipe is enough to line a 10-inch pie pan.

½ cup light brown sugar

½ cup light or dark molasses

1 egg

2 cups water

2 cups plus 1 tablespoon all-purpose flour

1 teaspoon vanilla

1 unbaked 10-inch pie shell

1 cup granulated sugar

½ cup lard or butter, at room temperature

1 teaspoon baking soda

Preheat oven to 350°F.

In a saucepan, combine the brown sugar, molasses, egg, water, 1 tablespoon flour, and vanilla. Place over medium heat and bring to a boil, stirring constantly, until slightly thickened. Pour hot mixture into the pie shell. In a bowl, combine 2 cups flour, the granulated sugar, lard or butter, and baking soda. Mix until coarse crumbs are formed. Carefully spoon the crumb mixture over the molasses mixture in the pie shell. Place on a rimmed baking sheet to save spillovers in the oven. Bake 35 minutes, or until the pie does not jiggle when moved. Cool before cutting.

Southern Creamy Chess Pie

MAKES ONE 9-INCH PIE

Chess pies were originally a cake or tart of light pastry that contained a cheese filling. Over the years, the cheese disappeared from the recipe and lemon or orange and almonds were substituted. The word *chess* is a corruption of *cheese.*

1 *cup sugar*
¼ *cup butter, melted*
3 *eggs, lightly beaten*
1 *cup light cream*
2 *tablespoons lemon juice*
½ *teaspoon grated fresh lemon rind*
1½ *teaspoons all-purpose flour*
1½ *teaspoons cornmeal*
1 *unbaked 9-inch pie shell (see recipes)*

Preheat oven to 400°F.

In the large bowl of an electric mixer, combine the sugar, butter, eggs, cream, lemon juice, and lemon rind. Beat until thick and light. Add the flour and cornmeal to the lemon mixture at medium speed, until blended. Spoon filling into the pie shell. Bake at 400°F. for 10 minutes; reduce temperature to 300°F. and bake 50 minutes longer, until set.

All-American Cakes

For all the references to Austrian, German, Swiss, and French cakes in the names for these creations, most are a result of the creativity of American bakers. The three-layer, stacked, and frosted cake as we know it is truly an American invention. The closest European counterparts are tortes that are baked in deep, straight-sided pans; after baking, they are split into layers, filled, and frosted. The 8- or 9-inch layer cake pan, the 9-by-13-inch pan, and even the square cake pan are all the contribution of American technology and standardization. Even the Bundt pan, so popular lately, is an American shape, made to look like a fancy tube pan of Austrian heritage. But this Bundt pan is not known in Europe, nor are the great variety of moist cakes baked in it. An older tube-type pan, which we use for baking angel food cakes, and the large center-tube pan traditionally used for sponge cakes are also American inventions.

American cakes can be divided into five general categories: butter cakes, foam cakes, coffee cakes, cheesecakes, and shortcakes. Cheesecake American style is not found as such in other parts of the world, although many American cheesecakes are definitely inspired by foreign flavors, ingredients, and combinations.

Butter cakes include all those made with solid fat—butter, margarine, lard, or homogenized shortening. The simple one-egg cake, as well as an elaborate many-tiered wedding cake, belongs to this category. There are dozens of versions and variations, from silver cake to gold cake, to sweet chocolate cake and devil's food cake. Spice cakes and cakes that include fruits and nuts belong to this category. All are American.

Americans have often been better bakers than cooks. Baking powder, an American invention, helped. With this leavening agent, a whole new category of cakes that are light and moist was developed. The baking-powder biscuit and fruit shortcakes became possible with the advent of baking powder.

Before baking powder, in the late 1700s, baking soda, known as "saleratus," had simplified the process of baking. Combined with acidic ingredients, such as sour milk or buttermilk, it produced carbon dioxide that, when given off during baking, made the batter rise. Introduced in 1856, baking powder combined both the basic and acidic ingredients in one powder that, when moistened in a batter, started reacting and giving off carbon dioxide to make it rise during baking.

American bakers have traditionally baked cakes for the creativity of it. In the mid 1900s, when the cake mix was introduced, it was a totally complete mix. Nothing was needed but water. Cake mixes failed. However, with the aid of marketing psychology, the egg was removed from the mix, and with the addition of the egg by the baker, consumers accepted it. With the use of a cake mix, American bakers continued on with their creative formulations, making exotic varieties of cakes from voluptuous sounding double chocolate fudge ripple cake to fanciful cakes based on the idea of fancy alcoholic drinks like piña colada and Harvey Wallbanger pound cakes.

A distinction needs to be made at this point between "mix" cakes and "scratch" cakes. We will not use cake mixes in this chapter; instead, all cakes will be made from scratch. Traditional butter cakes are usually baked in 8- or 9-inch layer pans, 9-by-13-inch oblong pans, or 8- or 9-inch-square pans that are buttered and floured or often buttered and sugared, depending on the effect the baker desires. They must be cooled in the pan at least 10 minutes before removing onto a cake rack.

Two of the "foam cakes," sponge and angel food, contain no fat; they consist of flour, sugar, eggs, and flavoring. The leavening agent is air beaten into eggs, as opposed to baking powder or baking soda and an acid ingredient. Angel food cake, an American invention made with the foam of egg white, is the counterpart to sponge cake, which is made with the foam of the whole egg. Another foam cake, chiffon, is a cross between a chemically leavened cake and an egg-foam-leavened cake. Chiffon cakes were developed in the mid-1900s as the result of the perfecting of liquid shortenings (vegetable oils). All foam cakes are baked in ungreased pans, generally in tube-type pans. After baking, they are inverted and allowed to cool "hanging" in the pan. They should not be removed from the pan until thoroughly cooled, or their own weight will compact the texture.

Coffee cakes may resemble butter cakes in preparation procedures, but they have a texture similar to that of quick breads. They are best when served hot out of the oven.

One of the most classic of American desserts is strawberry shortcake. Fresh wild strawberries, sugared and spooned onto split, warm biscuits and served with thick whipped cream, are among the first treats of the summer season. The typical American shortcake is made with a very unsweet biscuit dough, usually leavened with baking powder. The shortcakes may be cut into individual cakes or baked in a large round or square that is cut into individual servings. As the summer fruit season rolls on, other fruits are substituted for strawberries, although, strawberry shortcake is still the American favorite.

Cheesecake is another all-American dessert that sometimes seems strange and exotic to foreign visitors. Europe knows nothing quite like it. New York cheesecake and Lindy's cheesecake named after the famed New York restaurant, are known nationwide, although in recent years many variations and complexities have been added to the cheesecake repertoire of our country.

Basic Yellow Cake or 1-2-3-4 Cake

MAKES THREE 8- OR 9-INCH LAYERS

This old-fashioned cake appeared in church cookbooks through many decades. The name makes the formula for the cake easy to remember: 1 cup shortening, 2 cups sugar, 3 cups flour, and 4 eggs is the basic recipe. Originally it was a pound cake that contained no liquid. But, over the generations, with the addition of baking powder, salt, milk, and vanilla, it has evolved into a basic yellow layer cake, more typical of American tastes.

1 cup butter
2 cups sugar
4 eggs
3 cups all-purpose flour, stirred before measuring
½ teaspoon salt
3 teaspoons baking powder
1 cup milk
1 teaspoon vanilla
Rich Custard Filling (see following recipe)
Whipped Cream Frosting (see recipe)

Preheat oven to 350°F. Butter and flour three 8- or 9-inch-round cake pans.

Cream butter and sugar until blended. Add the eggs and beat until light. Combine the flour, salt, and baking powder. Add the flour mixture alternately with the milk to the creamed mixture, mixing until smooth and creamy. Blend in the vanilla.

Divide the batter among the cake pans and smooth to even. Bake 25 to 30 minutes, or until cakes shrink away from the sides of the pans and are golden. Remove from oven and cool 5 minutes before turning out of pans. Spread 2 layers with Rich Custard Filling; stack, placing the layer without filling on top. Frost the cake with Whipped Cream Frosting.

Rich Custard Filling

MAKES ABOUT 2½ CUPS

3 egg yolks
2 tablespoons butter
1 tablespoon cornstarch
2 tablespoons sugar
2 cups half-and-half or light cream
1 teaspoon vanilla

In a heavy saucepan, combine the egg yolks, butter, cornstarch, sugar, and half-and-half. Bring the mixture to a boil over medium to low heat, whisking constantly; cook until thickened, about 1 minute. Remove from heat and cool, covered. Stir in the vanilla.

Whipped Cream Frosting

MAKES ABOUT 4 CUPS

By adding a little gelatin to the whipped cream, the cream will hold up for several hours when refrigerated and at least 2 hours at room temperature once the cake is being served.

1 teaspoon unflavored gelatin
2 tablespoons water
2 cups heavy cream
2 to 3 tablespoons powdered sugar
1 teaspoon vanilla

In a small metal bowl, soften the gelatin in the water. Place over a pan of hot water and stir until the gelatin is dissolved and clear. In a large chilled bowl, beat the cream until it holds soft peaks. Beat in the powdered sugar and dissolved gelatin. Flavor with the vanilla.

One-Egg Cake

MAKES ONE 9-INCH-SQUARE CAKE

This basic cake can be made in a square, into cupcakes, or as an upside-down cake. The "quick mix" method requires that the butter be soft but not melted.

¼ cup butter, at room temperature
1⅓ cups all-purpose flour, stirred before measuring
2 teaspoons baking powder
¼ teaspoon salt
¾ cup sugar
1 egg, beaten
½ teaspoon vanilla
½ cup milk

Preheat oven to 350°F. Butter a 9-inch-square cake pan.

In the large bowl of an electric mixer, combine the butter, flour, baking powder, salt, and sugar. Mix until butter is completely blended into the flour mixture. Add the egg, vanilla, and milk and beat until smooth. Pour into the prepared pan and bake 25 to 30 minutes, or until golden.

BLUEBERRY CAKE: Sprinkle with 1 cup fresh blueberries over batter in pan. Sprinkle with ¼ cup more sugar. Bake, cut into squares, and serve warm.

PINEAPPLE UPSIDE-DOWN CAKE: Melt ½ cup butter in a 10- to 11-inch cast-iron skillet over low heat. Add 1 cup tightly packed light or dark brown sugar and blend well. Arrange 5 slices fresh or canned pineapple, drained, and ¼ cup chopped pecans over the sugar. Pour batter into the skillet, covering the pineapple, nuts, and sugar mixture evenly. Bake in the skillet 25 to 30 minutes, or until the cake tests done. Invert immediately onto a serving dish. Cut in wedges to serve.

Basic Two-Egg Cake

MAKES TWO 8- OR 9-INCH LAYERS

One of the basic rules for making a butter cake is that all ingredients be at room temperature. If eggs are cold, place them in a bowl of hot tap water for a few minutes to warm them up. If the shortening or butter is cold, cut it into small pieces and beat in the large bowl of an electric mixer until light and fluffy. For the lightest-textured cake, use cake flour instead of all-purpose flour. If you do not have a sifter, put the cake flour from the box into a sieve placed over a bowl. With a spoon stir the flour until it is sifted into the bowl. Spoon into a dry-measure cup and, with the straight edge of a knife, level off the top.

½ *cup shortening or butter, at room temperature*
1 *cup sugar*
1 *teaspoon vanilla*
2 *eggs*
2 *cups sifted cake flour*
2½ *teaspoons baking powder*
½ *teaspoon salt*
¾ *cup milk*
Rich Custard Filling (see recipe)
Whipped Cream Frosting (see recipe)

Preheat oven to 350°F. Butter and flour two 8- or 9-inch layer cake pans.

In the large bowl of an electric mixer, cream the shortening or butter until light and fluffy. Add the sugar gradually and continue beating. Add the vanilla, then the eggs, one at a time, beating all the time. Combine the sifted flour, baking powder, and salt, and add to the creamed ingredients alternately with the milk. Beat to keep batter smooth.

Turn batter into the cake pans and spread until smooth and even. Bake 25 to 30 minutes, until tops of cakes are golden. Remove from oven, cool on rack 10 minutes, then remove from pans. Fill with Rich Custard Filling and frost with Whipped Cream Frosting, or fill and frost with your favorite icing.

CHOCOLATE-NUT FUDGE CAKE: Melt three 1-ounce squares unsweetened chocolate, and beat into the creamed mixture after adding the eggs. Increase the milk to 1 cup. Add ½ cup finely chopped walnuts to the dry ingredients when incorporating them in the creamed mixture.

Lady Baltimore Cake

MAKES ONE 3-LAYER CAKE

Lady Baltimore was a novel written by Owen Wister in 1906. He chose Charleston as the setting of the novel, and one of the former of the Charleston bells, Mrs. Alicia Rhett Mayberry, as the central character of the story. Mrs. Mayberry created a cake called "Lady Baltimore." When the novel was published, the cake became a famous American dessert. It is a basic silver cake made with egg whites instead of whole eggs and solid shortening instead of butter to keep a pure white crumb. (Using butter will work too, but will not yield as white a crumb.) The filling is made with fruits and nuts, which are mixed into part of the icing; the cake is then frosted with the remaining icing.

6 *egg whites*
1¾ *cups sugar*
1 *cup vegetable shortening or butter, at room temperature*
¼ *teaspoon salt*
3 *cups sifted cake flour*
4 *teaspoons baking powder*
1 *cup milk*
1 *teaspoon vanilla*
Lady Baltimore Filling (see following recipe)
Seven-Minute Icing (see recipe)

Preheat oven to 350°F. Butter three 9-inch-round cake pans.

Beat egg whites until stiff. Beat in 1 cup of the sugar, 2 tablespoons at a time, and set aside. Cream the shortening or butter and beat in the remaining sugar. Combine the dry ingredients, and add to the creamed mixture alternately with the milk. Fold in the egg whites, and add the vanilla. Divide batter among the cake pans and spread evenly. Bake 25 to 30 minutes, or until golden. Remove from oven, cool 10 minutes, and remove cakes from pans. Fill with the Lady Baltimore Filling and frost with Seven-Minute Icing.

Lady Baltimore Filling

MAKES ABOUT 2 CUPS

½ recipe Seven-Minute Icing (see following recipe)
½ cup toasted chopped pecans
3 dates, finely chopped
½ cup seedless raisins, chopped
½ teaspoon almond extract

Combine the seven-minute icing with the pecans, dates, raisins, and almond extract.

Seven-Minute Icing

MAKES ABOUT 4 CUPS

3 cups sugar
½ cup water
½ teaspoon cream of tartar
A few grains of salt
4 egg whites
4 teaspoons vanilla

Mix sugar, water, cream of tartar, salt, and egg whites in the top of a double boiler. Set over boiling water and beat with an electric mixer, for *exactly* 7 minutes, beating all the while. Blend in the vanilla.

Lord Baltimore Cake
or "Gold Cake"

MAKES ONE 3-LAYER CAKE

Lord Baltimore Cake is the counterpart to Lady Baltimore Cake, which uses only egg whites. Traditionally this is filled with Lord Baltimore Filling and frosted with Seven-Minute Icing. After baking the layers, prepare the Seven-Minute Icing first because you need to use half of it for the filling.

½ cup butter, at room temperature
1 cup sugar
1 egg
6 egg yolks
1¾ cups sifted cake flour
2½ teaspoons baking powder
¼ teaspoon salt
½ cup milk
½ teaspoon vanilla
Lord Baltimore Filling (see following recipe)
Seven-Minute Icing (see recipe)

Preheat oven to 350°F. Butter and flour three 8-inch-round cake pans.

In the large bowl of an electric mixer, cream the butter with the sugar. Blend in the egg and egg yolks and beat until light. Combine the cake flour, baking powder, and salt. Blend the flour mixture into the creamed mixture alternately with the milk, until the batter is smooth. Blend in the vanilla. Divide the batter among the cake pans and smooth the tops to make even layers. Bake 25 to 30 minutes, until golden. Remove from oven, cool 10 minutes, and remove cakes from pans. Fill with Lord Baltimore Filling and frost with Seven-Minute Icing.

Lord Baltimore Filling

MAKES ABOUT 2 CUPS

½ cup macaroon crumbs
¼ cup chopped toasted pecans
½ teaspoon grated orange rind
¼ cup chopped toasted, blanched almonds
12 candied cherries, cut into quarters
2 teaspoons lemon juice
1 tablespoon sherry
½ recipe Seven-Minute Icing (see recipe)

Mix the macaroon crumbs, pecans, orange rind, almonds, cherries, lemon juice, and sherry with the icing.

Country Spice Cake

MAKES ONE 9- TO 10-INCH TUBE CAKE

Packed with raisins and nuts, this cake is great served in thin slices with shavings of sharp Canadian Cheddar cheese.

1 *cup water*
1 *cup golden raisins*
1 *cup dark raisins*
1 *cup tightly packed dark brown sugar*
⅓ *cup butter, at room temperature*
½ *teaspoon cinnamon*
½ *teaspoon allspice*
½ *teaspoon nutmeg*
½ *teaspoon salt*
2 *cups sifted cake flour*
1 *teaspoon baking powder*
1 *teaspoon baking soda*
1 *cup chopped walnuts*
Powdered sugar

In a medium-size saucepan, combine the water, raisins, brown sugar, butter, spices, and salt. Bring to a boil and cook, stirring, for 3 minutes. Remove from the heat and cool to room temperature.

Preheat oven to 325°F. Butter and flour a 9- or 10-inch fancy tube pan.

In a large bowl, combine the flour, baking powder, baking soda, and walnuts. Stir in the raisin mixture until blended. Turn batter into the prepared pan. Bake 45 to 50 minutes, or until a wooden skewer inserted in the center comes out clean. The cake may sink slightly in the center, but this is not noticeable when it is inverted onto a serving plate. Cool 5 minutes in the pan, turn out onto a rack, and cool completely. Sprinkle with powdered sugar.

Spiced Crumb Cake

MAKES ONE 8-BY-12-INCH CAKE

In the 1930s this cake was often served for breakfast.

2 cups dark brown sugar
½ cup vegetable shortening
2 cups all-purpose flour
1 teaspoon baking powder
½ teaspoon baking soda
1 teaspoon cinnamon
½ teaspoon ground cloves
½ teaspoon salt
1 egg
1 cup buttermilk
1 teaspoon vanilla
½ teaspoon lemon extract

Preheat oven to 350°F. Butter an 8-by-12-inch oblong cake pan or a 9-inch-square pan.

In a large mixing bowl, blend the brown sugar, shortening, and flour until the mixture resembles coarse crumbs. Remove and reserve 1 cup of the crumbs. Add the baking powder, baking soda, cinnamon, cloves, and salt to the mixture in the bowl; blend. Add the egg, buttermilk, vanilla, and lemon extract. Beat at high speed for 2½ minutes. Pour batter into the prepared pan and smooth the top. Sprinkle with the reserved crumb mixture. Bake 35 minutes, or until a wooden skewer inserted in the center comes out clean.

Cocoa Cake

MAKES 10 TO 12 SERVINGS

This cake works the best when baked in a large jelly-roll pan and is perfect for serving a large group of people.

FOR THE CAKE

2 *cups all-purpose flour*
2 *cups granulated sugar*
½ *cup butter or margarine*
½ *cup vegetable shortening*
1 *cup water*
¼ *cup dark, unsweetened cocoa*
½ *cup buttermilk*
2 *eggs, lightly beaten*
1 *teaspoon baking soda*
1 *teaspoon vanilla*

FOR THE FROSTING

½ *cup butter or margarine*
4 *tablespoons milk*
2 *tablespoons dark, unsweetened cocoa*
3½ *cups powdered sugar*
1 *teaspoon vanilla*

Preheat oven to 400°F. Generously butter a 10½-by-15½-inch jelly-roll pan (cookie sheet with sides).

In a large bowl, combine the flour and granulated sugar. In a saucepan, bring ½ cup butter or margarine, shortening, water, and ¼ cup cocoa to a boil, stirring constantly, and cook until smooth, about 1 minute. Pour mixture over the dry ingredients and stir until

228

blended. Add the buttermilk, eggs, baking soda, and 1 teaspoon vanilla. Mix until very smooth and blended. Pour into the prepared pan. Bake 20 minutes, or until the cake tests done in the center.

While cake is baking, combine ½ cup butter, the milk, and 2 tablespoons cocoa in a medium-size saucepan; bring to a boil. Add the powdered sugar and 1 teaspoon vanilla. Pour the hot frosting over the hot baked cake.

Basic Chocolate Cake

MAKES ONE 10-INCH TUBE CAKE

A touch of baking soda gives chocolate cake a reddish tint and a rich, chocolatey flavor.

2 cups sifted cake flour
3 teaspoons baking powder
½ teaspoon baking soda
¼ teaspoon salt
½ cup unsalted butter
1 cup sugar
2 eggs, separated
3 squares (3 ounces) unsweetened chocolate, melted
1 teaspoon vanilla
1¼ cups milk
Chocolate Cream Frosting (see recipe)

Preheat oven to 350°F. Lightly grease and dust with flour a 10-inch tube pan.

Combine the flour with the baking powder, baking soda, and salt. In the large bowl of an electric mixer, cream the butter until light, and gradualy add the sugar; continue beating until mixture is smooth. Beat in the egg yolks, chocolate, and vanilla. With rubber spatula, fold in the flour mixture along with the milk, until blended. In another bowl, beat the egg whites until stiff, and quickly fold into the batter with the rubber spatula. Pour mixture into the prepared pan and bake 55 minutes, or until a cake tester comes out clean. Remove cake from oven and cool on a wire rack 10 minutes before removing from the pan. Cool and frost with Chocolate Cream Frosting.

Devil's Food Cake

MAKES ONE 2-LAYER 9-INCH CAKE,
OR ONE 9-BY-13-INCH CAKE

It is the characteristic of baking soda to impart a reddish tint to a chocolate cake batter. To reinforce the red color, there was a popular recipe that circulated during the 1950s that called for a whole bottle of red food coloring. If you wish to try it, simply replace some of the water with the food coloring (pour a 1-ounce bottle of red food coloring into a measuring cup and add water to equal 1⅓ cups).

2/3 *cup vegetable shortening*

1 2/3 *cups sugar*

3 *eggs*

2/3 *cup dark, unsweetened cocoa*

1 1/3 *cups cold water*

2 *cups all-purpose flour, stirred before measuring*

1/2 *teaspoon baking powder*

1 1/4 *teaspoons baking soda*

1/4 *teaspoon salt*

1 *teaspoon vanilla*

Seven-Minute Icing (see recipe) or Fluffy Chocolate Frosting (see
following recipe)

Preheat oven to 350°F. Grease two 9-inch-round cake pans or one 9-by-13-inch oblong pan.

In the large bowl of an electric mixer, cream the shortening and sugar until smooth. Beat in the eggs until mixture is fluffy. In a small bowl, blend the cocoa with the cold water. In another small bowl, combine the flour, baking powder, baking soda, and salt. Add the flour mixture alternately with the cocoa-water mixture to the creamed mixture, blending until smooth. Add the vanilla. Pour batter into the prepared pans or pan. Bake 30 to 35 minutes for layers, or 35 to 45 minutes for the oblong pan, or until the cake tests done. Cool. Spread with Seven-Minute Icing or with Fluffy Chocolate Frosting.

Fluffy Chocolate Frosting

MAKES ABOUT 2 CUPS

2 tablespoons water
¼ cup granulated sugar
2 squares (2 ounces) unsweetened chocolate
1 egg
2⅓ cups powdered sugar
½ cup butter, at room temperature
1 teaspoon vanilla

In a medium-size heavy saucepan, combine the water and granulated sugar. Bring to a boil, stirring, and boil 1 minute. Remove from the heat. Add the chocolate and stir until chocolate is melted. In the large bowl of an electric mixer, beat the egg until frothy; add the powdered sugar and beat until blended. Beat in the chocolate mixture and the butter. Beat at high speed until the frosting is fluffy. Add the vanilla. Use the frosting immediately.

Kentucky Bourbon Pecan Cake

MAKES ONE 9-BY-13-INCH CAKE,
OR ONE 10-INCH TUBE CAKE

This is a chocolate cake that has been made in Kentucky for generations. Flavored with bourbon and studded with pecans, the native nut, it is baked either as a sheet cake or a tube cake.

2 *cups sifted cake flour*
2 *teaspoons baking powder*
¼ *teaspoon salt*
½ *cup unsalted butter*
2 *cups granulated sugar*
4 *squares (4 ounces) unsweetened chocolate, melted*
2 *eggs, separated*
1 *teaspoon vanilla*
3 *tablespoons bourbon*
1½ *cups milk*
1 *cup chopped pecans*
Powdered sugar (optional)

Preheat oven to 350°F. Butter a 9-by-13-inch oblong cake pan or a 10-inch tube pan.

In small bowl, combine the flour, baking powder, and salt. In the large bowl of an electric mixer, cream the butter with the granulated sugar until smooth. Add the melted chocolate and egg yolks; beat until light. Add the vanilla and bourbon. Blend the flour mixture into the creamed mixture alternately with the milk, mixing until smooth. Whip egg whites until stiff. Fold in the egg whites and pecans. Turn batter into the prepared pan. Bake 25 to 30 minutes in the oblong pan, or 55 minutes to 1 hour in the tube pan, or until the cake tests done. This is a very moist cake, and it will stick slightly to a cake tester. Do not overbake or the cake will be dry. Remove from oven and cool on rack. If desired, dust with powdered sugar.

Sour Cream Spice Cake

MAKES ONE 8- OR 9-INCH-SQUARE CAKE

2 eggs, separated
½ cup butter, at room temperature
1½ cups tightly packed brown sugar
2 cups all-purpose flour
1 teaspoon baking soda
1 teaspoon cinnamon
½ teaspoon salt
½ teaspoon ground cloves
1 cup sour cream
1 teaspoon vanilla
½ cup chopped nuts
Araby Spice Frosting (see following recipe) (optional)

Preheat oven to 350°F. Butter an 8- or 9-inch-square cake pan.
In a medium-size bowl, beat the egg whites until stiff but not dry;
set aside. In another bowl, cream the butter and sugar, and beat in the
egg yolks. Combine the flour with the baking soda, cinnamon, salt,
and cloves. Blend the sour cream with the vanilla. Add the dry ingredients to the creamed mixture alternately with the sour cream.
Fold in the egg whites. Pour batter into the prepared pan. Sprinkle
with the nuts. Bake 45 minutes, or until the cake tests done. Cut in
squares and serve warm. Or, cool and frost with Araby Spice Frosting,
if desired.

Araby Spice Frosting

MAKES ABOUT 2½ CUPS

½ *cup butter, at room temperature*
1 *egg yolk*
3 *cups powdered sugar*
1½ *tablespoons unsweetened cocoa*
1 *teaspoon cinnamon*
1 *to 2 tablespoons strong hot coffee*

In the large bowl of an electric mixer, beat the butter and egg yolk until fluffy. Slowly add the powdered sugar, cocoa, cinnamon, and enough hot coffee to make a smooth, spreadable frosting.

Coconut Butter Cake

MAKES 12 SERVINGS

Coconut and bourbon mark the flavors of this classic Southern cake.

1 *cup butter*
1 ½ *cups granulated sugar*
4 *eggs*
2 ½ *cups all-purpose flour*
2 ½ *teaspoons baking powder*
1 *cup milk*
1 *teaspoon vanilla*
1 *cup flaked or shredded coconut*
9 *tablespoons bourbon*
2 *cups heavy cream*
⅓ *cup unsweetened cocoa*
½ *cup powdered sugar*
1 *teaspoon vanilla*
1 *cup toasted pecans, chopped*

Preheat oven to 350°F. Butter and flour three 9-inch-round layer cake pans.

Cream the butter and granulated sugar together until light. Beat in the eggs until fluffy. Sift the flour with the baking powder. Add the flour mixture to the creamed mixture alternately with the milk. Add the vanilla. Fold in the coconut. Divide the batter among the prepared pans. Bake 20 to 30 minutes, or until the cakes test done in the center. Cool on racks. Remove from pans and split each layer horizontally.

To assemble the cake, place a split layer onto a cake plate. Spoon about 1 ½ tablespoons bourbon onto each layer. In large bowl of electric mixer, combine the cream, cocoa, powdered sugar, and vanilla. Beat until mixture holds stiff peaks. Top each layer with about ⅓ cup of the chocolate-cream mixture. Sprinkle each layer with toasted pecans, and stack the layers. Frost the top and sides of the cake with the remaining frosting. Chill until ready to serve. Serve cut into thin wedges.

Fresh Apple Cake

MAKES 12 TO 16 SERVINGS

A moist cake made with fresh raw apples has been an American favorite for generations.

1 *cup sugar*
½ *cup butter*
2 *eggs*
1½ *cups all-purpose flour*
2 *teaspoons unsweetened cocoa*
1 *teaspoon baking soda*
1 *teaspoon cinnamon*
½ *teaspoon ground cloves*
2 *cups chopped fresh pared apple*
½ *cup chopped pitted dates*
1 *cup chopped walnuts or pecans*
½ *cup cold coffee*
Old-fashioned Caramel Frosting (see following recipe)

Preheat oven to 350°F. Butter a small 6½-cup tube pan or ring mold, or a 9-by-13-inch cake pan.

Cream the sugar with the butter until blended, add the eggs, and beat until light. Combine flour, cocoa, baking soda, cinnamon, and cloves. In a small bowl, combine the chopped apple, dates, and nuts. Add 2 tablespoons of the flour mixture to apples and mix. Add the remaining flour mixture to creamed mixture alternately with coffee, and mix until batter is smooth. Fold in the apple mixture. Turn batter into the prepared pan and bake 45 to 55 minutes for the tube pan, 35 to 40 minutes for the 9-by-13-inch pan. Turn out cake baked in tube pan and cool on a wire rack. Cake baked in flat pan can cool in pan. Prepare frosting, and frost cake when cool.

Old-fashioned Caramel Frosting

MAKES ABOUT 2 CUPS

¼ *cup butter*
½ *cup tightly packed brown sugar*
2 *tablespoons milk*
1½ *cups powdered sugar*
1 *teaspoon vanilla*

In a small saucepan, melt the butter. Add brown sugar and stir over low heat for 2 minutes. Add milk and heat to a boil, stirring. Remove pan from heat and gradually add powdered sugar, mixing until smooth and creamy. Add vanilla. If necessary, add a few drops more milk.

Applesauce Cake

MAKES ONE 9-BY-13-INCH CAKE

Applesauce cake has been credited to the Yankee kitchen of early Colonial days. Apples were a mainstay in the diet of our early settlers, and to this day they remain a favorite fruit for cooking and baking. Applesauce cake has many different variations, having been baked in layers and tube pans as well as in oblong or square pans.

½ cup butter or shortening
1½ cups sugar
1 egg
1½ cups applesauce
2 teaspoons baking soda
2 cups all-purpose flour
1 teaspoon cinnamon
¼ teaspoon ground cloves
¼ teaspoon salt
¾ cup chopped pitted dates
¼ cup raisins
1 cup chopped walnuts
Lemon Icing (see following recipe)

Preheat oven to 350°F. Butter a 9-by-13-inch baking pan.

In the large bowl of an electric mixer, cream the butter or shortening with the sugar. Add the egg and beat until light. Mix the applesauce with the baking soda. Combine the flour, cinnamon, cloves, and salt. Add the dry ingredients to creamed mixture alternately with the applesauce. Stir in the dates, raisins, and walnuts. Pour batter into the prepared pan. Bake 40 to 45 minutes, until the cake pulls away from the sides of the pan and the center tests done. Frost with Lemon Icing.

Lemon Icing

MAKES ABOUT 2½ CUPS

4 *tablespoons melted butter*
3 *tablespoons lemon juice*
1 *tablespoon grated lemon rind*
3 *cups powdered sugar*

Blend the melted butter with the lemon juice. Add the lemon rind and powdered sugar and beat until smooth. Spread on the cooled cake.

Orange Butter Cake

MAKES ONE 9-BY-13-INCH CAKE

This is a delicate orange cake that has a syrup made of orange juice and sugar poured over it as it comes from the oven. The cake keeps well and seems to improve in flavor for up to three days.

THE ORANGE CAKE

1 *cup sugar*
1 *cup butter*
2 *eggs*
Grated rind of 2 medium oranges
1 *teaspoon baking soda*
1 *teaspoon baking powder*
2½ *cups all-purpose flour*
1 *cup chopped dates*
1 *cup chopped walnuts*
1 *cup buttermilk*

THE ORANGE SYRUP

Juice of 2 oranges (about 1 cup)
1 cup sugar

Butter a 9-by-13-inch cake pan or a 9½- to 10-inch Bundt pan. Preheat oven to 350°F.

Cream 1 cup sugar with butter until smooth. Beat in the eggs, until mixture is light and lemon-colored. Add grated orange rind. In a bowl, stir together the baking soda, baking powder, and flour. Put dates and walnuts into another bowl. Add 1 tablespoon of the flour mixture to dates and nuts and mix until coated. Add the rest of the flour mixture to the creamed mixture alternately with the buttermilk, until a smooth batter forms. Add the flour-dusted dates and nuts. Turn the batter into the prepared pan. Bake 35 minutes for a 9-by-13-inch cake pan, or 55 minutes to 1 hour for a Bundt pan, or until cake tests done.

While cake bakes, combine the orange juice and 1 cup sugar in a saucepan. Stir and bring to a boil. Pour the hot glaze evenly over the hot baked cake. Cool thoroughly in the pan. Invert cake baked in Bundt pan onto a serving plate. Serve oblong cake from the pan, cut into squares.

Banana Cake

MAKES TWO 8- OR 9-INCH LAYERS

Bananas have been imported to the United States from the West Indies since the early 1800s. Available everywhere today, and often allowed to get too ripe, bananas have been turned into banana breads and banana cakes by inventive American bakers.

2 *cups all-purpose flour*
1¼ *cups sugar*
2 *teaspoons baking powder*
½ *teaspoon baking soda*
½ *teaspoon salt*
¾ *cup unsalted butter or vegetable shortening*
2 *eggs*
1½ *cups mashed ripe bananas*
1 *teaspoon vanilla, or* ½ *teaspoon rum extract*
Sliced bananas
Whipped cream

Preheat oven to 350°F. Butter and flour two 8- or 9-inch layer cake pans.

In the large bowl of an electric mixer, combine the flour, sugar, baking powder, baking soda, and salt. Add the butter or shortening and blend until the mixture resembles cornmeal. Blend in the eggs and ½ cup of the bananas. Beat 2 minutes at medium speed, scraping the sides of the bowl often. Add the remaining bananas and vanilla or rum extract. Beat 1 minute longer. Turn batter into baking pans and bake 30 to 35 minutes, or until tops of cakes are golden. Cool. Place sliced bananas between layers and frost with whipped cream or your choice of frosting.

Molasses Gingerbread

MAKES ONE 9-BY-13-INCH CAKE

Molasses and ginger were essential ingredients in early American cooking. Only the very wealthy could afford to use sugar, so most people used molasses as a sweetener. It was twenty years after Abraham Lincoln's assassination before the price of sugar dropped, due to more efficient processing methods. In this recipe, brown sugar is used to replace some of the molasses.

½ cup butter, at room temperature
½ cup tightly packed brown sugar
2 eggs
2 cups all-purpose flour
1 teaspoon ginger
1 teaspoon baking soda
½ teaspoon salt
½ cup sour cream
½ cup light or dark molasses
Whipped cream or vanilla ice cream

Preheat oven to 350°F. Butter a 9-by-13-inch pan.
In a large mixing bowl, cream the butter with the brown sugar. Beat in the eggs until mixture is light. Combine the flour, ginger, baking soda, and salt. Combine the sour cream and molasses. Add the flour mixture alternately with the sour cream–molasses mixture to the creamed mixture. Pour the batter into the prepared pan. Bake 35 to 40 minutes, or until a toothpick inserted in the center comes out dry. Serve warm with whipped cream or vanilla ice cream.

Chocolate Beer Cake

MAKES ONE 2-LAYER 9-INCH CAKE,
OR ONE 9-BY-13-INCH CAKE

This old Colonial recipe must have been developed by those who brewed their own beer. Deep, rich, and moist, this cake has an especially good chocolate flavor. The cake keeps well and actually improves in flavor for up to three days.

⅔ cup butter, at room temperature
2 cups sugar
2 eggs
2 squares (2 ounces) unsweetened chocolate, melted
2¼ cups all-purpose flour
2 teaspoons baking soda
1 teaspoon salt
¾ cup buttermilk
1 cup beer
Chocolate Cream Frosting (see following recipe)

Preheat oven to 350°F. Butter and flour two 9-inch-round cake pans or one 9-by-13-inch pan.

In the large bowl of an electric mixer, cream the butter and sugar until smooth. Add the eggs and beat until light and creamy. Mix in the melted chocolate. In another bowl, stir together the flour, baking soda, and salt. Add dry ingredients to the creamed mixture along with the buttermilk and beer, mixing until the batter is smooth. Turn the batter into the prepared pan or pans. Bake 25 to 30 minutes for the layers, 40 to 45 minutes for the oblong pan. Cool. Frost with the Chocolate Cream Frosting.

Chocolate Cream Frosting

MAKES ABOUT 1 CUP

½ cup heavy cream
1 cup sugar
2 squares (2 ounces) unsweetened chocolate

Combine the cream and sugar in a saucepan. Bring to a boil and boil 1 minute, stirring. Add the chocolate and stir until melted.

Country Carrot Cake

MAKES ONE 9-INCH 3-LAYER CAKE,
OR ONE 9-BY-13-INCH CAKE

Carrot cakes are a recent classic. A rich, moist, spicy cake, this is sometimes used for wedding cakes today.

THE CAKE

2 cups granulated sugar
1½ cups vegetable oil
4 eggs
2 teaspoons baking soda
2 teaspoons cinnamon
1 teaspoon salt
2 cups all-purpose flour
2 tablespoons rum or vanilla
3 cups shredded carrots
1 cup chopped dates
1 cup chopped pecans

THE CREAM CHEESE FROSTING

One 8-ounce package cream cheese, at room temperature
½ cup butter
3 to 3½ cups powdered sugar
2 tablespoons rum or vanilla extract
1 cup chopped pecans

Preheat oven to 350°F. Butter and flour three 9-inch-round cake pans or one 9-by-13-inch oblong pan.

In the large bowl of an electric mixer, beat the granulated sugar, oil, and eggs together, until light and fluffy. Add the baking soda, cinnamon, and salt while beating the mixture. Blend in the flour. Beat until smooth. Stir in 2 tablespoons rum or vanilla, the carrots, dates, and 1 cup pecans. Pour into the prepared pans or pan. Bake 30 to 35 minutes for layers, or 35 to 45 minutes for the oblong pan, or until the cake tests done. Cool 5 minutes, loosen edges, then invert onto racks to cool.

To make the frosting, blend the cream cheese and butter and beat in the powdered sugar and 2 tablespoons rum or vanilla extract, until mixture is light. Stir in 1 cup pecans. To make a 3-layer cake, spread about ½ cup of the frosting on each of two layers as you stack them; spread remaining frosting on top and sides. For the oblong cake, spread all frosting on top and sides.

Lazy-Daisy Cake

MAKES ONE 9-BY-13-INCH CAKE

As the nineteenth century progressed, many changes took place in American kitchens. When the range with the built-in broiler came into use, creative home bakers were quick to think of all sorts of ways in which to take advantage of the new convenience. A cake that was first baked, then topped with a brown-sugar-and-butter topping became the rage in the 1930s, when it was first acceptable to admit to "laziness."

THE CAKE

½ cup milk

2 tablespoons butter

2 eggs

1 cup granulated sugar

1 teaspoon vanilla

1 teaspoon baking powder

½ teaspoon salt

1 cup all-purpose flour

THE CARAMEL-COCONUT TOPPING

5 tablespoons brown sugar

3 tablespoons heavy cream

3 tablespoons melted butter

½ cup flaked or shredded coconut

Preheat oven to 350°F. Butter a 9-by-13-inch cake pan.

Put milk and butter into a saucepan over low heat. While it is scalding, beat the eggs, granulated sugar, and vanilla, until very light and fluffy. Stir in the baking powder, salt, and flour. Mix in the scalded milk, until batter is smooth. Pour batter into prepared pan. Bake 25 minutes, until cake is golden and pulls away from edges of the pan.

Meanwhile, combine topping ingredients in a bowl. Spread hot baked cake with the topping and place under broiler until golden, about 2 minutes.

Eggless, Milkless, Butterless Cake or "War Cake"

MAKES ONE 9-BY-13-INCH CAKE

This unusual recipe was called several names, including "hillbilly cake" and "spice cake." The Royal Baking Powder Company in 1918 put together a little booklet, *Best War-Time Recipes,* which included a recipe similar to this one.

THE CAKE

1 *cup granulated sugar*
1 *cup cold water*
1 *teaspoon cinnamon*
½ *teaspoon salt*
½ *teaspoon ground cloves*
½ *teaspoon allspice*
½ *cup shortening or lard*
1 *cup dark raisins*
½ *cup chopped walnuts*
2 *cups all-purpose flour*
1 *teaspoon baking soda*

THE BROILED TOPPING

⅓ *cup melted butter*

⅔ *cup tightly packed brown sugar*

3 *tablespoons heavy cream*

½ *cup shredded or flaked coconut*

Preheat oven to 350°F. Butter a 9-by-13-inch cake pan and dust lightly with flour.

In a saucepan, combine the granulated sugar, water, cinnamon, salt, cloves, allspice, shortening or lard, raisins, and walnuts. Bring to a boil and cook, stirring, 1 minute. Let the mixture cool for 15 minutes. Add the flour and baking soda, mixing well. Turn batter into the prepared cake pan and bake 25 to 30 minutes, until the cake tests done in the center.

While cake bakes, blend the topping ingredients. Spread mixture over the top of the hot cake. Broil, about 6 inches from the source of the heat, for 2 to 3 minutes, until the top bubbles and begins to brown in spots. Watch carefully so it does not burn.

Country Pound Cake

MAKES 2 LOAVES, OR ONE 10-INCH TUBE CAKE

The lush central Tennessee bluegrass country leads the state in dairy production. It's not surprising to find some of the best pound cakes in the country here. Strawberries are grown here, too. Picture a screened farmhouse porch with a table set for afternoon coffee, tea, or lemonade, with a bowlful of shiny strawberries and thin slices of this rich, tender pound cake. It is important that all ingredients be at room temperature, or the butter-sugar-egg mixture will appear curdly. After adding the flour, do not overmix, or the cake may develop tunnels during baking; if undermixed, there will be dry spots in the cake.

1 *cup butter*

2 *cups sugar*

6 *eggs*

1 *cup sour cream*

1/4 *teaspoon baking soda*

3 *cups all-purpose flour*

1 *teaspoon vanilla*

Preheat oven to 325°F. Butter two 8 1/2-by-4 1/2-by-2 3/4-inch loaf pans, or one 10-inch tube pan, fancy or plain, or one 11-cup ring mold.

In the large bowl of an electric mixer, cream the butter and sugar until smooth. Add the eggs, 1 at a time, beating until fluffy. Stir in the sour cream. Combine the baking soda and flour, and stir into the sour cream mixture. Beat at low speed until well mixed and smooth; beat in vanilla. Spoon batter into the prepared pans or pan. Bake 1 hour, or until the cake tests done. Let stand in the pan for 10 minutes, then remove and cool on a rack.

St. Louis Angel Food Cake

MAKES ONE 10-INCH CAKE

Among the culinary refinements of St. Louis, Missouri, is angel food cake. St. Louis in the antebellum years was a mecca for travelers on the floating palaces that plied the Mississippi. The clientele demanded—and could easily afford—the best of everything, and the steamers that gilded the river between New Orleans and St. Louis spared no cost or effort to see that it was made abundantly available.

¾ *cup all-purpose flour*

1½ *cups sugar*

12 *egg whites (about* 1½ *cups), at room temperature*

1½ *teaspoons cream of tartar*

¼ *teaspoon salt*

1½ *teaspoons vanilla*

Preheat oven to 375°F.

Combine the flour and ¾ cup sugar. In a large bowl whip the egg whites until frothy; add the cream of tartar and salt and beat until mixture forms soft peaks. (You may start out beating with an electric mixer, but after addition of the cream of tartar, finish with a whisk for best results.) Whisk the remaining sugar into the egg whites, 1 tablespoon at a time, working vigorously until stiff peaks form. Fold in the vanilla. Spoon flour mixture into the egg whites, ¼ cup at a time, and fold gently just until blended. Pour batter into an ungreased 10-inch angel food cake pan. Cut through batter gently to remove any large air bubbles. Bake 30 to 35 minutes, until the crust is golden and the cracks are dry. Invert and let hang suspended, until completely cooled. Do not remove from pan until completely cool.

Chocolate Angel Food Cake

MAKES ONE 10-INCH CAKE

This is an old-fashioned cake that requires you to sift the sugar, cocoa, and flour many times. The easiest way is to use two bowls and one sieve, placing the sieve over a bowl, sieving the ingredients into one bowl, then repeating it over a second bowl.

2 cups sugar
½ cup dark unsweetened cocoa
1 cup sifted cake flour
12 egg whites (about 1½ cups), at room temperature
A pinch of salt
1½ teaspoons cream of tartar
1 teaspoon vanilla
Vanilla Custard Filling (see following recipe)
Cocoa (optional)

Preheat oven to 375°F.

Sift sugar and ½ cup cocoa together 4 times until evenly blended; then add the cake flour and sift together another 6 times until ingredients look homogeneous. In a large bowl, whip the egg whites with a pinch of salt until frothy; add the cream of tartar and beat with a wire whisk until whites form stiff peaks. (You may start out the beating with an electric mixer, but after addition of the cream of tartar, finish with a whisk for best results). Using the whisk, blend in the vanilla and the cocoa mixture, adding a heaping ¼ cup of the dry ingredients at a time. Fold in, using 15 strokes of the whisk for each addition. Turn batter into an ungreased 10-inch angel food cake pan. Bake 40 minutes, until cake is dry on top and has dry-looking, rather deep cracks. Invert and let hang suspended, until completely cooled.

While cake cools, prepare the Vanilla Custard Filling, and allow it to cool.

Remove the cake from pan. Wash the pan. Invert cake onto breadboard. Cut it into 4 layers. Spoon about one-fourth of the Vanilla Custard Filling into the bottom of the cake pan. Place one layer (what was the bottom of the cake) with the cut side up onto the layer of filling. Top next with more Vanilla Custard Filling, then another layer; repeat using the last of the filling on top of the third layer. Top with last layer (which is the top of the baked cake). Wrap cake and refrigerate several hours.

Before serving, loosen cake around the edges of the pan. Loosen center tube, and remove tube and cake from the pan. Slide a spatula around the bottom of the cake. Invert cake onto a serving plate. Dust with cocoa, if desired.

Vanilla Custard Filling

MAKES ABOUT 5 CUPS

4 egg yolks
⅔ cup sugar
2 tablespoons all-purpose flour
1½ cups milk
1 package (1 tablespoon) unflavored gelatin
¼ cup cold water
1 teaspoon vanilla
2 cups heavy cream

In a small bowl, beat the yolks lightly with a whisk. Mix in the sugar and flour. Pour the milk into a saucepan and heat just to a boil. Blend in the sugar-egg mixture. Cook until thickened. Dissolve the gelatin in cold water, and add to the hot custard. Add the vanilla. Cool. Stir once in a while, until mixture is syrupy. Beat the cream until stiff, and fold into the custard. Spread the filling on the cake as directed.

Sponge Cake

MAKES ONE 10-INCH CAKE, OR TWO 9-INCH LAYERS

Leavened with beaten whole egg, sponge cake has been a basic the longest time of all. Often, it is used as a base for a shortcake, but there are other uses, too, such as in layered refrigerated desserts.

4 *eggs, separated*
⅔ *cup cold water*
1 *cup sugar*
1½ *cups all-purpose flour*
¼ *teaspoon salt*
1 *teaspoon lemon extract*
1 *teaspoon cream of tartar*

Preheat oven to 325°F.

In the large bowl of an electric mixer, beat the egg yolks with the water on high speed for 5 minutes, scraping the bowl often. Gradually add the sugar, and continue beating for another 4 minutes. Sift together the flour and salt, and add to the egg yolk mixture with the mixer on lowest speed. Add the lemon extract. In another bowl, beat the egg whites until frothy; beat in the cream of tartar and continue beating until the whites hold stiff peaks but are not dry. Fold whites into the egg yolk mixture. Turn into an ungreased 10-inch tube-type sponge cake pan. Bake 1 hour to 1 hour and 5 minutes, or until the cake tests done in the center. Invert onto rack and cool completely. Remove from cake pan.

To bake into layers, pour batter into two 9-inch cake pans with removable bottoms; or butter bottoms of cake pans, line with parchment rounds, but do not butter the sides of the pans. Bake 30 to 35 minutes.

Chiffon Cake

MAKES ONE 10-INCH TUBE CAKE

The basic chiffon cake is the youngest of the American-born foam cakes. It was developed after liquid shortening or vegetable oil came into wide use. The cake is really a cross between a sponge cake and a butter cake, and it takes well to a variety of flavor combinations.

2 cups all-purpose flour
1½ cups sugar
3 teaspoons baking powder
1 teaspoon salt
½ cup vegetable oil
5 egg yolks
¾ cup cold water
2 teaspoons vanilla
1 cup egg whites (about 7 to 8 large whites)
1 teaspoon grated lemon rind
Powdered sugar or lightly sweetened whipped cream

Preheat oven to 325°F.

In a large bowl, combine the flour, sugar, baking powder, and salt. In another bowl, stir together the oil, egg yolks, water, and vanilla. Add liquids to the dry ingredients and beat until very smooth. In a large, dry bowl, whip the egg whites with clean beaters until frothy; add the lemon rind and whip until the whites hold soft but firm peaks (do not overbeat). Fold the whites into the yolk mixture until blended. Turn batter into an unbuttered 10-inch tube pan. Bake 55 minutes, or until cake springs back when touched in the center. Remove from the oven and invert and let hang, suspended, until cooled. Remove from the pan and dust with powdered sugar or frost with lightly sweetened whipped cream.

ORANGE CHIFFON CAKE: Omit lemon rind. Add 3 tablespoons grated orange rind to the egg yolk mixture.

CHIFFON SPICE CAKE: Omit vanilla and lemon rind. Add 1 teaspoon cinnamon, ½ teaspoon nutmeg, ½ teaspoon allspice, and ½ teaspoon ground cloves to the dry ingredients.

CHOCOLATE CHIP CHIFFON CAKE: Grate 3 squares semisweet chocolate, and fold into the cake last of all.

PINEAPPLE CHIFFON CAKE: Use pineapple juice in place of the water. Add ½ cup very well drained, finely crushed pineapple to the mixture along with the oil and egg yolks.

Old-fashioned Lemon-Nut Coffee Cake

MAKES ONE 8- OR 9-INCH-SQUARE CAKE

Coffee cakes were important for the mid-morning coffee breaks taken by workers in the Midwestern fields. Although they have a definite Old World character, they are not found anywhere in the Old World.

1 *cup all-purpose flour*
⅓ *cup tightly packed light or dark brown sugar*
⅓ *cup granulated sugar*
¾ *teaspoon baking powder*
¼ *teaspoon baking soda*
½ *cup butter, chilled*
⅓ *cup chopped walnuts or pecans*
1 *egg*
⅓ *cup buttermilk*
2 *teaspoons freshly grated lemon rind or* ½ *teaspoon lemon extract*

Preheat oven to 350°F. Butter an 8- or 9-inch-square cake pan.

In a large mixing bowl, combine the flour, brown sugar, granulated sugar, baking powder, and baking soda. Cut in the butter until mixture resembles coarse crumbs. Add the nuts. Remove and reserve ⅓ cup of the mixture. In another bowl, beat the egg, buttermilk, and lemon rind or lemon extract together. Stir the egg mixture into dry ingredients. Do not overmix. Batter will not be smooth-looking. Turn batter into the prepared cake pan. Sprinkle reserved crumb mixture over the top. Bake 25 minutes, until golden. Serve warm.

Cinnamon Sour Cream Coffee Cake

MAKES ONE 10-INCH TUBE CAKE

A ripple of cinnamon and walnuts through the center of this coffee cake gives it a wonderful aroma as it bakes. It is best served hot out of the oven.

1 *cup butter, at room temperature*
1¼ *cups plus 2 tablespoons granulated sugar*
2 *eggs*
1 *cup sour cream*
1½ *teaspoons baking powder*
½ *teaspoon baking soda*
2 *cups all-purpose flour*
1 *teaspoon vanilla*
¾ *cup finely chopped walnuts*
1 *teaspoon cinnamon*
Powdered sugar

Preheat oven to 350°F. Butter or grease a 10- to 12-cup fancy tube cake pan. Dust with sugar.

In the large bowl of an electric mixer, cream the butter and 1¼ cups granulated sugar; add the eggs and beat until light. Add the sour cream, blend in the baking powder and baking soda, then mix in the flour until blended. Stir in the vanilla. Spoon half of the batter into the prepared pan. Sprinkle with walnuts. Mix the cinnamon and 2 tablespoons granulated sugar, and sprinkle over the walnuts. Top with the remaining half of batter. Bake 55 minutes to 1 hour, or until the cake tests done. Allow to cool in the pan for 10 minutes, invert onto cake rack, and remove from pan. Dust with powdered sugar.

Strawberry Shortcake

MAKES 6 TO 8 SERVINGS

Strawberry shortcake can be done two different ways. Either the shortcake base is baked in a whole round or square, being cut into individual servings later, or the dough is cut into rounds like baking-powder biscuits and baked, then split and filled.

THE RICH BISCUIT BASE

2 *cups all-purpose flour*
2 *tablespoons sugar*
1 *tablespoon baking powder*
1 *teaspoon salt*
½ *cup butter or shortening*
⅔ *to* ¾ *cup milk*
Additional butter to dot between layers of biscuit

THE STRAWBERRY FILLING

1 quart fresh strawberries, preferably wild berries, hulled
¾ to 1 cup sugar

Lightly sweetened whipped cream

Preheat oven to 450°F. Grease an 8- or 9-inch cake pan well.

In a large bowl, combine the flour, 2 tablespoons sugar, baking powder, and salt. Cut in the butter or shortening, until the mixture resembles coarse crumbs. With a fork, stir in just enough milk to make a dough that will hold together. On a floured surface, knead the dough 2 or 3 turns to mix. Divide the dough into 2 parts. Pat half of the dough into the pan, dot with butter, and pat the other half on top. Bake 15 minutes, or until golden. Split the layers. Place the bottom layer on a serving plate.

If wild strawberries are unavailable, very large strawberries should be sliced. Combine the strawberries and ¾ to 1 cup sugar, and spoon half of the mixture over the bottom layer. Top with second layer and the remaining strawberry mixture. Cut into wedges and serve with the sweetened whipped cream.

For individual shortcakes, roll the dough out to ½-inch thickness and dot with butter. Fold over. Press layers together and cut into 3-inch rounds. Place rounds on an ungreased cookie sheet and bake at 450°F. for 10 to 12 minutes. Split shortcakes and fill them with half the strawberry filling, serve with the remaining strawberry filling and whipped cream.

PEACH SHORTCAKE: Substitute 1 quart peeled, sliced, fresh ripe peaches for the strawberries and use 1 cup sugar in the filling.

RASPBERRY SHORTCAKE: Substitute 1 quart fresh raspberries for the strawberries and use ¾ cup sugar in the filling.

Strawberry-topped Cheesecake

MAKES 12 SERVINGS

Lindy's, the New York restaurant famous for its cheesecake, probably has more to do with the promotion of this classic Jewish-American dessert than any other single establishment. The cheesecake is basic and the topping is classic.

THE COOKIE CRUST

1 *cup all-purpose flour*
4 *tablespoons sugar*
1 *teaspoon grated lemon rind*
½ *cup unsalted butter, at room temperature*
1 *egg yolk*

THE FILLING

Three 8-ounce packages cream cheese, at room temperature
½ *cup sugar*
2 *tablespoons all-purpose flour*
1 *teaspoon grated lemon rind*
1 *teaspoon vanilla*
3 *whole eggs, plus* 1 *egg yolk*
¼ *cup heavy cream*

THE TOPPING

1 *quart fresh strawberries*
⅓ *cup sugar*
1 *tablespoon cornstarch*
¼ *cup cold water*
Red food coloring (optional)

To prepare the crust, combine 1 cup flour, 4 tablespoons sugar, and 1 teaspoon lemon rind in a large mixing bowl. Cut in the butter until the mixture resembles soft crumbs. Blend in the egg yolk until the mixture makes a cookielike dough. Shape the dough into a ball, and dust with flour. Chill 30 minutes.

Preheat oven to 400°F.

Pat chilled dough into an ungreased 9- or 10-inch springform pan to cover the bottom and come up 2 inches on the side of the pan. Bake 10 minutes, until set and pale gold in color. Place on rack to cool.

Reduce oven to 250°F.

Beat the cream cheese in a large mixing bowl until smooth and creamy. Add ½ cup sugar, 2 tablespoons flour, 1 teaspoon lemon rind, the vanilla, eggs and egg yolks, and cream. Mix until well blended. Pour filling into the pan with the baked crust. Place in the center of the oven, and bake 1 hour. Remove from the oven and cool in pan on a rack.

Wash and hull the berries. Press enough of the berries through a sieve to get ¾ cup strawberry purée. Blend ⅓ cup sugar, the cornstarch, and cold water in a saucepan over medium heat, and bring to a boil; cook 2 minutes, stirring, until thickened. Mix thickened sauce with the strawberry purée. Bring to a boil over high heat and stirring frequently, boil 1 minute. Remove from the heat. (Add a few drops red food coloring, if desired, to deepen the color.)

Arrange the remaining berries on top of the cheesecake, and spoon the thickened purée over the berries. Chill at least 4 hours before serving.

Cinnamon-Apple Cheesecake

MAKES 12 SERVINGS

This farm-style cheesecake is pretty because the apple slices bake right into the cheesecake filling, with a cinnamon-sugar glaze on top.

THE CRUST

½ cup butter

⅓ cup sugar

1 cup all-purpose flour

THE CHEESECAKE FILLING

Two 8-ounce packages cream cheese, at room temperature

½ cup sugar

2 eggs

1 teaspoon vanilla

THE CINNAMON-APPLE TOPPING

3 large Golden Delicious apples, pared

⅓ cup sugar

1 teaspoon ground cinnamon

½ cup orange marmalade, melted

Preheat oven to 400°F.

To prepare the crust, cream the butter and ⅓ cup sugar, and add the flour and blend until mixture resembles coarse crumbs. Pat crumbs into the bottom and 1 inch up the sides of a 10-inch springform pan. Bake 10 minutes, until golden. Cool.

In the large bowl of an electric mixer, cream the cream cheese and ½ cup sugar together until blended, scraping down the sides of the bowl several times. Mix in the eggs and vanilla. Pour the mixture evenly over the baked crust.

Core apples and cut into thin even slices. Arrange apple slices in overlapping layers over the cream cheese filling. Mix ⅓ cup sugar and the cinnamon, and sprinkle over top of the apples. Bake 35 minutes, until the apples are tender and the cheesecake layer is set. Cool, then chill. Before serving, spoon the warm orange marmalade over the top.

Cookie-Jar Cookies and Pan Bars

Cookies are truly American. In other parts of the world they are "little cakes," "little breads," "biscuits," or named individually, like "macaroons," "florentines," or "shortbread." The actual word "cookie" or "cooky" probably was derived from the Pennsylvania Dutch word *koekje,* which is pronounced "cookie."

American cooks have, over the years, created hundreds and hundreds of different cookies. In the 1700s, two forms of ovens developed around the fireplace, one of them being a portable reflector. The ovens were used mainly for baking roasts, puddings, pies, and cakes. In order to check the oven temperature, little "test cakes" were dropped on baking pans and baked. They were then given to the children to eat.

As a result, in America, all little cakes, regardless of their nationality, have been called cookies rather than the name used in their country of origin. They can be divided into five general categories: rolled, molded, refrigerator, drops, and pan bars, which are cut into squares and rectangles after baking.

Traditionally, at Christmastime, cookies have been baked by the dozens in every home, often using treasured old cookie cutters shaped like animals, which were brought from the Old World. Sand tarts, Lebkuchen, gingerbreads, and a wide variety of butter cookies can usually be traced right back to their European roots, where they were called by more specific names. In early America, cookies were usually a big production, being delicately shaped with cutters, fancy molds, and by hand into fanciful hand-rolled shapes. The Puritans baked them, as did the Shakers, the Italians, the English, the Germans, and even the very sober Amish, who loved eating cookies with a glass or two of wine at Christmas.

As the history of cookie baking progressed, Americans took to simplifying the cookie-making process with drop cookies, refrigerator cookies, and pan bars. This made it possible to make dozens of cookies using a mass-production method. Cookies were no longer just a holiday specialty, but were made and eaten throughout the year. A glass of milk and a cookie after school became a favorite snack for kids. With the advent of "kid-filler" cookies (chocolate chip, oatmeal, peanut butter cookies) came such a variety that fancy Christmas cookies, as we know them, are today in a category by themselves.

Included in this chapter are the basic, all-time favorite American cookies. Crispy, sugar-topped Sugar Cookies, spicy Gingerbread Boys, and Moravian Easter Rabbit Cookies are all part of the America's heritage. From Jumbles to Brownies, a historic path has been paved from the time when kids first enjoyed the test cakes from the hearth to the huge assortment readily available today. The recipes have been molded and changed, improved upon and defined over the years. Many of these cookies have been developed and mass produced to the point where the average child today thinks they cannot be made anywhere but in a cookie factory.

Grandmother's Sugar Cookies

MAKES ABOUT 5 DOZEN 3-INCH COOKIES

The dough for sugar cookies is easiest to roll out when it is first chilled. To prevent sticking to the rolling pin, slip a canvas cover over the board and a stockinette over the rolling pin. Rub flour into both covers. The crispiest cookies are made when the dough is rolled very thin. Dip the cookie cutter in flour, then shake off excess and use it to cut out rounds. To save time, you may drop the dough onto cookie sheets and flatten it very thin with a glass dipped in sugar.

½ *cup unsalted butter, at room temperature*

¾ *cup sugar*

1 *egg*

1 *tablespoon buttermilk, or 2 teaspoons lemon juice*

1 *teaspoon vanilla or lemon extract, or a combination of both*

1¼ *cups all-purpose flour*

¼ *teaspoon baking soda*

¼ *teaspoon salt*

Sugar

In a large bowl, cream the butter with the sugar, and add the egg. Mix in the buttermilk or lemon juice and vanilla or lemon extract or a combination of both. Stir together the flour, baking soda, and salt, and blend into the dough. Chill 30 minutes to several hours.

Preheat oven to 375°F. Cover cookie sheets with parchment paper or lightly grease them.

Roll out dough very thin (¹⁄₁₆ inch). Cut into rounds or other desired shapes. Place cutouts on the prepared cookie sheets and sprinkle with sugar. Bake 5 to 7 minutes, until pale gold and crisp.

Gingerbread Boys

MAKES TWELVE 8-INCH GINGERBREAD BOYS

"Run, run as fast as you can, you can't catch me, I'm the Ginger-bread Man!" We all grew up with this little fairy tale about the Gingerbread Man (or Boy) that came to life. Use a cookie cutter, or trace the shape of a gingerbread boy on a piece of plain white paper. Place the paper on the rolled-out dough and cut around it with a sharp-tipped knife. To make "dancing" gingerbread boys, bend the legs and arms into action positions as you place them on the cookie sheet. Baked cookies can be stored in an airtight container for 2 weeks.

⅔ *cup butter, at room temperature*
¾ *cup tightly packed dark brown sugar*
1 *tablespoon cinnamon*
2 *teaspoons ginger*
1½ *teaspoons ground cloves*
1½ *teaspoons baking soda*
¼ *cup water*
2½ *cups all-purpose flour*
Almond Royal Icing (see following recipe)

In a large mixing bowl, blend the butter, brown sugar, cinnamon, ginger, cloves, and baking soda until smooth. Add the water and flour, mixing until a smooth dough forms. Wrap in plastic wrap and chill 30 minutes.

Preheat oven to 350°F.

On a floured board or pastry cloth, roll out dough to about ¼-inch thickness. Using cookie cutters or a pattern cut from paper, cut out gingerbread-boy shapes. Place cookies on an ungreased baking sheet and bake 10 to 15 minutes, until they are firm to the touch. Remove from the oven and cool.

To decorate the cookies, press the icing through a pastry bag equipped with a writing tip. Allow icing to harden, then wrap cookies in plastic wrap and store in an airtight container.

Almond Royal Icing

MAKES ABOUT 2 CUPS

1 egg *white*
3 *cups powdered sugar*
½ *teaspoon almond extract*

Whisk the egg white and powdered sugar together until smooth and free of lumps. Blend in the almond extract. If necessary, add more powdered sugar if the icing is too thin, or add water, a teaspoonful at a time, if the icing is too stiff.

Moravian Easter Rabbit Cookies

MAKES 4 TO 5 DOZEN COOKIES

The Pennsylvania Dutch introduced the Easter egg and its proud parent, the Easter bunny. They used to bake a big cookie rabbit in the act of laying an egg. Eggs were important to Easter celebrations, and an egg laid on Good Friday was a treasure. It was to be eaten on that day, the shell saved to drink water from on Easter morning. At the Moravian Easter service, every worshiper received an egg marked "The Lord is Risen."

¼ *cup tightly packed dark brown sugar*
½ *teaspoon baking soda*
¼ *teaspoon salt*
½ *teaspoon ginger*
½ *teaspoon ground cloves*
½ *teaspoon cinnamon*
¼ *teaspoon nutmeg*
¼ *teaspoon allspice*
½ *cup dark molasses*
¼ *cup vegetable shortening, at room temperature*
2 *cups all-purpose flour*

In a mixing bowl, blend the brown sugar with the baking soda, salt, and spices. Heat the molasses just to the boiling point, but do not boil. Stir in the shortening until absolutely smooth. Cool, and beat in the sugar-spice mixture. Blend in the flour, until the dough holds together. (This is easily done in a food processor with the steel blade in place.) Shape dough into a ball, wrap in plastic wrap, and chill until firm. Dough will keep for several weeks, so you can bake cookies a few at a time, if you wish.

Preheat oven to 375°F.

Break off pieces of the dough and roll to ¹⁄₁₆-inch thickness on a lightly floured board or pastry cloth. Using a bunny-shaped cookie cutter, cut out the shapes and place on a lightly greased cookie sheet. Bake 6 to 8 minutes, until lightly browned.

Ginger Crinkles

MAKES 4 DOZEN COOKIES

The great variety of ginger-and-molasses cookies and little cakes is understandable. In early Colonial days, molasses was the common sweetener. The legacy of ginger and molasses has given us ginger snaps, ginger cakes, and crunchy and chewy crinkles in great variety. These are thick, chewy, and spicy, with a crinkly sugar topping.

¾ *cup unsalted butter or vegetable shortening*
1 *cup tightly packed light or dark brown sugar*
1 *egg*
¼ *cup dark molasses*
2¼ *cups all-purpose flour*
2 *teaspoons baking soda*
1 *teaspoon cinnamon*
1 *teaspoon ginger*
½ *teaspoon ground cloves*
¼ *teaspoon salt*

Preheat oven to 375°F.

In a large mixing bowl, cream the butter or shortening with the brown sugar, until blended. Mix in the egg and molasses. Combine the flour, soda, cinnamon, ginger, cloves, and salt, and blend into the creamed mixture until the dough is stiff. If the dough is very soft, chill for 30 minutes. Shape into balls the size of large walnuts. Dip tops in sugar, and place with sugared side up 3 inches apart on lightly greased cookie sheets. Sprinkle each cookie with 2 to 3 drops of water to create the crackly surface. Bake 10 to 12 minutes, until just set, not hard.

Snickerdoodles

MAKES 5 DOZEN COOKIES

These crinkly topped cookies have had many different names, depending on where they were made. "Schneckenoodles" would indicate a Germanic or Dutch history, as does "Snipdoodles." According to the late James Beard, snickerdoodles is a name that appears in cookbooks throughout the Midwest, while in New England, where it was common to attach odd names to foods, Graham Jakes, Jolly Boys, Brambles, Tangle Breeches, and Kinkawoodles are other names for the same cookie.

THE COOKIE DOUGH

1 *cup butter, at room temperature*

1½ *cups sugar*

2 *eggs*

2¾ *cups all-purpose flour*

1 *teaspoon baking soda*

1 *teaspoon cinnamon*

¼ *teaspoon salt*

1 *cup finely chopped walnuts (optional)*

½ *cup currants (optional)*

½ *cup raisins (optional)*

THE CINNAMON SUGAR

2 *tablespoons sugar mixed with 2 teaspoons cinnamon*

Preheat oven to 400°F.

In a large mixing bowl, cream the butter with the sugar; beat in the eggs until smooth. Combine the flour, baking soda, cinnamon, and salt. Blend the flour mixture into the creamed mixture. Add the walnuts, currants, and raisins, if desired. If dough is soft, chill 30 minutes. Roll out dough into balls the size of small walnuts. Roll each ball in the cinnamon sugar. Place balls about 2 inches apart on ungreased cookie sheets. Bake until lightly browned but still soft.

Peanut Butter Cookies

MAKES 3 DOZEN COOKIES

Peanut butter is a health food that originated in St. Louis in 1890. For the benefit of his patients, a physician developed this spreadable butter because it was an easily digested form of protein. The idea was welcomed by food faddists, but it has clearly outlived the life of a fad and has become a blessing for mothers of young children. Cookies made with peanut butter are a cookie jar staple. They are a "molded" cookie and are always identified by the crisscross pattern made by flattening the dough mounds with a fork. They should not be over-baked or they will be hard.

½ cup butter or vegetable shortening, or a combination of both
½ cup peanut butter, creamy or chunk-style
⅓ cup granulated sugar
⅓ cup tightly packed brown sugar
1 egg
1 ¼ cups all-purpose flour
½ teaspoon baking powder
½ teaspoon baking soda
¼ teaspoon salt

Preheat oven to 375°F. Lightly grease cookie sheets.

In a large mixing bowl, cream the butter or shortening with the peanut butter, granulated sugar, brown sugar, and egg. Blend together the flour, baking powder, baking soda, and salt. Mix the dry ingredients into the creamed ingredients until well blended. If the dough is soft, chill for 30 minutes.

Roll the dough into balls the size of large walnuts. Place about 3 inches apart on the prepared cookie sheets. With a fork dipped in flour, flatten the balls, making a crisscross pattern on each cookie. Bake 10 to 12 minutes, until set but not hard.

Old-fashioned Sugar Jumbles

MAKES 3 DOZEN COOKIES

Jumbles are among the oldest of American cookies, and probably the simplest, too. Made with flour, butter, sugar, and eggs, sometimes seasoned with nutmeg or mace, they were made into soft drops or into cookies that were rolled out and cut into shapes. One version calls for a glass of brandy, while Jackson Jumbles is made with sour cream and is a thick rolled-out cookie. This version is a simple drop cookie with suggested variations.

1/4 cup butter, at room temperature
1/4 cup shortening, at room temperature
1/2 cup sugar
1 egg
1 teaspoon vanilla
1 cup plus 2 tablespoons all-purpose flour
1/4 teaspoon baking soda
1/2 teaspoon salt

Preheat oven to 375°F. Lightly grease the cookie sheets.

In a large mixing bowl, cream the butter and shortening with the sugar; beat in the egg and vanilla, until the mixture is smooth and light. Combine the flour, baking soda, and salt, and mix into the creamed mixture. Drop rounded teaspoonfuls of dough onto the cookie sheets, about 2 inches apart. Bake 8 to 10 minutes, or until pale gold in color; the cookies should still be soft. Cool, then remove from the cookie sheets.

COCONUT JUMBLES: Mix 1 cup flaked or shredded coconut into the cookie dough.

CHOCOLATE CHIP JUMBLES: Add 1/4 cup brown sugar to the dough along with the granulated sugar, and blend in 1/2 cup chopped walnuts and one 6-ounce package chocolate chips.

ORANGE-GLAZED JUMBLES: Blend 2 teaspoons grated orange rind and 1 cup chopped walnuts or almonds into the cookie dough. Combine 1/3 cup powdered sugar with 1 teaspoon grated orange rind and 3 tablespoons orange juice. While baked cookies are still hot, dip tops in this mixture.

PECAN JUMBLES: Blend 2 cups chopped pecans into the cookie dough.

CINNAMON JUMBLES: Combine 1/4 cup sugar and 1 teaspoon cinnamon. Sprinkle cookies with cinnamon sugar before baking.

Old-fashioned
Icebox Cookies

MAKES 10 DOZEN COOKIES

The convenience of icebox cookies was discovered early, when homes had the ice-chilled storage box near the back door of the kitchen. Due to the sugar, shortening, and spice content of the mixture, the dough keeps well when shaped into logs and wrapped thoroughly. The logs should be 3 inches in diameter, and can be sliced and baked whenever freshly baked cookies are desired. Icebox cookies were the classic accompaniment to homemade ice cream for dessert.

1 *cup butter, at room temperature*
1 *cup vegetable shortening*
1 *cup granulated sugar*
1 *cup tightly packed dark brown sugar*
3 *eggs*
5 ½ *cups all-purpose flour*
1 *teaspoon cinnamon*
½ *teaspoon nutmeg*
½ *teaspoon ground cloves*
1 *teaspoon baking soda*
1 *tablespoon hot water*
1 *teaspoon vanilla*
1 *cup whole pecans or walnuts*

In a large mixing bowl, cream the butter, shortening, granulated sugar, and brown sugar. Blend in the eggs. Combine 3 cups of the flour with the cinnamon, nutmeg, and cloves. Blend the baking soda with the water. Blend the flour mixture and soda-water into the creamed mixture, until well mixed. Add the vanilla. Blend in the remaining flour and the nuts. Divide dough into 4 parts and shape each into a roll 3 inches in diameter. Wrap rolls in plastic wrap or wax paper, and refrigerate overnight.

Preheat oven to 400°F. Cut dough into ¼-inch-thick slices. Place rounds on ungreased cookie sheets and bake 7 to 10 minutes, or until crisp.

CHOCOLATE-NUT ICEBOX COOKIES: Omit the cinnamon, nutmeg, and cloves. Into the creamed mixture, blend 5 squares (5 ounces) melted unsweetened chocolate. Increase the nuts to 2 cups.

Basic Butter Drop Cookies

MAKES 3 DOZEN COOKIES

This is considered to be the forerunner of the Toll House Cookie, and it appears in many old American cookbooks. When chocolate-covered candy bars became popular in the mid-1900s, creative cooks added those confections, cut into pieces, to this basic dough. Baby Ruth, Butterfinger, and Heath Bars were used most often.

½ *cup butter, at room temperature*
⅓ *cup granulated sugar*
⅓ *cup tightly packed brown sugar*
1 *egg*
½ *teaspoon vanilla*
1 *cup plus 2 tablespoons all-purpose flour*
½ *teaspoon salt*
½ *teaspoon baking soda*

Preheat oven to 375°F. Lightly grease 2 or 3 cookie sheets.

In a large mixing bowl, cream the butter with the granulated sugar, brown sugar, egg, and vanilla. Combine the flour, salt, and baking soda. Blend the flour mixture into the creamed mixture, until well mixed. Drop teaspoons of the dough on the cookie sheets, about 2 inches apart. Bake 8 to 10 minutes, or until lightly browned. Do not overbake.

CURRANT DROPS: Blend 1 cup currants into the basic dough.

PEANUT BUTTER CHIP COOKIES: Blend one 6-ounce package peanut butter chips into the basic dough.

BUTTERSCOTCH CHIP COOKIES: Blend one 6-ounce package butterscotch chips into the basic dough.

CANDY BAR COOKIES: Add 1 cup chopped chocolate-and-nut candy bars, such as Baby Ruth, Butterfinger, Heath Bar, or almond or plain milk chocolate bars to the basic cookie dough.

Toll House Cookies

MAKES ONE HUNDRED 2-INCH-DIAMETER COOKIES

In 1930, Ruth Wakefield, owner of the Toll House Inn, cut a bar of semisweet chocolate into bits and added it to a basic butter cookie recipe. She expected the bits to melt and blend into the dough, but instead they held their shape, softening just a bit. The recipe was soon put on the wrapper of the chocolate bar, and it gained in popularity. Soon the chocolate bar was being manufactured specially scored to make it easy for the cookie baker to make chocolate "bits." In 1939, the chocolate pieces were first available in convenient "chips" or "morsels." The following is Mrs. Wakefield's original recipe.

1 *cup butter, at room temperature*
¾ *cup granulated sugar*
¾ *cup tightly packed light brown sugar*
2 *eggs*
1 *teaspoon vanilla*
2¼ *cups all-purpose flour*
1 *teaspoon baking soda*
½ *teaspoon salt*
12 *ounces semisweet chocolate morsels*
1 *cup chopped walnuts or pecans*

Preheat oven to 375°F.

In a large mixing bowl, cream the butter with the granulated sugar and brown sugar, until light. Add the eggs and vanilla and beat until creamy. In a small bowl, blend the flour, baking soda, and salt. Mix the flour mixture into the creamed mixture, until smooth and blended. Stir in the chocolate morsels and nuts. Drop rounded teaspoons onto ungreased cookie sheets. Bake 8 to 10 minutes, until pale gold in color.

Hermits

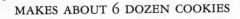

MAKES ABOUT 6 DOZEN COOKIES

Hermits are a spicy, chewy, old-fashioned drop cookie with raisins and nuts. Many old recipes call for sour cream in the cookies, and Southern recipes often include molasses. The choice of nuts depended on what was available. It could be that the name "hermit" comes from the fact that the cookies improve after being stored away by themselves in an airtight container for a few days.

1 *cup butter or vegetable shortening, at room temperature*
2 *cups tightly packed light or dark brown sugar*
1 *egg*
½ *cup sour cream, or* ¼ *cup sour cream and* ¼ *cup molasses*
3 *cups all-purpose flour*
1 *teaspoon cinnamon*
1 *teaspoon nutmeg*
1 *teaspoon baking soda*
½ *teaspoon salt*
½ *teaspoon ground cloves*
½ *teaspoon allspice*
2 *cups light or dark raisins or chopped dates*
1 ½ *cups chopped walnuts, pecans, filberts, or almonds*

In a large mixing bowl, cream the butter or shortening with the sugar, egg, and sour cream (and molasses, if used); beat until creamy. In another bowl, combine the flour, cinnamon, nutmeg, baking soda, salt, cloves, and allspice. Blend the dry ingredients into the creamed mixture thoroughly. Add the raisins or dates and nuts. Chill 1 hour.

Preheat oven to 400°F. Lightly grease cookie sheets. Drop rounded teaspoons of the dough on the cookie sheets, 2 inches apart. Bake 8 to 10 minutes, until just set. Do not overbake. Cool on racks, then store in airtight containers.

Oatmeal Cookies

MAKES 5 DOZEN COOKIES

Although the world of oatmeal cookies offers a great variety, this is probably the all-time favorite. It is a "cookie-jar filler" that is not too sweet, is chewy, keeps well, and is just right with a glass of milk when the kids come home from school. Baked with butter, the flavor is the best. Vegetable shortening gives a lighter texture and a shorter crumb, but does nothing for the flavor.

¾ cup butter or vegetable shortening
1 cup tightly packed light or dark brown sugar
½ cup granulated sugar
1 egg
¼ cup water
1 teaspoon vanilla
3 cups uncooked rolled oats, old-fashioned or quick
¾ cup all-purpose flour
¼ teaspoon salt
½ teaspoon baking soda

Preheat oven to 350°F. Lightly grease cookie sheets.

In a large bowl, blend the butter or shortening, brown sugar, granulated sugar, egg, water, and vanilla, until creamy. Combine the oats, flour, salt, and baking soda, and blend into the creamed mixture. Drop rounded teaspoons onto the cookie sheets, about 2 inches apart. Bake 10 to 12 minutes, until lightly browned. Remove from cookie sheets and cool on racks.

OATMEAL-NUT COOKIES: Add 1 cup chopped walnuts or pecans to the dough.

OATMEAL–CHOCOLATE CHIP COOKIES: Add one 6-ounce package chocolate chips to the dough.

OATMEAL-COCONUT COOKIES: Add 1 cup flaked or shredded coconut to the dough.

OATMEAL-RAISIN COOKIES: Add 1 cup dark raisins to the dough.

Brownies

MAKES ONE 9-BY-13-INCH PAN, ABOUT 2½ DOZEN
BROWNIES

How do you like your brownies? Moist and chewy? Fudgy? Light
and cakey? If we took a vote, the traditional American favorite probably would turn out to be "moist and fudgy." That's what these are.

1 *cup unsalted butter*
4 *squares (4 ounces) unsweetened chocolate*
4 *eggs*
2 *cups sugar*
1 *teaspoon vanilla*
⅛ *teaspoon salt*
½ *cup all-purpose flour*
1 *cup walnuts, coarsely chopped*
Chocolate Cream Frosting (see recipe) (optional)

Preheat oven to 350°F. Butter and flour a 9-by-13-inch baking
pan.

In a saucepan or the top half of a double boiler, melt the butter
and chocolate together over boiling water. Let cool to room temperature.

In a large bowl, beat the eggs until fluffy and slowly beat in the
sugar, until the mixture is light and lemon-colored. Add the vanilla
and salt. Blend the chocolate mixture into the egg mixture, and carefully fold in the flour. Blend in the nuts. Pour batter into the prepared
pan and bake 25 to 30 minutes, until the center is just set. Do not
overbake or brownies will become hard. Cool in the pan before
cutting into bars. Frost with Chocolate Cream Frosting, if desired.

Matrimonial Cakes
(Date-Oatmeal Squares)

MAKES ONE 9-BY-13-INCH PAN, ABOUT 2½ DOZEN BARS

Fruit fillings between nutty, rich crumb crusts were the beginning of a number of bar cookies so popular today. This is one of the oldest of the favorites. These are sometimes called "date bars."

THE DATE FILLING

3 *cups chopped pitted dates*
¼ *cup granulated sugar*
1½ *cups water*

THE OAT CRUST

¾ *cup butter, at room temperature*
1 *cup tightly packed brown sugar*
1¾ *cups all-purpose flour*
½ *teaspoon baking soda*
½ *teaspoon salt*
1½ *cups uncooked rolled oats, old-fashioned or quick*

To prepare the filling, combine the dates, granulated sugar, and water in a heavy saucepan. Place over low heat and cook, stirring constantly, until thickened, about 10 minutes. Cool.

Preheat oven to 400°F. Butter and flour a 9-by-13-inch baking pan.

In a large bowl, cream the butter and brown sugar. Mix the flour, baking soda, and salt together, and blend into the creamed mixture. Add the rolled oats and mix until crumbly. Press half of the crumb mixture into the prepared pan and flatten with hands to cover the bottom of the pan. Spread crumb mixture with the cooled filling. Cover with the remaining crumb mixture. Pat lightly to compress the layers. Bake 25 to 30 minutes, until lightly browned. While warm, cut into bars and remove from pan.

Index

Almond:
   Burnt-, Cream, California, 177
   -Crunch, Chocolate, Parfaits, 180
   Peach Crisp, 32
   Poppy-seed and, Filling, *for*
      Pennsylvania Dutch *Apfelstrudel,*
      119
   Royal Icing, 267
   Toasted-, Fudge Ice Cream, 161–62
Amana Village Plain Chocolate Bread
      Pudding, 89–90
Ambrosia, Orange, 11
American Cream Pie, 207
Angel food cakes, *see* Cake(s)
Angel Parfait Cream, 180
Apfelstrudel, Pennsylvania Dutch, 117–19
Apple(s):
   Baked, Stuffed with Dates and
      Walnuts, 25
   in Bird's Nest Pudding, 45–46

Cinnamon-, Cheesecake, 261–62
Crunch, 33
dried:
   to cook, 121
   in Southwestern Fruit *Empanadas,*
      121
Duff, New England, 37–38
Dumplings:
   Baked, 53
   Rosy, Shaker, 114–15
in Dutch Fruit Fritters, 126
Filling, *for Kolaches,* 123
Fresh, Cake, 237
Grunt, Early American, 47–48
jelly, *in* Fruit Jelly Ice, 156
in Mormon Bachelor's Pudding,
      91–92
Mystery Pudding, York County Farm,
      51–52
in Old-fashioned Fruit Cobbler, 34–35

283

Apple(s) (*cont'd*)
in Old-fashioned Fruit Tumble, 16–17
Pancakes, Dutch, 124
Pandowdy, 44–45
in Pennsylvania Dutch *Apfelstrudel*, 117–19
pies, *see* Pie(s)
Poached, with Maple Cream, 21–22
-and-Rhubarb Dumplings, Michigan, Stina's, 116
Roly-poly, 113–14
in Shaker Dessert Omelet, 181
Slump, Louisa May Alcott's, 50
Snow, Yankee, 12
in Stewed Fruits, 22–23
Strudel Squares, 119–20
see also Applesauce
Applesauce:
Cake, 239
in Cooked Fruit Fool, 8–9
Crisp, 31
Homemade, 24–25
Apricots:
candied, *in* Tutti-frutti Ice Cream, 165–66
in Cooked Fruit Fool, 8–9
dried:
to cook, 121
in Southwestern Fruit *Empanadas*, 121
in Winter Fruit Soup, 70
in Stewed Fruits, 22–23
Araby Spice Frosting, 235

Baked Alaska, 152–53
Baked Apple Dumplings, 53
Baked Apples Stuffed with Dates and Walnuts, 25
Baked Carrot Pudding, 96–97
Baked Country Custard, 170
Baked Honey Custard, 176
Baked Lemon Pudding, 42
Baked Peaches Flambé, 28
Baked Pears with Mint Cream, 26
Baked Pie Plant (Rhubarb), 29
Baklava, 132–34
Banana(s):
Cake, 241–42
Cream Pie, 207
in Dutch Fruit Fritters, 126
Foster, 30
in Orange Ambrosia, 11
Basic Bread Pudding, 84
Basic Butter Drop Cookies, 275
Basic Chocolate Cake, 229–30
Basic Two-Egg Cake, 220–21
Basic Yellow Cake or 1-2-3-4 Cake, 217
Batter Cake, Blueberry, Old Maine, 43
Bavarian Cream, 61

Beer, Chocolate, Cake, 244
Beignets, New Orleans, 125
Berries:
notes on, 6
see also names of specific berries
Betty(s):
Brown, Blueberry, 35
see also Cobbler(s); Crisp(s)
Bird's Nest Pudding, 45–46
Bismarks, 111
Blackberry(ies):
Duff, 38–39
Flummery, 67
in Fresh Berry Tumble, 9
Mush, Pennsylvania Dutch, 68
in Old-fashioned Fruit Cobbler, 34–35
in Scandinavian Berry Pudding, 69
Blueberry(ies):
Batter Cake, Old Maine, 43
Bread-and-Butter, Pudding, 90–91
Brown Betty, 35
Cake, 220
Flummery, 66
in Fresh Berries and Vanilla Cream Sauce, 6–7
in Fresh Berry Tumble, 9
Grunt, Cape Cod, 49
in Old-fashioned Fruit Cobbler, 34
in Old-fashioned Fruit Tumble, 16–17
in Scandinavian Berry Pudding, 69
Wild, or Huckleberry Pie, 195
see also Huckleberry(ies)
Bourbon Pecan Cake, Kentucky, 232–33
Brandy:
Butter Sauce, 41
Sauce, 105
Colonial Plum Pudding with, 103–105
Bread puddings, *see* Pudding(s)
Brownies, 280
Buckle, Oregon Huckleberry, 93–94
Burnt-Almond Cream, California, 177
Burnt-Sugar Ice Cream, Old–fashioned, 167
Butter:
Brandy, Sauce, 41
Bread-and-, Pudding, Blueberry, 90–91
cakes, *see* Cake(s)
Drop Cookies, Basic, 275
Pecan Ice Cream, 162
Butterscotch:
Chip Cookies, 275
Pudding, 58
Buttery Pastry for Pies, 187–88
Butt'ry Sauce, 102
Carrot Pudding with, 100–102

Cabinet Pudding, 141–42
Cake(s):
　Angel food:
　　Chocolate, 252–53
　　St. Louis, 251
　Applesauce, 239
　Baked Alaska, 152–53
　Banana, 241
　Blueberry, 220
　　Batter, Old Maine, 43
　Bourbon Pecan, Kentucky, 232–33
　Brownies, 280
　butter:
　　Coconut, 236
　　notes on, 215
　　Orange, 240–41
　Carrot, Country, 245–46
　Chiffon, 255–56
　　Chocolate Chip, 256
　　Orange, 255
　　Pineapple, 256
　　Spice, 256
　Chocolate:
　　Angel Food, 252–53
　　Basic, 229–30
　　Beer, 244
　　Chip Chiffon, 256
　　Icebox, Old-fashioned, 150
　　-Nut Fudge, 221
　Cocoa, 228–29
　coffee, see Coffee cake(s)
　Crumb, Spiced, 227
　Devil's Food, 230–31
　Doughnuts, 112–13
　Eggless, Milkless, Butterless or "War
　　Cake," 248–49
　flour, to measure, 95
　Fresh Apple, 237
　"Gold," Lord Baltimore Cake or, 224
　Icebox:
　　Chocolate, Old-fashioned, 150
　　Lemon, 143–44
　　Pumpkin Cream Roll, 144–45
　Lady Baltimore, 222
　Lazy-Daisy, 247–48
　Lemon Icebox, 143–44
　Lord Baltimore or "Gold Cake," 224
　Matrimonial (Date-Oatmeal Squares), 281
　mixes, notes on, 215
　Molasses Gingerbread, 243
　One-Egg, 219–20
　1-2-3-4, Basic Yellow Cake or, 217
　Orange:
　　Butter, 240–41
　　Chiffon, 255
　Pineapple:
　　Chiffon, 256
　　Upside-Down, 220
　Pound, Country, 250

Pumpkin Cream Roll, Icebox, 144–45
Spice:
　Chiffon, 256
　Country, 225–26
　Sour Cream, 234
Sponge, 254
Two-Egg, Basic, 220–21
Upside-Down, Pineapple, 220
"War," Eggless, Milkless, Butterless
　Cake or, 248–49
Yellow, Basic, or 1-2-3-4 Cake, 217
see also Cheesecake(s); Shortcake
California Burnt-Almond Cream, 177
Calliope Coffee, 147
Caramel:
　Frosting, Old-fashioned, 238
　Sauce, Hot, 10–11
　　Frozen Cranberries with, 9–10
Carrot:
　Cake, Country, 245–46
　Pudding:
　　Baked, 96–97
　　with Butt'ry Sauce, 100–102
Cantaloupe(s)
　in Iced Cantaleupes, 14–15
　in Old-fashioned Fruit Tumble, 16–17
Candy:
　Apple Pie, 192
　Bar Cookies, 276
Cape Cod Blueberry Grunt, 49
Champagne, Strawberries in, 17–18
Charlotte, Maple, 142–43
Cheesecake(s):
　Cinnamon-Apple, 261–62
　Strawberry-topped, 260–61
Cherry(ies):
　Black, Michigan, Dessert, 18
　candied, in Tutti-frutti Ice Cream,
　　165–66
　Filling, for Pennsylvania Dutch
　　Apfelstrudel, 118
　Fresh Red, 198
　in Old-fashioned Fruit Cobbler, 34–35
Chess Pie, Southern Creamy, 213
Chiffon cakes, see Cake(s)
Chilled Chocolate Pudding, 71
Chocolate:
　Almond-Crunch Parfaits, 180
　cakes, see Cakes
　Chip:
　　Chiffon Cake, 256
　　Ice Cream, 164
　　Jumbles, 272
　　Oatmeal-, Cookies, 279
　Cream Frosting, 245
　Frosting, Fluffy, 232
　Glaze, 112
　Ice Cream, 161
　Mocha Icebox Pudding, 148

Chocolate (*cont'd*)
  -Nut Icebox Cookies, 274
  puddings, *see* Pudding(s)
  Rum:
    Russe, 149
    Sauce, 95
  Spanish Cream, 60
  see also Fudge
Choux paste, notes on, 109
Cider Sauce, 182
Cinnamon:
  -Apple Cheesecake, 261–62
  Hard Sauce, 54
  Jumbles, 273
  Sour Cream Coffee Cake, 257–58
  Wild Rice Pudding, 98–99
Cobbler(s):
  Fruit, Old-fashioned, 34–35
  see also Betty(s); Crisp(s)
Cocoa:
  Cake, 228–29
  Cornstarch Pudding, 59
Coconut:
  Butter Cake, 236
  Cream Pie, 208
  Ice Cream, 164–66
  Jumbles, 272
  Oatmeal-, Cookies, 279
  Pudding, 58
Coffee:
  cakes, *See* Coffee cake(s)
  Ice Cream, 161
  Spanish Cream, 60
Coffee cake(s):
  Cinnamon Sour Cream, 257–58
  Lemon-Nut, Old-fashioned, 256
  Spiced Crumb Cake, 227
Colonial Molasses Pecan Ice Cream,
    166–67
Colonial Plum Pudding with Brandy
    Sauce, 103–105
Compote, Honeydew and Fresh Peach,
    15–16
Cooked Fruit Fool, 8–9
Cookies:
  Butterscotch Chip, 275
  Candy Bar, 276
  Currant Drops, 275
  Drop, Basic Butter, 275
  Easter Rabbit, Moravian, 267–68
  Gingerbread Boys, 266
  Ginger Crinkles, 269
  Hermits, 277–78
  Icebox:
    Chocolate-Nut, 274
    Old-fashioned, 273–74
  Oatmeal, 278–79
    –Chocolate Chip, 279
    -Coconut, 279

  -Nut, 279
  -Raisin, 279
  Peanut Butter, 271
    Chip, 275
  Snickerdoodles, 270
  Sugar, Grandmother's, 265
  Toll House, 276–77
  see also Jumbles
Cornstarch:
  puddings, *see* Pudding(s)
  as thickener, problems with, 56–57
Cottage Pudding, Chocolate Rum,
    Old-fashioned, 94–95
Country Carrot Cake, 245–46
Country Kitchen Custard Pie, 201
Country Pound Cake, 250
Country Spice Cake, 225–26
Cow Lake Township Funeral Pie, 199
Cranberry(ies):
  Frozen, with Hot Caramel Sauce,
    9–10
  in Fruit Jelly Ice, 156
  Pie, 196
  Pudding, 40
Cream:
  Chocolate, Frosting, 245
  Custards, 172
  desserts, *see* Cream(s); Fool(s);
    Parfait(s)
  pies, *see* Pie(s)
  Pudding(s):
    Norwegian, 72–73
    Tapioca, 62
  Puffs, 130
  Roll, Pumpkin, Icebox, 144–45
  Sauce, Vanilla, Fresh Berries in, 6–7
  Sherbet, Orange, 158
  sour, *see* Sour cream
  Waffles, 136–37
  Whipped:
    Frosting, 218–19
    Topping, 208
Cream(s):
  Bavarian, 61
  Burnt-Almond, California, 177
  Maple, Poached Apples with, 21–22
  Mint, Baked Pears with, 26
  Rice:
    Pineapple, 64
    Vanilla, 64
  Shaker Floating Islands, 179
  Spanish, 60
    Chocolate, 60
    Coffee, 60
  see also Fool(s); Parfait(s)
Crème de Menthe Parfaits, 180
Creole Sweet Potato Pie, 203
Crisp(s):
  Almond Peach, 32

Crisp(s) (cont'd)
  Applesauce, 31
  see also Betty(s); Cobbler(s)
Crumb Cake, Spice, 227
Crumb Pie, Quaker Town, 212
Cup Custards, 171
Currant(s):
  in Cooked Fruit Fool, 8-9
  Drops, 275
  Orange and, Bread Pudding, 85
  red, in Fresh Berry Tumble, 9
Custard(s):
  Baked:
    Country, 170
    Honey, 176
  Cream, 172
  Cup, 171
  Filling(s):
    Rich, 218
    Vanilla, 253
  Ice Cream, Vanilla, 160
  Maple, 174
  Mission Flan, 178
  Pie, Country Kitchen, 201
  Pudding, Rice, Fluffy, 81-82
  Pumpkin, 175
  Sauce, Rum, 88-89
    Whole Wheat Chocolate Bread
      Pudding with, 87-88
  Soufflé, Old Salem, 173

Danish Puff, 128-29
Date(s):
  Oatmeal Squares, 281
  and Walnuts, Baked Apples Stuffed
    with, 25
Denver Fudge Pudding, 97-98
Dessert Omelet, Shaker, 181
Devil's Food Cake, 230-31
Doughnuts:
  Bismarks, 111
  Cake, 112-13
  Fritters, Dutch Fruit, 126
  Long Johns, 111
  New Orleans Beignets, 125
  Spudnuts, 126-27
  Yeast-raised, 110-11
Duff(s):
  Apple, New England, 37-38
  Blackberry, 38-39
  Plum, 36
Dumplings, Apple:
  Baked, 53
  Rosy, Shaker, 114-15
  -and-Rhubarb, Stina's Michigan, 116
Durgin Park Indian Pudding, 77
Dutch Apple Pancakes, 124
Dutch Apple Pie, 192
Dutch Fruit Fritters, 126

Early American Apple Grunt, 47-48
Easter Rabbit Cookies, Moravian,
  267-68
Easy Pastry with an Electric Mixer or
  Food Processor, 189-90
Eclairs, 131
Egg(s):
  One-, Cake, 219-20
  Two-, Cake, Basic, 220-21
Eggless, Milkless, Butterless Cake or
  "War Cake," 248-49
Eggnog Sauce, 39-40
Empanadas, Southwestern Fruit, 121

Fancy Pears, 19
Figs, in Stewed Fruits, 22-23
Filling(s):
  Apple, for Kolaches, 123
  Cherry, for Pennsylvania Dutch
    Apfelstrudel, 118
  Lady Baltimore, 223
  Lord Baltimore, 225
  Poppy-seed and Almond, for
    Pennsylvania Dutch Apfelstrudel,
    119
  Rich Custard, 218
  Vanilla, 132
    Custard, 253
Flan, Mission, 178
Floating Islands, Shaker, 179
Florida Key Lime Pie, 204
Flour:
  cake, to measure, 95
  as thickener, problems with,
    56-57
Fluffy Chocolate Frosting, 232
Fluffy Rice Custard Pudding, 81-82
Flummery(ies):
  Blackberry, 67
  Blueberry, 66
  Strawberry, 65-66
Foamy Sauce, 37
Fool(s):
  Cooked Fruit, 8-9
  Fresh Berry, 7-8
  Tumble, 9
Fresh Apple Cake, 237
Fresh Red Cherry Pie, 198
Fritters, Dutch Fruit, 126
Frosting(s):
  Caramel, Old-fashioned, 238
  Chocolate:
    Cream, 245
    Fluffy, 232
  Spicy, Araby, 235
  Whipped Cream, 218-19
  see also Glaze(s); Icing(s); Topping(s)
Frozen Cranberries with Hot Caramel
  Sauce, 9-10

Fruit(s):
Cobbler, Old-fashioned, 34
Cooked, Fool, 8–9
dried:
  in Southwestern Fruit *Empanadas*,
      121
  mixed, *in* Winter Fruit Soup, 70
Empanadas, Southwestern, 121
Fritters, Dutch, 126
Jelly Ice, 156
mixed candied, *in* Tutti-frutti Ice
    Cream, 165–66
Soup, Winter, 70
Stewed, 22–23
Tumble, Old-fashioned, 16–17
see also names of specific fruits
Fudge:
Cake, Chocolate-Nut, 221
Chocolate, Ice Cream, 163
Pudding, Denver, 97–98
Toasted-Almond, Ice Cream, 161–62
Funeral Pie, Cow Lake Township, 199

Ginger:
Crinkles, 269
Lemon-, Ice Cream, 161
Gingerbread:
Boys, 266
Molasses, 243
Glaze(s):
Chocolate, 112
Honey, 112, 128
Powdered Sugar, 111–12
see also Frosting(s); Icing(s);
    Topping(s)
"Gold Cake" or Lord Baltimore Cake,
    224
Golden Brown Sugar Sauce, 92
Gooseberries, *in* Cooked Fruit Fool, 8–9
Grandmother's Sugar Cookies, 265
Grape jelly, *in* Fruit Jelly Ice, 156
Grunt(s):
Apple, Early American, 47–48
Blueberry, Cape Cod, 49

Hard Sauce, 106
Cinnamon, 54
Hasty pudding, *see* Pudding(s)
Hazelnut Icebox Pudding, 140
Hermits, 277–78
Homemade Applesauce, 24–25
Honey:
Custard, Baked, 176
Glaze, 112, 128
Rhubarb Pie, 197
Honeydew and Fresh Peach Compote,
    15
Hot Caramel Sauce, 10–11
Frozen Cranberries with, 9–10

Hot-Water Pastry, 190–91
Huckleberry(ies):
Buckle, Oregon, 93–94
notes on, 93
in Scandinavian Berry Pudding, 69
Wild Blueberry or, Pie, 195
see also Blueberry(ies)

Ice(s):
Fruit Jelly, 156
notes on, 155
see also Ice cream(s); Sherbet(s)
Icebox cakes, *see* Cake(s)
Icebox cookies, *see* Cookies
Icebox puddings, *see* Pudding(s)
Ice cream(s):
in Baked Alaska, 152–53
Burnt-Sugar, Old-fashioned, 167
Butter Pecan, 162
Chocolate, 161
  Chip, 164
  Fudge, 163
Coconut, 164–65
Coffee, 161
Lemon-Ginger, 161
Molasses Pecan, Colonial, 166–67
Peppermint Chip, 164
Pistachio, 161
Rum-Raisin-Nut, 164
Southern-Style, 162–63
Strawberry, 163
Toasted-Almond Fudge, 161–62
Tutti-frutti, 165–66
Vanilla:
  Custard, 160–61
  Philadelphia, 163–64
see also Ice(s); Parfait(s); Sherbet(s)
Iced Cantaleupes, 14–15
Icing(s):
Lemon, 240
Royal, Almond, 267
Seven-Minute, 223
see also Frosting(s); Glaze(s);
    Topping(s)
Indiana Persimmon Pudding, 99–100

Jelly, Fruit, ice, 156
Jumbles:
Chocolate Chip, 272
Cinnamon, 273
Coconut, 272
Orange-glazed, 273
Pecan, 273
Sugar, Old-fashioned, 272

Kentucky Bourbon Pecan Cake, 232–33
Key lime(s):
notes on, 204
Pie, Florida, 204

Kiss Pudding, 73
Kolaches, 122–23

Lady Baltimore Cake, 222
Lady Baltimore Filling, 223
Lazy-Daisy Cake, 247–48
Lemon:
  Cream Sherbet, 159–60
  -Ginger Ice Cream, 161
  Icebox Cake, 143–44
  Icing, 240
  Meringue Pie, 208–209
  -Nut Coffee Cake, Old-fashioned,
    256–57
  Pastry, No-Fail, 188–89
  Pudding, Baked, 42
  Sauce, 103
Lime(s):
  key, *see* Key lime(s)
  Sherbet, 157
Loganberries:
  in Fresh Berry Tumble, 9
  in Old-fashioned Fruit Cobbler, 34–35
  in Scandinavian Berry Pudding, 69
Long Johns, 111
Lord Baltimore Cake or "Gold Cake,"
  224
Lord Baltimore Filling, 225
Louisa May Alcott's Apple Slump, 50

Maple:
  Charlotte, 142–43
  Cream, Poached Apples with, 221–22
  Custard, 174
  syrup, notes on, 174
Marshmallows:
  in Coffee Mallow, 146
  notes on, 146
Matrimonial Cakes, 281
Meringue, Lemon, Pie, 208–209
Michigan Black Cherry Dessert, 18
Milk:
  Sherbet, Strawberry, 158–59
  sweetened condensed, notes on,
    139–40, 155–56
Mint Cream, Baked Pears with, 26
Minted Orange Cup, 16
Mission Flan, 178
Mocha, Chocolate, Icebox Pudding, 148
Molasses:
  Gingerbread, 243
  notes on, 76, 243
  Pecan Ice Cream, Colonial, 166–67
  Pie, White House, 205
Moravian Easter Rabbit Cookies,
  267–68
Mormon Bachelor's Pudding, 91
Mush-Apple Pie, 193

Nesselrode Pudding, 151–52
New England Apple Duff, 37
New England Hasty Pudding, 79
New England Indian Pudding, 78
New England Nutmeg Sauce, 51
New Orleans *Beignets,* 125
New Orleans Bread Pudding with
  Whiskey Sauce, 86
No-Fail Lemon Pastry, 188–89
Norwegian Cream Pudding, 72
Nut(s), *see names of specific nuts*
Nutmeg Sauce, New England, 51

Oatmeal:
  cookies, *see* Cookies
  Date-, Squares, 281
Old Arkansas Vinegar Pie, 210
Old-fashioned Burnt-Sugar Ice Cream,
  167
Old-fashioned Caramel Frosting, 238
Old-fashioned Chocolate Icebox Cake,
  150
Old-fashioned Chocolate Rum Cottage
  Pudding, 94–95
Old-fashioned Country-Style Apple Pie,
  191–92
Old-fashioned Fruit Cobbler, 34
Old-fashioned Fruit Tumble, 16–17
Old-fashioned Icebox Cookies, 273–74
Old-fashioned Lemon-Nut Coffee Cake,
  256–57
Old-fashioned Strawberry Whip, 12–13
Old-fashioned Sugar Jumbles, 272
Old Maine Blueberry Batter Cake, 43
Old Oregon Baked Pears, 27
Old Salem Custard Soufflé, 173
Old Virginia Hasty Pudding, 80
Old Williamsburg Golden Pecan Pie,
  211
Old Williamsburg Raisin Rice Pudding,
  82–83
Omelet(s):
  Dessert, Shaker, 181
  Soufflé, 182
One-Egg Cake, 219–20
1-2-3-4 Cake, Basic Yellow Cake or,
  217
Orange:
  Ambrosia, 11
  Butter Cake, 240–41
  Chiffon Cake, 255
  Cream Sherbet, 158
  Cup, Minted, 16
  and Currant Bread Pudding, 85
  -glazed Jumbles, 273
Oregon Huckleberry Buckle, 93–94
Original Injun' Puddin', 77
Original Pumpkin Pie, 202

INDEX

Pandowdy, Apple, 44–45
Pancakes, Dutch Apple, 124
Parfait(s):
Angel Cream, 180
Chocolate Almond-Crunch, 180
Crème de Menthe, 180
Strawberry-Stripe, 180
Pastry, pie:
Buttery, for Pies, 187–88
Easy, with an Electric Mixer or Food
Processor, 189–90
Hot-Water, 190–91
Lemon, No-Fail, 188–89
Pastry(ies):
Apple Roly-poly, 113–14
Apple Strudel Squares, 119–20
Baklava, 132–34
Cream Puffs, 130
Cream Waffles, 136–37
Danish Puff, 128–29
Eclairs, 131
Kolaches, 122–23
Pennsylvania Dutch Apfelstrudel,
117–19
Potica, 134–36
Southwestern Fruit Empanadas, 121
Peach(es):
Almond, Crisp, 32
Baked, Flambé, 28
candied, in Tutti-frutti Ice Cream,
165–66
dried:
to cook, 121
in Southwestern Fruit Empanadas,
121
in Dutch Fruit Fritters, 126
Fresh, Honeydew and, Compote,
15–16
in Old-fashioned Fruit Cobbler, 34–35
in Old-fashioned Fruit Tumble, 16–17
Shortcake, 259
in Stewed Fruits, 22–23
Peanut Butter:
Chip Cookies, 275
Cookies, 271
Pear(s):
Baked:
with Mint Cream, 26
Old Oregon, 27
Fancy, 19
Poached, with Raspberries, 23–24
in Stewed Fruits, 22–23
Walnut Pudding, 106–107
Pecan(s):
Apple-, Pie, 192
Bourbon, Cake, Kentucky, 232–33
Butter, Ice Cream, 162
in Chocolate-Nut Icebox Cookies, 275
Golden, Pie, Old Williamsburg, 211

Jumbles, 273
Molasses, Ice Cream, Colonial,
166–67
in Oatmeal-Nut Cookies, 279
in Old-fashioned Lemon-Nut Coffee
Cake, 256–57
Pennsylvania Dutch Apfelstrudel, 117–19
Pennsylvania Dutch Blackberry Mush,
68
Pennsylvania Dutch Shoofly Pie,
205–206
Peppermint Chip Ice Cream, 164
Persimmon, Indiana, Pudding, 99–100
Philadelphia Vanilla Ice Cream, 163–64
Pie(s):
Apple:
Candy, 192
Dutch, 192
Mush-, 193
Old-fashioned Country-Style,
191–92
-Pecan, 192
-Raisin, 192
Streusel, 192
Wisconsin, 192
Chess, Southern Creamy, 213
Cranberry, 196
Cream:
American, 207
Banana, 207
Coconut, 208
Crumb, Quaker Town, 212
Fresh Red Cherry, 198
Funeral, Cow Lake Township, 199
Key Lime, Florida, 204
Lemon Meringue, 208–209
Molasses, White House, 205
pastry for, see Pastry
Pecan, Golden, Old Williamsburg,
211
Pumpkin, Original, 202
Rhubarb, 197
-Strawberry, 194
Shoofly, Pennsylvania Dutch, 205–206
Sugar, 200
Sweet Potato, Creole, 203
Vinegar, Old Arkansas, 210
Wild Blueberry or Huckleberry, 195
Pie plant, see Rhubarb
Pineapple:
candied, in Tutti-frutti Ice Cream,
165–66
Chiffon Cake, 256
jelly, in Fruit Jelly Ice, 156
Upside-Down Cake, 220
Pistachio Ice Cream, 161
Plum(s):
Duff, 36
jelly, in Fruit Jelly Ice, 156

Plum(s) (*cont'd*)
  Pudding, Colonial, with Brandy
    Sauce, 103–105
  in Stewed Fruits, 22–23
Poached Apples with Maple Cream,
  21–22
Poor Man's Rice Pudding, 83
Poppy seed(s):
  and Almond Filling, *for* Pennsylvania
    Dutch *Apfelstrudel,* 119
  in Kolaches, 122–23
Potato, Sweet, Pie, Creole, 203
Potica, 134–36
Pound Cake, Country, 250
Powdered Sugar Glaze, 111–12
Prunes:
  to cook, 121
  in Southwestern Fruit *Empanadas,* 121
Pudding(s):
  Apple:
    Mystery, York County Farm, 51–52
    Pandowdy, 44–45
    Slump, Louisa May Alcott's, 50
  Berry, Scandinavian, 69
  Bird's Nest, 45–46
  Bread:
    Basic, 84
    -and-Butter, Blueberry, 90–91
    Chocolate, Plain, Amana Village,
      89–90
    New Orleans, with Whiskey Sauce,
      86
    Orange and Currant, 85
    Whole Wheat Chocolate, with Rum
      Custard Sauce, 87
  Butterscotch, 58
  Cabinet, 140
  Calliope Coffee, 147
  Carrot, Baked, 96–97
  Chocolate, 58
    Chilled, 71
    Mocha Icebox, 148
    Rum Cottage, Old-fashioned, 94–95
    Rum Russe, 149
    see also Pudding(s), bread, *above*
  Coconut, 58
  Coffee Mallow, 146
  Cornstarch:
    Cocoa, 59
    Vanilla, 57
  Cranberry, 40
  Cream:
    Norwegian, 72–73
    Tapioca, 62
  Fudge, Denver, 97–98
  Hasty:
    New England, 79
    Old Virginia, 80
    sliced and fried, 79

Icebox:
  Chocolate Mocha, 148
  Hazelnut, 140–41
Indian:
  Durgin Park, 77
  New England, 78
  Original Injun' Puddin', 77
  Rhode Island, 77
Indiana Persimmon, 99–100
Kiss, 73
Lemon, Baked, 42
Maple Charlotte, 142–43
Mormon Bachelor's, 91–93
Old Maine Blueberry Batter Cake,
  43
Oregon Huckleberry Buckle, 93–94
Pear Walnut, 106–107
Pennsylvania Dutch Blackberry Mush,
  68
Plum, Colonial, with Brandy Sauce,
  103–105
Rice:
  Custard, Fluffy, 81–82
  Poor Man's, 83
  Raisin, Old Williamsburg, 82–83
  Simmered, 63
  Wild, Cinnamon, 98–99
Rhubarb, 54–55
Winter Fruit Soup, 70
see also Cream(s); Custard(s); Duff(s);
  Flummery(ies); Grunt(s)
Pumpkin:
  Cream Roll, Icebox, 144–45
  Custard, 175
  Pie, Original, 202

Quaker Town Crumb Pie, 212
Quinces, *in* Stewed Fruits, 22–23

Raisin(s):
  Apple-, Pie, 192
  to cook, 121
  Rice Pudding, Old Williamsburg,
    82–83
  Oatmeal-, Cookies, 279
  Rum-, -Nut Ice Cream, 164
  in Southwestern Fruit *Empanadas,* 121
Raspberry(ies):
  in Fresh Berries and Vanilla Cream
    Sauce, 6–7
  in Fresh Berry Fool, 7–8
  in Fresh Berry Tumble, 9
  Ice Cream, 163
  jelly, *in* Fruit Jelly Ice, 156
  Pears Poached with, 23–24
  in Scandinavian Berry Pudding, 69
  Shortcake, 259
Red currants, *in* Fresh Berry Tumble, 9
Rhode Island Indian Pudding, 77

Rhubarb:
  Apple-and-, Dumplings, Stina's
      Michigan, 116
  in Baked Pie Plant, 29
  notes on, 183
  Pudding, 54–55
  Soufflé, 183–84
  in Stewed Fruits, 22–23
  -Strawberry Pie, 194
Rice:
  Cream:
      Pineapple, 64
      Vanilla, 64
  puddings, *see* Puddings
  wild, *see* Wild rice
Rich Custard Filling, 218
Roly-poly, Apple, 113–14
Rosewater, notes on, 115
Royal Icing, Almond, 267
Rum:
  Chocolate:
      Cottage Pudding, Old-fashioned,
          94–95
      Russe, 149
      Sauce, 95
  Custard Sauce, 88–89
      Whole Wheat Chocolate Bread
          Pudding with, 87–88
  -Raisin-Nut Ice Cream, 164

St. Louis Angel Food Cake, 251
Sauce(s):
  Brandy, 105
  Butter, 41
      Colonial Plum Pudding with,
          103–105
  Butt'ry, 102
      Carrot Pudding with, 100–102
  Caramel, Hot, 10–11
      Frozen Cranberries with, 9–10
  Chocolate Rum, 95
  Cider, 182
  Cream, Vanilla, 7
      Fresh Berries and, 6–7
  Eggnog, 39
  Foamy, 37
  Hard, 106
      Cinnamon, 54
  Lemon, 103
  Nutmeg, New England, 51
  Rum Custard, 88–89
      Whole Wheat Chocolate Bread
          Pudding with, 87
  Sour, 47
  Strawberry, Shaker, 13–14
  Sugar, Golden Brown, 92
  Whiskey, 87
      New Orleans Bread Pudding with, 86
  Wine, 81

Scandinavian Bread Pudding, 69
Seven-Minute Icing, 223
Shaker Dessert Omelet, 181
Shaker Floating Islands, 179
Shaker Rosy Apple Dumplings, 114–15
Shaker Strawberry Sauce, 13–14
Sherbet(s):
  Lemon Cream, 159–60
  Lime, 157
  Milk, Strawberry, 158–59
  see also Ice(s); Ice Cream(s); Parfait(s)
Shoofly Pie, Pennsylvania Dutch,
      205–206
Shortcake:
  Peach, 259
  Raspberry, 259
  Strawberry, 258–59
Simmered Rice Pudding, 63
Slump, Apple, Louisa May Alcott's,
      50
Snickerdoodles, 270
Soufflé(s):
  Custard, Old Salem, 173
  Rhubarb, 183–84
Soup, Winter Fruit, 70
Sour Cream:
  Cinnamon, Coffee Cake, 257–58
  Spice Cake, 234
Sour Sauce, 47
Southern Creamy Chess Pie, 213
Southern-Style Ice Cream, 162–63
Southwestern Fruit *Empanadas,* 121
Spanish creams, *see* Cream(s)
Spice:
  cakes, *see* Cake(s)
  Frosting, Araby, 235
Spiced Crumb Cake, 227
Sponge Cake, 254
Spudnuts, 126–27
Stewed Fruits, 22–23
Stina's Michigan Apple-and-Rhubarb
      Dumplings, 116
Strawberry(ies):
  in Champagne, 17–18
  Flummery, 65–66
  in Fresh Berries and Vanilla Cream
      Sauce, 6–7
  in Fresh Berry Fool, 7–8
  in Fresh Berry Tumble, 9
  Ice Cream, 163
  jelly, *in* Fruit Jelly Ice, 156
  Milk Sherbet, 158–59
  in Old-fashioned Fruit Tumble,
      16–17
  Rhubarb-, Pie, 194
  Sauce, Shaker, 13–14
  in Scandinavian Berry Pudding, 69
  Shortcake, 258–59
  -Stripe Parfaits, 180

Strawberry(ies) *(cont'd)*
  -topped Cheesecake, 260–61
  Whip, Old-fashioned, 12–13
Streusel Apple Pie, 192
Strudel:
  Apple, Squares, 119–20
  Pennsylvania Dutch *Apfelstrudel,*
    117–19
Sugar:
  Burnt-, Ice Cream, Old-fashioned,
    167
  Cookies, Grandmother's, 265
  Jumbles, Old-fashioned, 272
  notes on, 76
  Pie, 200
  Powdered, Glaze, 111–12
  Sauce, Golden Brown, 92
Sweetened condensed milk, notes on,
  139–40, 155–56
Sweet Potato Pie, Creole, 203

Tapioca:
  Cream Pudding, 62
  notes on, 62
Toasted-Almond Fudge Ice Cream,
  161–62
Toll House Cookies, 276–77
Topping(s):
  Whipped Cream, 208
  see also Frosting(s); Glaze(s); Icing(s);
    Sauce(s)
Tumble(s):
  Fresh Berry, 9
  Fruit, Old-fashioned, 16–17
Tutti-frutti Ice Cream, 165–66
Two-Egg Cake, Basic, 220–21

Upside-Down Cake, Pineapple, 220

Vanilla:
  Cornstarch Pudding, 57–58
  Cream Sauce, 7
    Fresh Berries in, 6–7
  Filling, 132
    Custard, 253

Ice Cream:
  Custard, 160–61
  Philadelphia, 163–64
  Rice Cream, 64
Vinegar Pie, Old Arkansas, 210

Waffles, Cream, 136–37
Walnut(s):
  in Chocolate-Nut Icebox Cookies, 275
  in Chocolate-Nut Fudge Cake, 221
  Dates and, Baked Apples Stuffed with,
    25
  in Oatmeal-Nut Cookies, 279
  in Old-fashioned Lemon-Nut Coffee
    Cake, 256–57
  Pear, Pudding, 106–107
  in Rum-Raisin-Nut Ice Cream, 164
  "War Cake," Eggless, Milkless,
    Butterless Cake or, 248–49
Whip, Strawberry, Old-fashioned,
  12–13
Whipped Cream:
  Frosting, 218–19
  Topping, 208
Whiskey Sauce, 87
  New Orleans Bread Pudding with,
    86
White House Molasses Pie, 205
Whole Wheat Chocolate Bread Pudding
  with Rum Custard Sauce, 87–88
Wild Blueberry or Huckleberry Pie,
  195
Wild rice:
  Cinnamon, Pudding, 98–99
  to cook, 99
Wine Sauce, 81
Winter Fruit Soup, 70
Wisconsin Apple Pie, 192

Yankee Apple Snow, 12
Yeast-raised Doughnuts, 110–11
Yellow Cake, Basic, or 1-2-3-4 Cake,
  217
York County Farm Apple Mystery
  Pudding, 51–52